BIBLICAL ENCOUNTER
WITH
JAPANESE CULTURE

Charles Corwin, Ph.D.

Christian Literature Crusade

2, 1-3 Surugadai, Kanda, Chiyodaku, Tokyo

II

TO NONIE

— mine is the inestimable privilege
of being her son —

Printed in Japan — Kishimoto, Himeji

PREFACE

"I don't know what the Japanese really mean when they say 'love'," was the frank admission of a fellow missionary several days ago. While writing out a Japanese message he bogged down at this point. Most of us readily contrast Greek words when explaining Biblical love but are seized with doubts over their Japanese equivalents. Can Japanese love (*ai*) mean both human and divine love? Does it contain the self-giving and sacrifice of *agape*? With such misgivings the Japan missionary pours his Biblical message into the Japanese symbol system and hopes for the best. But he is never quite sure what mental images his words flash upon the screen of the Japanese mind. For example, when he uses the Japanese word for righteousness (*gi*), do his hearers picture a man alone before God or merely a good neighbor? Does Japanese faith (*shinkō*) mean trust in a person or assent to creeds or religious zeal? When the Japanese talk of reality (*genjitsu*), do they mean the stuff of experience or principles behind it? When they speak of truth (*shinjitsu*), are they hewing to some line of logic or appealing to individual emotional feelings? When the Japanese disc jockey signs off with "I'm praying for you", is there a divine person in his thinking or is he merely saying, "Good luck"? Sooner or later the Japan missionary pauses to consider the *words* made available to him by Japanese culture for conveying the Biblical revelation.

For those who have been asking such questions this book is written. My hope is that it will be pulled down from the shelf whenever the missionary wishes to present the distinctives of the Christian message in the Japanese tongue. Knowledge comes through discrimination; the more sharply Biblical concepts are set apart from non-Christian ones, the more deeply will they be inscribed on Japanese hearts.

Here is a resumé of the contents. The *Introduction* explains how basic concepts of Japanese thought are (1) *discovered* through semantic groupings of words and phrases from the common language, and (2) *understood* by observing semantic change through the centuries. Following this methodology, the main body examines thirty-three concepts of human experience as seen in the Japanese tradition and in the Biblical tradition. Earliest meanings of the Chinese ideographs, as understood by Japanese scholars when adopted, are first examined. Semantic changes within the Japanese words, to which the characters were affixed, are next noted, giving special attention to changes occuring during the Nara-Heian periods. To mark which semantic changes have been preserved in the present-day language, the *Modern Range of Meaning* is listed. This includes the pre-modern era as well, since older lexical works, such as *Gensen* (Spring of Words), and *Daigenkai* (Great Sea of Words) are cited. Buddhist concepts and

IV

English idiom parallels are also listed. Here we leave our data uncorrelated and explore meanings of equivalent Hebrew-Greek words in the Biblical context. Thus the stage is set for contrasting Biblical and Japanese cultural thinking in the *Encounter* section. In the *Conclusions*, I critically evaluate the methodology and attempt to discover a *concept-clearing-center* in the Japanese psyche which either resists hostile ideas altogether or generates semantic changes in words. Lastly, *five canons for Bible translators are listed*—canons hammered out of this approach to cultural thinking through language.

For assistance in reading Japanese dictionaries, my heartfelt thanks to Renta Kidera and the students of Tyrannus Hall (Tokyo Christian Gakuryō), where I am ministering. For helpful criticism during the preparation of the manuscript, my deep appreciation to Dr. Cyrus Peake, Dr. John Hutchison, and Dr. Hans Ruyter, under whom I studied at Claremont Graduate School. In tracing down semantic changes and checking findings, Prof. Susumu Ōno of the Peers University, Tokyo, gave of his valuable time and experience unstintingly. *Arigatō gozaimasu.*

Perhaps this study will bring us closer to the Japanese people, still eager to learn from the West but asking in exchange sympathetic understanding of her deeper emotions. Being brought closer, let us present Biblical truth in clearer light and sharper perspective. For, if we have nothing to say to Japan's culture, why are we here?

Tokyo, Japan
January 26, 1967

Charles Corwin
Tyrannus Hall

TABLE OF CONTENTS

ABBREVIATIONS

Arnt, A Greek-English Lexicon of the New Testament
BD, Japanese-English Buddhist Dictionary
DGK, Daigenkai
DNKJ, Dainihonkokugojiten
EB, Encyclopaedia Brittanica
Gk., Greek
GS, Gensen
ISBE, International Standard Bible Encyclopaedia
KCJ, Kanwachūjiten
KGJ, Kanjigogenjiten
KJ, Kōjien
lit., literally
LXX, Septuagint
NT, New Testament
OT, Old Testament
Sk., Sanskrit
TDNT, Theological Dictionary of the New Testament
TWBB, Theological Word Book of the Bible
tr., translated or translation

INTRODUCTION

Students of Japanese culture have walked hitherto through the gallery of Japanese thought, gazing at pictures hung there by a handful of artists — the scribes of Japanese religion, history, and literature. They tried to penetrate Japanese thinking through interpretive works penned by Kōbō-Daishi, Shinran, Nichiren, Motoori, Hearn, Nitobe, *et al.*, and learned much. But the time has come to step into another hall in the gallery and view the works of common man. The one cultural monument which the Japanese people have shaped together out of their cumulative tradition is their *language*. This book, together with its companion volume, *Handbook of Japanese-English Idiomatic Equivalents*,[1] will serve as guide into this spacious room. For it follows the premise that *man's concepts of reality can be pieced together by examining the verbal symbol system he employs to express this reality*. We shall not view the verbal symbol system of the specialists nor the scholars but that of the man on the street. Hence, our findings will be gleaned not from Japanese and English interpretive works on Japanese thinking but from lexical data. I have arbitrarily chosen the Hebrew-Greek system as found in pages of Holy Writ to serve as a point of reference in the transcultural comparison. And to insure that we are in fact examining the symbol system of the average Japanese man, we shall make use of a semantic catagorizing of Japanese-English equivalent words, phrases, and idioms culled from Japanese literature, school textbooks and dictionaries.

But why step into the *room of language* to make a transcultural comparison of Japanese-Biblical thought? Language is a system of sounds and symbols that defines and delineates human experience. Reality and phenomena, both objective and subjective, are examined, differentiated and interpreted; word symbols are then selected to describe these phenomena. Language then becomes an arbitrary system of symbols that springs from the mind of man as he encounters reality and tries to differentiate the stuff of experience. Different cultures explain the same phenomenon differently. For example, the English language divides the spectrum into six major colors, the Rhodesian language into four, the Bassa language into two.[2] Carried into the sphere of human relationships perhaps language can shed light on cultural thinking. More, language itself might be *the* clue as to why two cultures observing the same slice of human experience view it differently. So differently that misunderstanding is the rule, genuine empathy the rarity in the transcultural encounter.

---

1 Soon to be published by Kōdansha International, Tokyo.

2 H.A. Gleason, *An Introduction to Descriptive Linguistics* (New York: Henry Holt and Co., 1955), p. 4.

However, if language be the tool for examining cultural thought, we could hardly have chosen more radically divergent symbol systems than Japanese and Biblical languages. Dr. James Hepburn, pioneer of Japanese-English lexicography and Bible translation during the Meiji era, bemoaned his first frustrations in learning the Japanese language:

> I know well, and we all know here, what it is to learn this language without a dictionary or any material help. It is a very laborious work; learning French is mere pastime to it. There are few of us, indeed I doubt if there is a foreigner in Japan that can now, after five years of study, extemporize two consecutive grammatical and idiomatical sentences in the Japanese, without some study.[3]

I can think of three reasons why the Japanese language baffles attempts at its mastery by the Western mind: (1) the essential Altaic character of the Japanese language, (2) confusion added to the Japanese language by the adaptation of Chinese ideographs during the Nara-Heian periods (A.D. 710-1159), (3) the non-technical, emotive character of the language. Let us discuss these in the above order.

Essential Altaic characteristics of the Japanese language

The Japanese language developed from Jōmon times from two distinct cultural sources, the Altaic and the Polynesian language groups. Relationship between languages is demonstrated by similarity of grammatical structure and vocabulary. From examination of linguistic data from the third to the ninth centuries Susumu Ōno points out vowel harmony of Japanese with the Altaic group.[4] The same vowels of Japanese (a, o, u, e, ö, ü) are also found in Turkish, Tungus, Manchu, Hungarian, Finnish, and archaic Korean. (However, this vowel similarity disappeared after the ninth century.) Other similarities with the Altaic group listed by Ōno are:

1. No sharp distinction exists between singular and plural.
2. There is no distinction between masculine, neuter, and feminine.
3. There are no articles.
4. Postprepositions are used.
5. The distinction between nouns and the stems of adjectives is not clear.
6. There are no comparative or superlatives of adjectives.
7. Basic forms of verbs are used as nouns and imperatives of verbs.
8. An interrogative sentence is formed by placing an interrogative word at the end.[5]

Despite this strong morphological similarity, Japanese has little or no cognate vocabulary with this group, except with Korean. Ōno lists some of the two hundred cognate words found in Korean, e.g. *kama* (kiln), *taba* (bundle), etc.

---

3 James Hepburn, ''Letter to Rev. J. C. Lowrie, Nov. 28, 1864,'' *The Letters of Dr. J. C. Hepburn*, ed. M. Takaya (Tokyo: Toshin Shobō, 1955), pp. 79-80.

4 Susumu Ōno, ''The Japanese Language: Its Origins and Sources,'' *Japanese Culture*, ed. Robert Smith and Richard Beardsley (Chicago: Aldine Publishing House, 1962), p. 19.

5 *Ibid.*

Concerning Polynesian strains in the Japanese language, Ōno has pointed out mythological analogues with Indonesia; also customs of tooth blackening, tattooing are parallel. Linguistic similarities discovered in writings of the Heian period are:

1. Polynesian also has five distinct vowels.
2. Polynesian words are also regularly ended with an open syllable.
3. When two vowels come in succession, one is often dropped in Polynesian, as in Japanese.
4. Cognate words exist for parts of the body, in Polynesian or Malayan, e.g., *ma* (eye), *kutsu* (mouth), *hara* (abdomen), *hoso* (navel), *hoho* (cheek).[6]

Summing up the linguistic effects of these two strains upon Japanese, Ōno says:

> Through Jōmon times a language of southern origin with a phonetic system like that of present day Polynesia was widespread throughout Western Japan. About 300 B.C., along with rice cultivation, use of metals, weaving, and eventually tumuli that distinguished Yayoi culture, a new language of northern derivation with grammar and vowel harmony of Altaic character arrived and spread south and east from northern Kyushu.[7]

Though the above analysis is generally accepted today there are some obvious weaknesses to the theory. First, if there is a true vowel harmony, then there should be more cognate words with the Altaic group, for the phonemes of any language are basic to the structure and meaning of words.[8] Secondly, the cognate words Ōno mentions could very well be loan words, i.e., words which find their way into languages by the simple processes of cultural exchange. Thirdly, Ōno does not consider the influence of Ainu language upon Japanese, but Kindaiichi mentions Ainu words like *magemono* (cherry bark), which are found in the Manyōshū.[9] Perhaps there was a substratum language, now completely lost, a primitive language, upon which these imported languages were built.

From the above discussion, it can be seen how far removed Japanese syntax and vocabulary are from English. The Altaic characteristics mentioned above find no common ground with English. Further, there are forty-six basic phonemes in English, only twenty-three in Japanese, which makes pronunciation relatively manageable for foreigners but an ordeal for Japanese learning English. Hearn sums up the difficulty Westerners face:

> Any one of their ordinary phrases, translated into Western speech, makes hopeless nonsense; and the literal rendering into Japanese of the simplest English sentence would scarcely be comprehended by any Japanese who had never studied a European

---

6 *Ibid.*, p. 20.

7 *Ibid.*

8 A phoneme is a "minimum feature of the expression system of a spoken language by which one thing that may be said is distinguished from any other thing which might have been said." Gleason, p. 9.

9 K. Kindaiichi, "Ainu Life and Legends," *Tourists Library* (Tokyo: Board of Tourist Industry, 1941), p. 19.

tongue. Could you learn all the words in a Japanese dictionary, your acquisition would not help you in the least to make yourself understood in speaking, unless you had learned also to think like a Japanese — that is to say, to think backwards, to think upside down and inside out, to think in directions totally foreign to Aryan habit. Experience in the acquisition of European languages can help you to learn Japanese as much as it would help you to acquire the language spoken by the inhabitants of Mars.[10]

Confusion added to the Japanese language by the adaptation of Chinese ideographs during the Nara-Heian periods (A.D. 710-1159)

Aston believes the introduction of Chinese characters began in the third century, as scholars came from Korea to the Imperial Court.[11] At first, Chinese calligraphy did not catch the interest of the nobility, and scribes were employed to write the characters in imperial accounts and registers. But with the exchange of embassies between China and Japan under the aegis of Prince Shōtoku in the early seventh century and the coming of Chinese Buddhist scholars, Chinese calligraphy became the object of interest at the court. Shōtoku himself began copying sutras; it became a temple fad.

> The records state that scribes were assembled in a temple in Yamato in 673 and set to copying the whole canon, the voluminous Tripitaka; but the oldest extant copy of a complete sutra seems to be one dating 686 ... by the middle of the Nara period, enthusiasm for sutra copying had grown to a fever.[12]

But there were secular stimuli as well. During the Taika Reform (A.D. 645-710) as the T'ang system of laws, government, taxation was adopted, registration of local families for taxation was enforced. Chinese ideographs were used phonetically to write down Japanese surnames in the registers. Overawed by the impressive calligraphy of the Chinese tradition and its literary attainments, these court scholars began adapting Chinese calligraphy to the Japanese spoken language. Actually these scholars were attempting the near-impossible. Chinese is monosyllabic and tonal, each character representing one word. It differs from Japanese in vocabulary, syntax, and idiom. Japanese is polysyllabic, highly agglutinated. The fact that four different methods of adaptation were used alternatively during the Nara-Heian period reveals the frustration and perplexity the Japanese scholars were experiencing. The four ways in which Chinese characters were adapted into the Japanese language are as follows: 1. adopting the Chinese character with its same meaning and sound into the Japanese vocabulary. This was a one-to-one correspondence, the simplest and most accurate; but if done wholesale it would have been tantamount to abandoning the Japanese language for the Chinese. At first nouns were adopted — especially nouns of abstract thought (since there were no translatable words in the Japanese vocabulary) — which were learned by the scholars and thus sifted down to the common people. Example: The Chinese word *tao* (way) came to

---

10 Lafcadio Hearn, *Japan, An Interpretation* (New York: Grosset and Dunlap, 1904), p. 14.

11 G. Aston, *Grammar of the Japanese Written Language* (London: Trubner and Co., 1877), p. ii.

12 G. B. Sansom, *Japan: A Short Cultural History* (London: The Cresset Press, 1932), p. 137.

be *dō* or *tō* in Japanese and was represented by the Chinese character 道. Thus we have Shin*tō'* (the way of the gods), a term strictly of Chinese origin. The *Kojiki*, the first book of which we have any record, was written this way. The Japanese story was simply written in Chinese. 2. Adopting the Chinese character for representing a synonymous Japanese word. In this case the Chinese sound is lost; only the meaning of the ideograph is kept. Example: The Chinese ideograph for spring, 春 is used for the Japanese word *haru* (spring). In the above two cases, the Chinese character has an ideographic value; when used thus it is called *mana* 真名 (true name). 3. Adopting the Chinese character for the sound of a Chinese syllable. In this case the phonetic value is used, with no correspondence in meaning or sound to the Japanese. Example: The Chinese character 天 (heaven), is used to denote *te*; 山 (mountain), to denote *san* 4. Adopting the Chinese character for the mere sound of a Japanese syllable. The Chinese character becomes thus a phonetic symbol for representing Japanese sounds; no consideration is given to the meaning of the ideograph. Example; The Chinese ideographs 夜 *ya* (night) and 魔 *ma* (demon) are put together to convey the Japanese word *yama* (mountain). In this way, the *manyōgana*, as they were called, were used in the *Manyōshū*.

In cases 3 and 4, the characters so used are called *kana* 仮名 (borrowed names). Here again the confusion was compounded by the bringing of different sounds for these characters from different locales and periods in China. Sounds first adopted came from the provinces of *Go* (Wu in Chinese) of southeastern China during the fifth and sixth centuries This *Go-on* was the pronunciation used by Buddhist priests in their litanies. Reasons for adopting this pronunciation were three: (1) this province was in closest touch with Japan at the time, (2) it was the most flourishing part of the empire, (3) the pronunciation most closely approached Japanese pronunciation. The second pronunciation system is known as the *kan-on*, the pronunciation system of the seventh and eighth centuries in north China. From this word come *kanji* (ideographs) and *kambun* (Chinese composition). There was also the *Jōko-on*, or the archaic sound of the Chinese characters. Thus we see that one Chinese character might have three possible pronunciations: (1) the Chinese word sound, (2) the Japanese phonetic sound, and (3) either the *Go-on* or the *Kan-on*. Help was afforded for determining the pronunciation of Chinese characters in the form of a phonetic dictionary, like the *Tenrei Banshō Myōgi* (A.D. 800), or the *Shinsen Jikyō* (A.D. 895). Of course the number of homophones in Chinese was great; thus in the *Manyōshū*, for example, there are twenty-three Chinese characters which phonetically convey the Japanese エ (e), forty-five characters for キ (ki).

It was during this period that through simplification of some Chinese characters a purely Japanese phonetic system was developed. *Hiragana* were certain characters written in a simplified cursive style; *katakana* were developed from parts of certain characters. Hence three types of symbols may be found in Japanese writing today: (1) *Chinese ideographs* — used for all words of Chinese origin and for roots of more important Japanese words, (2) *hiragana* — used for grammatical terminations and for the less important words of Japanese origin, such as the particles (*te-ni-o-ha*), (3) *katakana* — used for foreign words and names, interjections, onomatopoeia. Sansom called this clumsy development of the Japanese writing system a "tragedy of history":

> It is perhaps one of the tragedies of history that the Japanese genius did not a thousand years ago rise to its invention [i.e., of their own phonetic script]. Certainly when one considers the truly appalling system which in the course of the centuries did evolve, that immense and intricate apparatus of signs for recording a few dozen little syllables, one is inclined to think that the Western alphabet is perhaps the greatest triumph of the human mind.[13]

Japanese frustration is doubly felt by the foreigner attempting to use their dictionaries, running down a column of words listed under a key Chinese ideograph. The words may or may not be related to the meaning of the ideograph. Also the laborious task of learning Chinese characters by Japanese children promises more than it yields; the characters may or may not give clues to the meaning of the words. It probably can be demonstrated that Chinese ideographs today serve as sight differentiators, among the vast number of homophones, for detecting the meaning of the words, thereby facilitating rapid reading by eliminating silent pronunciation. It may also be possible to demonstrate that the etymological meanings of the characters themselves do not enter the thought processes of the Japanese readers.

The non-technical, emotive character of the Japanese language

"The expressive forms of Japanese sentences put more emphasis upon emotive factors than on cognitive."[14] In other words, Nakamura says, the development of the Japanese language has been along emotional or aesthetic lines, not logical or rational. The language is built up of one idiomatic phrase upon another, making vocabulary lists and grammatical rules irrelevant to its mastery. Watsuji Tetsurō expresses it thus: "In Japanese, the expression of feeling and will come to the foreground."[15]

Discovering Core Concepts through Semantic Categorizing

The Japanese language thus being highly complex and far removed from Biblical languages, not to mention English, how can we possibly circumscribe this vast field of lexical data for meaningful investigation? Research which led to the writing of this book *sought for core concepts through a semantic categorizing of Japanese words and expressions*. The semantic approach is built upon the observed fact that "the speakers of a language intuitively feel a relationship between certain pairs or sets of words which is not accounted for by any overt phonological or grammatical similarity."[16] Just how did such

---

13 *Ibid.* p. 134.

14 Hajime Nakamura, *The Ways of Thinking of Eastern Peoples* (Honolulu: East-West Center Press, 1964), p. 531.

15 *Ibid.*, p. 486.

16 Uriel Weinreich, "Lexicographical Definition in Descriptive Semantics," *Problems in Lexicography*, ed. Fred Householder and Sol Saporta (Indiana: Indiana University, 1960) p. 25.

a semantic categorizing facilitate finding core cultural concepts? First, by fixing on universal categories recognized as the common lot of human experience, *viz.*, *love*, *hatred*, *fear*, *danger*, etc., clusters of words and phrases gathered naturally around them, revealing nuances, meaning ranges, and finally core ideas. Secondly, such semantic groupings revealed the amazing ability of the Japanese language for developing symbols to express human sentiment — symbols that approach in meaning many English symbols. That is, though Japanese and English are entirely unrelated in words and syntax, they have developed parallel expressions independently for explaining delicate human emotional experience. Thirdly, semantic categorizing (without initial concern for Chinese characters), overcame the difficulty in tracing down meanings which was created by Chinese characters. Because of various uses to which characters were put in the development of the written language, word lists formed under characters will reveal many illogical entries, meaning-wise. Lastly, semantic categorizing afforded an easy method for classifying idiomatic phrases. The Japanese language literally abounds with phrases in which core words have no bearing upon the overall meaning of the phrase. Classifying such phrases solely by meaning enables the researcher to quickly grasp ideas underlying idiomatic phrases.

Determining Core Concepts through Semantic Change

Relation of linguistics to our research

Though we shall search for conclusions throughout this investigation, the nature of this research will be tinged with subjectivity because of the object of our research — language. It is not strictly logical. We make contact with each other, or our nervous systems bridge gaps between us, by sound waves. A stimulus causes a person to speak to another; these sounds produce a reaction in the hearer. Hence, language is voluntary, emotional, human, reflective, symbolical. Sapir says: "Language is a purely human and non-instinctive method of communicating ideas, emotions, and desires by means of a system of voluntarily produced symbols."[17] Let me now make clear to the reader by way of definition what field of linguistics we will be pursuing.

Linguistics. — The phenomenological study of the way man expresses his thoughts through sounds is called linguistics. It is simply "the study of language."[18] It is precise in the sense that its findings and rules are adaptable to new languages and cultures. However, there are many aspects of linguistics: etymology, comparative linguistics, philology, historical linguistics and descriptive linguistics. Since our attention will be directed to discovering Japanese thought patterns in contrast with Hebrew-Christian thought, we shall attempt to trace original meanings of words, semantic variations caused by cultural changes, and present range of meanings. Hence our linguistic approach will attempt to follow the general canons of etymology, philology, and historical

[17] Edward Sapir, *Language* (New York: Harcourt, Brace, and World, Inc., 1949), p. 8.
[18] Leonard Bloomfield, *Language* (London: George Allen and Unwin Ltd., 1962), p. 3.

linguistics. We have ruled out comparative linguistics, which is the finding of linguistic relationships between two languages, such as Sanskrit and Latin, as being beyond the scope of our endeavor. Also, descriptive linguistics is not relevant to our research. Descriptive linguistics attempts to discover basic principles of speech and grammar inherent in all modes of human speech and hence enables translators to reduce languages to writing. The one drawback of descriptive linguistics would be fatal to our study: "One of the greatest shortcomings of descriptive work with the expressive aspect of language has been the lack of understanding of the relationships between expression and content."[19]

Etymology. — "That part of linguistics which deals with the origin or derivation of words"[20] is called etymology. The word itself comes from the Greek word *etumos* (true) and *logos* (account). "The word *etumos* as applied to words, referred to meaning rather than to the origin."[21] Etymological study is thus concerned with tracing down older forms of a part of speech. In our brief investigation into the origins of Chinese characters, we will not follow all of Skeat's canons of etymology, but only the most obvious ones, i.e., "ascertain the earliest form and use of the words."[22] Skeat also holds as important the origin of the several parts of a word, to which Chinese ideographs do lend themselves readily. But we will not lay heavy stress upon present meanings as having direct relation to etymological findings.

> It is not often that a consciousness of a word's etymology helps to an understanding of its present meaning, and in many cases such knowledge is actually a hindrance.... Etymology is a valuable study, but we should not expect it to help us very much in understanding our mother tongue.[23]

Hence our concern with etymology of Chinese ideographs is simply to fix a starting point in meaning of present-day symbols so as to illucidate semantic change, if there has been any, and cultural drift, which expresses itself in these symbols.

Philology. — This is closer to our ken, though I am not qualified to make thorough philological studies of the symbol systems. Philology is simply the science of language, with an emphasis upon structure development. Those who have worked in this field, Cassirer, Humbolds, Vossler, have tried to "connect grammar with the state of civilization in general and of literature in particular, interpreting linguistic development and grammatical peculiarities in terms of national psychology."[24] The point of interest with us is that philology has attempted to ascertain "relations between the language of a race and its culture and mental characteristics."[25]

---

19 Gleason, *An Introduction...*, p. 3.

20 Etymology, *Encyclopaedia Britannica*, 17th ed., Vol. VIII. (Cited hereafter as EB.)

21 *Ibid.*

22 *Ibid.*

23 E. H. Sturtevant, *Linguistic Change* (Chicago: The University of Chicago Press, Phoenix Edition, 1961), pp. 97, 98.

24 "Philology," *EB*, Vol. XVII.

25 *Ibid.*

Relation of language to culture

Edward Sapir formulated a general principle covering the relationship of culture and language back in 1921. He said:

> The relation between language and experience is often misunderstood ... Language does not just catalogue what happens to us, but is also a self-contained creative symbolic organization, which not only refers to experience acquired without its help, but actually defines experience for us by reason of its formal completeness of our unconscious projections of its implicit expectations into the field of experience.[26]

This paragraph is basic to my whole approach. What it says is that language is not merely an indifferent mechanism for cataloguing men's experience but the language itself affects the cataloguing process. Thus, not only does language reflect a culture and its development but it is conceivable that language colors one's universe.

Sapir's principle was elaborated and developed by his pupil Benjamin Whorf who said, "language constitutes a sort of logic, a general frame of reference, and so molds the thought of its habitual users."[27]

But these linguists are not asserting that *language form* is an index to cultural thinking. Neither shall we in our pursuit of Japanese cultural thinking infer peculiar Japanese psychological qualities or cultural patterns from the syntactical character — absence of pronouns, use of honorifics, etc. — of the Japanese language. Sapir stated bluntly that mere "form of a language" has no connection with national temperament:

> It is impossible to show that *form of a language* [italics mine] has the slightest connection with national temperament.... I am convinced that it is futile to look in linguistic structure for differences corresponding to the temperamental variations which are supposed to be correlated with race... In this connection it is well to remember that the emotional aspect of our physical life is but meagerly expressed in the build of a language... When it comes to linguistic form, Plato walks with the Macedonian swineherd, and Confucius with the head-hunting savage of Assam.[28]

If these conclusions are valid, and I believe they are with minor modifications, then Nakamura's approach in understanding Japanese ways of thinking is freighted with difficulties. Max Mueller's view, *viz.*, that language tyrannized culture and men's thinking is also cast in critical light. Landar summarizes Mueller's views:

> When men of a certain culture framed a religious theory, he [Max Mueller] thought their language marked the system of ideas with deterministic finality. Hence to know the Indo-European religion, one had to study the meanings of the reconstructed roots.[29]

Durkheim countered Mueller, saying,

> Language is not merely the external covering of a thought; it is also its internal

---

26 Edwin Sapir, cited by Paul Henle, (ed.) *Language, Thought, and Culture* (Ann Arbor: The University of Michigan Press, 1965), p. 1.

27 *Ibid.*, p. 1.

28 Sapir, *Language*, pp. 217-219.

29 Herbert Landar, *Language and Culture* (New York: Oxford University Press, 1966), p. 230.

framework. It does not confine itself to expressing this thought after it has once been formed; it also aids in making it.[30]

What contemporary linguists are saying is that the language system of each culture is a fluid factor in culture; it varies with each generation and serves as a clue to its thinking as well as actually coloring and molding this thinking. Whorf says:

> We dissect nature along lines laid down by our native language. The categories and types that we isolate from the world of phenomena we do not find there because they stare every observer in the face. We cut nature up, organize it into concepts, and ascribe significance as we do, largely because we are parties to an agreement to organize it in this way — an agreement that holds throughout our speech community and is codified in the patterns of our language.[31]

There are formidable linguists who do find some relation of language form to cultural thinking. Hoijer detected in the verbal forms of the Navaho language a clue to Indian thinking. He noted, for instance, that the idea of "position" is rendered by words which mean "withdrawal of motion." Thus he makes the following cultural inference: "The Navaho are fundamentally a wandering, nomadic folk, following their flocks from one pasturage to another."[32] That is, to the Navaho the only way to conceive the idea of "stationary" or "position" is to think of a cessation of wanderings. From this the cultural linguist (philologist), without any knowledge of Navaho culture, could assume that the Navahos are a nomadic people. I am impressed with this type of reasoning until I attempt to apply the principle to Japanese language and culture. For instance, Nakamura concludes a peculiar cultural type of Japanese thinking from the use of honorifics in the language. The honorific "o" is attached to such common things as water or tea or stomach (*omizu, ocha, onaka,* resp.). Of this he says:

> Probably there is no other nation on earth that uses an honorific expression prefixed to the names of everyday objects.... We should not regard it merely as an honorific expression but rather consider it as a manifestation of the way of thinking that seeks a raison d'etre and sacredness in everything that exists.[33]

Such thinking might have existed when these honorifics were first attached to common objects, but it would be a fallacious deduction to assume that such Shintō philosophy is a general concept today. The word for "tea" in common parlance is *ocha*; to ask for *"cha"* (leaving off the honorific), would be asking someone to bring something of the *color* of tea; *omizu* today is "drinking water," distinguished from *mizu*, plain water. *Onaka* is simply stomach; to complain to a doctor that one's *naka* is in pain would be a meaningless expression. Similarly, Yamagiwa, finds in the levels of usage of Japanese (honorific, polite, ordinary, and humble forms) a pointer to a stratified society. He says:

---

30 Quoted by Landar, p. 230.
31 Quoted by Joseph Bram, *Short Studies in Sociology*, No. 8 (New York: Doubleday, 1955), p. 24.
32 Henle, p. 22.
33 Nakamura, p. 360.

Undeniably spoken Japanese has traditionally contained a great wealth of expressions which denote relative social position... Every expression made by one person to another automatically sets the speaker in a relationship to the second as being superior, inferior, or equal...[34]

Yamagiwa feels that Nakamura infers too much from this peculiar tendency of the Japanese but he generally follows the linguistic principle that structural form of a language gives a clue to cultural thinking. But it appears to me as just a cultural reading into the language what one has learned on other grounds. This interplay of honorifics, polite and ordinary forms actually makes it clear who is the subject and who is the object in each sentence without the use of pronouns. The use of pronouns in the Japanese language did not come in vogue until the Meiji era and even today such usage makes the language seem stilted and unnatural. The honorifics and the interplay of the verb forms make Japanese sentences capable of running at great length, without periods or stops; no one is ever confused as to who is doing the acting, though such equivalent words as "I, he, you" never appear. It probably never occurs to Japanese children learning their own language that the involved form of "you read" (*oyomi ni naru*) is honorific, while the shortened form "I read" (*yomimasu*) is humble. He probably just learns that the long form means the other person reads, while the short form means he himself reads, thus eliminating pronouns.

Rather, I would find it safer to approach cultural thinking through the *meaning* of language. Henle says: "Shared concepts are the meanings expressed in the common language. To learn a language involves forming the concepts expressed by it."[35] That is, peculiar cultural concepts lie submerged beneath the external symbol system. These serve as guardians or preservers of values from one generation to another. Thus we are warranted in first analyzing a particular language, for within it many clusters of words and synonymous phrases will give traces of cultural concepts. Walloch says:

If the concepts we have influence our perception, then the possession of a given language determines, to some extent, at least, what kind of a world we perceive around us... One key to the concepts which are shared by the members of a given culture is the common language used by them, and we can take changes in their languages as evidence(though perhaps not conclusive proof) of changes in the concepts they share.[36]

Searching for Core Concepts

Having fixed our destination—cultural thinking revealed through language meaning—we set sail across a sea of Japanese words, phrases, idioms, colloquial expressions, proverbial sayings. We crossed the sea the average Japanese man traverses in his daily social interactions. There being such a vast expanse of

---

34 Joseph K. Yamagiwa, "Language as an Expression of Japanese Culture," *Twelve Doors to Japan*, (ed.) John W. Hall and Richard Beardsley (New York: McGraw-Hill Book Company, 1965), p. 205.

35 Henle, p. 40.

36 Quoted by Henle, p. 41.

lexical data, we first attempted to group this sea of words into smaller oceans, 222 of them to be exact, which we called *General Thought Categories*.[37] At this point our procedure can be challenged; for we made *a priori* selections of *Thought Categories* of human experience from accepted Western sources. This then could be a reading back into the Japanese language a general concept held in the West. To this I answer that (1) such a process served as temporary means for categorising the lexical data, (2) some Western categories simply did not fill up with Japanese expressions and were eliminated, (3) new categories were added, such as "Resignation," for expressions of this concept piled up for which we had no category selected, (4) we form no conclusions through simple groupings of the words and phrases, but examine the core word of the category alone. That is, so many expressions gathered under the core word "love," that we are warranted in analyzing the word "love" to determine the Japanese concepts of love.

Such categories, to change the metaphor, become stars around which idiomatic and colloquial expressions orbit. In syntax, in Chinese character relationship, in word order, they appear superficially as unrelated comets whirling about the Japanese mind. But on closer scrutiny, they line up in meaningful order, honed to general concepts, orbiting around in such a way as to evidence an important Japanese sentiment. These word clusters with their slight nuances give clues to concepts that have grown out of the cumulative experience of the group. Thus we may be on objective ground; what Japanese poets and writers have said about the Japanese in the past may represent what only a segment of society believes. In fact, the Japanese literary tradition until the Tokugawa period was largely an aristocratic, court-centered tradition. We know little of the common man, save the glimpses afforded us by the courtiers peering out through castle windows. Because the Japanese have historically adopted Buddhism and Confucianism as national religions, we may be going beyond the bounds of scholarship to piece together Japanese thinking by an examination of cardinal doctrines of either of those religious systems. This will be discussed more fully below; my only point is that concepts derived from the common language of the people are those accepted by the majority.

But having localized these concepts by separating the sea of verbal symbols into smaller oceans and rendering these Japanese words into their nearest English equivalents by no means insures us that we have truly discovered general concepts or understood them. For our English words are symbols of English concepts and we may be simply transferring English concepts to Japanese verbal symbols. Alas, this is the common experience of most Japan missionaries (including myself); after learning a few Japanese equivalents for "righteousness" (*gi*), "sin" (*tsumi*), "God" (*kami*), we employ these words in Japanese sentences only to discover that the concepts these symbols express have made little impression upon Japanese thinking. For the Japanese verbal symbols were all the while orbiting around essentially Japanese concepts. How then can we go about an accurate search for the truly Japanese concepts

---

37 Full list of Japanese-English General Thought Categories will be found in the companion volume, *Handbook of Japanese-English Idiomatic Equivalents*.

which the verbal systems express? One method suggested by linguists, including Susumu Ōno as well as Henle, Sturtevant, and Bloomfield, is to observe the *semantic change* of a verbal symbol in different periods of cultural history.

But what is *semantic change*? Somehow, as Sturtevant points out, the meaning of a particular word symbol is given it by convention.[38] And this "convention" is an ever-changing phenomenon of human life. Our main interest will be in this area of linguistic analysis — the semantic change within the Japanese symbol system. All to the end that we may piece together the concepts of the average Japanese man. Bloomfield says that semantic change within a word symbol comes about in two ways: (1) expansion and obsolescences, and (2) cultural borrowing. By expansion and obsolescences, we mean that a word becomes used in one situation more and in another less. This affects its predominant meaning element. "The circumstances under which a word is used very often lead to a change of the predominant element in its meaning... a change of customs or environment sometimes makes a shift in emphasis inevitable."[39] Bloomfield expresses it:

> There is the dominant meaning element in a word which may shift to new situations by usage ... A semantic change then is a complex process. It involves favorings and disfavorings and as its crucial point, the extension of a favored form into practical applications which hitherto belonged to the disfavored form.[40]

Sturtevant's rule for this semantic change, that "the decrease in the logical content of the word involved an increase in its range of applicability,"[41] is what we will discover in use of Chinese ideographs and indigenous Japanese words. For example, the word for "time" (*jikan*), whose Chinese ideograph reveals the concept of the sun in motion, has finally developed into a range of meanings from time to season, occasion, the good time, and ephemerity of the world.

Cultural borrowing is the flow of ideas between cultures. "Cultural loans show us what one nation has taught another."[42] Bloomfield feels that cultural borrowing is normally a mutual thing, and is one-sided "only to the extent that one nation has more to give than another."[43] Waves of culture have been sweeping across Japan from prehistoric times; so much so that it is difficult to find within Japan's present psychological makeup that form of cultural behavior which makes him distinctly Japanese, as for example Confucianism sets off Chinese culture from all other cultures. Ōno gives the similar rule:

> When the opportunity arises for the structure of one word to come in contact with another word form, depending upon the weakness or strength of a culture, a change occurs in the language.... The word of the stronger culture is adapted into that of the weaker.[44]

---

[38] Sturtevant, p. 24.

[39] Sturtevant, p. 88.

[40] Bloomfield, p. 441.

[41] Sturtevant, p. 89.

[42] Bloomfield, p. 438.

[43] *Ibid.*, p. 461.

[44] Susumu Ōno, *Nihongo no Nenrin* (Tokyo: Yuki Shobō, 1960), p. 190.

Hence a semantic change from cultural contact gives significant clues to a people's thinking. For example, Ōno gives the illustration of the use of the word "sister" (*imōto*) in ancient times as a change of thinking regarding consanguineous marriage. The word can be traced to a cognate word in Polynesian, and prior to the introduction of Chinese culture into Japan, the word meant what it did in Hawaii, either, "sister" or "fiancée". Consanguineous marriage was practiced in both cultures at that time. However, after the introduction of Chinese culture in the Nara-Heian periods, with its frowning upon this custom, the superior Chinese culture effected a change in the semantic meaning of *imōto*. From then it was used to mean "sister" only; another word came to the fore to represent "fiancée".

This phenomenon of cultural borrowing is very marked in Japan, and as Ōno points out, Japan has consistently revealed a lack of confidence in her own developed culture to be a conveyer of new ideas. The newest fads or ideas in Japan today are usually introduced in Japanized foreign words. Meaningless English words, chosen over against Japanese words (perfectly capable of conveying the meaning) are mixed in Japanese advertisements. Ōno inveighs against this:

> It is because we Japanese have no confidence in our ability to create culture and have lost the ability to think on our own that we pride ourselves on something we have borrowed from others. If we do not develop our own culture with our own ability and power, the Japanese language will continue to be depreciated.[45]

Diagramming it, the thesis of this book says simply:

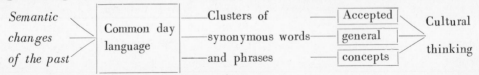

METHODOLOGY

Selection of words for analysis

From the General Thought Categories — Japanese-English list,[46] thirty-three topical words of the categories which pertain to the intellectual, emotional and religious aspects of Japanese experience were selected arbitrarily for analysis. Their counterparts in Greek and Hebrew were found and similarly examined within the Biblical context.

Chinese character etymology

By first presenting the findings of Japanese scholarship on the etymological studies of the Chinese ideographs employed for representing these topical words, we fix a point of reference for noticing semantic changes in Japan. That is, we set sail on our "semantic change" course from the most distant port conceivable. Since the Japanese people accepted these ideographs as representative of the meanings of their own words, or in some instances, actually

---

45 *Ibid.*
46 Found in *Handbook....*

imported Chinese characters with their words and concepts, we do have a beginning point for tracing semantic change. The *Kanjigogenjiten* (Etymological Dictionary of Chinese Characters), upon which we largely rely, draws upon the Sinologist Karlgren's work on archaic Chinese but also attempts to trace meanings to the eighth century A.D., the era of introduction into Japan. The meanings of the component parts as discovered by the editor Akiyasu Tōdō were probably not understood by the average Japanese but they may have been by the literary aristocrats of the time. What is germain to our study is that the meanings of characters did represent concepts of reality shared in common by both Chinese and Japanese — *the Oriental view*. Secondly, by the introduction of the characters with their meanings as understood by the Chinese transmitting and the Japanese receiving, these characters served to limit semantic change through the centuries. All findings in this section are given in English but are translations of Japanese sources. Any Japanese work cited in its Romanized title indicates that the work is not available in English.

Semantic changes in Japan

Earliest usage of the word in Japanese classical literature which I could detect in my sources is listed under this heading. Also information gleaned from personal interviews with Professor Ōno is given here. Again, these findings are presented in English but are my translations from Japanese sources.

Modern range of meaning

Main definitions or different usages of the word as listed in larger Japanese dictionaries are given here. Where there are one-word definitions, the Japanese equivalent will be given in parentheses, but where the definition is too long, only my English translations will be given.

English idiom parallels

These are culled from the lexical data of *Handbook of Japanese-English Idiomatic Equivalents*. They are listed to indicate the strikingly similar way both symbol systems have differentiated human experience.

Buddhist concepts

These findings are largely fom the new Japanese-English Buddhist Dictionary and serve to point out the religious significance (if any) of the words being discussed. By giving the Buddhist usage of the words and then comparing this with the modern range of meaning, it can be shown just how far Buddhism has affected Japanese thought. These findings are presented in English just as they appear in the Buddhist dictionary.

Biblical concepts

These are culled from the English sources indicated. Semantic changes of Greek and Hebrew words within the Biblical record are not traced; rather, following the work of the contributing scholars of Kittel's *Theological Dictionary of the New Testament*, we will observe how the Bible itself generates a semantic change upon words introduced from surrounding cultures.

Encounter

This is where Biblical and Japanese concepts collide. Clues for determining Japanese concepts of human experience were provided from the word meanings of the symbols examined, after having undergone centuries of semantic change and sifting into the modern vernacular. Just what ramifications such cultural thought plays upon Japanese life I have illustrated from personal observation.

CHAPTER I
CONCEPTS OF INTELLECTUAL EXPERIENCE

TIME 時間 *JIKAN*

Japanese Concepts of Time

Chinese character etymology

Jikan is comprised of two characters: 時 (time) and 間 (segment), hence *segment of time. Ji* has two components, but it is not agreed as to what these actually signified. *KGJ*: "two components are 'sun' and 'walking feet', hence the concept of the sun walking past the observer or the day in motion." *KGJ* quotes a Confucian work: "Time is quickly hastening on day and night."[1] *KCJ* finds within the earliest form of *ji* two possible concepts: (1) the sun stopped, or (2) an eagle in flight.[2]

Semantic changes in Japan

During the Nara-Heian periods Buddhist thought and the fleeting fortunes of the nobility brought the concept of the "ephemerity of the world" into the word. The world and its splendor was fast moving on and fading; hence time could be a synonymous expression for the *world* (世). Not all was pessimism however, for the *man of the hour (toki no hito)* was the man who seized present opportunities and became prosperous. However, his situation was tenuous at best; in the *Kokkinshū* (A.D. 905), the warning appears: "The man of the hour may suddenly fall into ruin."[3]

Modern range of meaning

KCJ: (1) that which flows from eternity to eternity, (2) segment of time, (3) measurement of time, i.e., seconds, minutes, hours, (4) four seasons of the year, (5) occasion (*ori*), (6) period of history, (7) particular time, (8) this, that, (9) philosophically, the total length of time commencing before history and continuing to its end.

GS: (1) passing of days and months, (2) time of day, (3) epoch of history, (4) season of the year, (5) chance, (6) that occasion, that moment, (7) good chance, (8) ephemerity of the world.

---

[1] *Kanjigogenjiten* (Etymological Dictionary of Chinese Characters), ed. Akiyasu Tōdō, (Tokyo: Gakutōsha, 1965), p. 73. [Cited hereafter as *KGJ*.]

[2] *Kanwachūjiten* (Chinese-Japanese Medium Dictionary), ed. Shigeki Kajitsuka, Iwatomo Fujino, and Shinobu Ono (Tokyo: Kadokawa Shoten, 1965). [Cited hereafter as *KCJ*.]

[3] *Gensen* (Spring of Words), ed. Naobumi Ochiai (5 vols., 2nd rev.; Tokyo: Okura Shoten, 1927), IV, 3118. [Cited hereafter as *GS*.]

DGK: (1) passing of time, (2) division of twenty-four hour day, (3) the age, (4) opportunity, (5) good time.[4]

KJ: (1) passing of days and months, (2) time of day, (3) the age, (4) that time, the right time, (5) ephemerity of the world, (6) proper time for succeeding.[5]

English idiom parallels

It can't be done in a day (*Itchō isseki ni... nai*). It's a matter of time (*jikan no mondai*). Time is precious (*Ikkoku senkin*). Time is money (*Toki wa kane nari*). Time waits for no man (*Saigetsu hito o matazu*).

Biblical Concepts of Time

Old Testament concepts

Hebrew concepts of time were more qualitative than quantitative. The word for "hour" (*shea*) does not occur until Daniel 4:33, and this is an Aramaic loan word. The sun dial of Ahaz (II Kings 20:9) indicates some division of the day into segments. The word for "day" (*yom*) is ambiguous, sometimes denoting an indefinite period of time (Gen. 2:4), sometimes a twenty-four hour day, from sunset to sunset. Months were lunar, similar to the Japanese present-day system, e.g., 1st month, 2nd month, etc., beginning with the appearance of the new moon and named by numbers (Jer. 36:9 39:2). What happened in a particular time or month was more important to the Hebrew than their chronological aspects. Hence we find the expressions "the month of ripening ears," "the month of rain," "the month of streams." Time is a period of fulfillment. To everything there is a right season (*eth*), provided for man by God, the Lord of time, and it behooves man to make good use of this opportunity. Natural events are of His ordaining. He gives rain (Deut. 11:14), harvests (Hos. 2:11), feeds creatures (Psa. 104:27). So when man responds to these times he is in effect responding to God. Thus history is not a fortuitous aggregation of events but a series of times with significant content, ordained of God and demanding man's response (Isa. 44:24-28, Deut. 30:19). Nature and history are endowed by God with rich content, for He is active in and through them (Psa. 31:15). Judgments come into history at the appointed times. Thus should men pray at the right time (Psa. 32:6, 69:13, Isa. 49:8). Forgiveness and restoration come as the consumation of history. The "day of the Lord" is precursor to this, in which God's intervention in history is paramount (Lam. 2:1, Isa. 61:2, Psalm 110:3). Marsh sums up the *OT* view of time:

---

4 *Daigenkai*, (Great Sea of Words), ed. Fumihiko Ōshiki (2nd ed. rev.; Tokyo: Toyama Sho, 1956). [Cited hereafter as *DGK*.]

5 *Kojien*, (Large Garden Dictionary), ed. Izuru Shimmura (17th ed. rev.; Tokyo: Iwanami Shoten, 1965), [Cited hereafter as *KJ*.]

The various words used for time in the OT are thus seen to express a view of history as made up of various times which are God's appointment. Their content may be varied but ultimately all times belong to Him and serve His purposes. Man experiences times of God's anger and judgment and times of His mercy and favor.[6]

New Testament concepts

The *NT* employs more words for time than the *OT*. It sustains the *OT* concepts that time is synonomous with opportunity vouchsafed to men by the Lord of time but also reckons with the scientific aspects of time units and chronological divisions. *Chronos* is measured time, duration. It may be long (Acts 13:18) or short (Luke 4:5). More important is *kairos*, the time of opportunity and fulfillment. Man's supreme opportunity, his *kairos*, came simultaneously with the coming of Christ (Mark 1:15, Luke 4:21). To accept the revelation of God in Christ in this *kairos* is salvation; to let the occasion slip by is inviting disaster. Contrary to the religious leaders who could not discern the *kairos* (Matt. 16:3, Luke 12:56), the Christians were characterized as those sensitive to it and apprised of its momentous implications (Rom. 13:11, Eph. 5:16, Col. 4:5). Hence history to the NT writers was a series of *kairois* or opportunities for man to respond to the activity of God. Beyond history and eternal in its significance was the *aion*.[7] Participation in the *aion* is qualified by man's obedience in the *kairos* (John 5:24, Rom. 8:18, I Pet. 1:4, 11, Heb. 12:28).

Other words, such as "hitherto," "henceforward," reveal the NT writers' view that history has been once for all divided by the Incarnation. They were living in the momentous "now," the hour (*hora*) (John 7:30, 8:20, 12:23, 13:1). The word *oikonomia*, tr. "dispensation" in the King James, really means an *economy*, but has a time significance in Eph. 1:10, 3:2. It has been used as a basis for dividing history into arbitary compartments, but this is importing more into the word than is there. Marsh adds:

> The word translates the Gk. word "economy," and is plainly a metaphor, expressing the belief that the *kairoi* that constitute history are part of God's economy or stewarding of the world by which the Divine purposes are effected.[8]

Encounter

Japanese thinking on time is more quantitative than qualitative, laying emphasis upon the chronological movement of the sun. Days move swiftly on as a man walking through the world. Supratemporal concepts have seeped into the modern range of meaning, but again this is just extended duration. The opportunity concept (*ori*), similar to the Hebrew *eth* and the Gk. *kairos*, is there, but this seems more a ripe opportunity for quick gain and material success rather than a response to an activity of God leading to salvation and

---

6 John Marsh, "Time," *A Theological Word Book of the Bible*, ed. Alan Richardson (New York: The Macmillan Co., 1950), p. 261. [Cited herafter as *TWBB*.]

7 Discussed more fully under "Eternity," pp. 37-40.

8 Marsh, *TWBB*, p. 264.

participation in the next *aion*. Sekine Masao has devoted an entire chapter to this divergence of thinking on time and sums up the Japanese view:

> Over all, we may say that the European or Greek concept of time was quantitative and chronological. The Hebrew concept is one of quality and content... The Japanese concept borders on the European concept.[9]

Marsh sums up the Biblical view:

> Once more we see that the Biblical conception of time is not that of evolution or progress, or even of chronological succession; it is at bottom one of promise and fulfillment, in which history consists of times bringing opportunities, the basic time and the decisive opportunity being that of the coming of Jesus Christ, in whom all the promises of God, prophetic and historical are yea, Amen.[10]

---

9 Sekine Masao, *Israerubito no Shisō to Sono Gengo* (The Thinking of the Israelites and Their Language), (Tokyo: Iwanami Shoten, 1958), p. 288.

10 Marsh, *TWBB*, p. 263.

BEGINNING 始 HAJIME

Japanese Concepts of Beginning

Chinese character etymology

Hajime is comprised of one character having two components: 女 (woman), and 台 (womb). *KGJ* sees earliest concept of beginning as (1) lineage originating from woman's womb, or (2) child formed in the womb begins family line. *KCJ* takes same view; life is first born from woman. Gradually the character came to mean simply *beginning*.

Semantic changes in Japan

No significant changes are noted in Nara-Heian periods. In the work *Yoshi Hogen* we find, "Whatever *begins* must end."[1] In the *Kojiki*, "When heaven and earth *began*."[2] Ōno finds a phonetic similarity with *haji* (edge); the beginning is that which begins at the edge.

Modern range of meaning

KCJ: (1) the beginning (*hajime*), (2) begin something (*hajimeru koto*), (3) basis, foundation, source (*moto, okori*), (4) foremost, chief (*hajimete*).

DNKJ: (1) begin something (*kaishi suru*), (2) make chief or prominent (*shu to suru*), (3) make first in order of importance (*daiichi ni suru*), (4) base, foundation (*moto*).[3]

KJ: (1) begin something (*hajimeru koto*), (2) origin, source (*okori*), (3) root, basis (*kongen*), (4) ahead, in front (*saki*), (5) first in order (*koto no shidai*).

English idiom parallels

Start over again with a clean slate (*hakushi ni kaesu*). Start over again from scratch (*shinki maki naoshi*). Start (*sutaruto*).

Biblical Concepts of Beginning

Old Testament concepts

Hebrew word *reshith* is used (1) to refer to some point of time in the distant past (Gen. 1:1), (2) to indicate an inauguration of a particular event

---

1 *GS*, IV, 3628.

2 *DGK*, p. 1579.

3 *Dainihonkokugo jiten*, (Great National Language Dictionary of Japan) ed. Mannen Ueda and Kanji Matsui (11 ed.: Tokyo: Fusanbo, 1956). [Cited hereafter as *DNKJ*.]

(Ex. 12:2), (3) of a headstone (Zech. 4:7), (4) as the foremost (Gen. 33:2, Esth. 1:14), (5) to indicate something former, like prophecies (Jer. 42:9).

New Testament concepts

Chief word is *arche*. In Gk. usage it denoted primacy, either in time or rank, and so its cognates express *rule*, such as *archo*, and *archaios*. In the temporal sense it denoted "the place in a temporal sequence at which something now which is also finite commences."[4] Gk. philosophic thought had a concept of boundlessness, summed up in the word *apeiron*. Everything proceeded from and led back to it. "All occurrence which can be measured in time is simply falling off from the *apeiron*.[5] This was the cyclical concept of time and against it stood the concept of *arche*, which more than temporal beginning denoted the "original material from which everything has evolved."[6] To express this concept *stoicheion* later came to the fore, appearing in the NT in Gal. 4:9, tr. "beggarly elements" in *KJV*, but "beggarly spirits of the elements" in the New English Bible. Both words served as symbols for the "fundamental laws which control the evolution of the world in great things and small."[7]

In the NT, *arche* is used to denote (1) the first point of time, according to context, whether of (a) creation (Heb. 1:10, Mt. 19:4, II Pet. 3:4), (b) first appearing of Christ (Luke 1:2, John 15:27), (c) first beginning of being a Christian (I John 2:24, II John 5:6). The point of beginning is not always clear. It can mean from birth or from all ages. In I John 3:8, the devil is the subject, hence it probably means *from all ages*, not implying eternity but existence prior to earthly time. In John 1:1 *arche* is used anarthrously of *logos*, speaking of Him who is before time. Used in this qualitative way, *arche* denotes the primacy and eternity of Christ. Delling says:

> With reference to Christ, this includes the assertion of eternity, for that which or He who was from all ages can only be that which or He who is included in the being of God. This gives us preexistence in the strict sense.[8]

Reference should be made to the phrase "I am Alpha and Omega, the beginning and the ending" found in Rev. 1:8, 21:6, *et passim*. It emphasizes that God or Christ is both initiator and consummator, having its root concepts in the *OT*, e.g., "I am the first and I am the last, and beside me there is no God" (Isa. 41:4, 44:6).

Encounter

The concept of beginning as being synonomous with source has been preserved in the Japanese word *Hajime*. But this source cannot be traced much beyond

---

4 Gerhard Delling, *"arche" Theological Dictionary of the New Testament*, ed. Gerhard Kittel, trans. Geoffrey Bromiley (Grand Rapids: Wm. B. Eerdmans Publishing Co., 1964), I, 479. [Cited hereafter as *TDNT*.]

5 *Ibid.*

6 *Ibid.*, p. 480.

7 *Ibid.*, p. 480.

8 *Ibid.*, p. 482.

man. The Chinese character also points to "beginning" as being *man's* beginning. The concept that the beginning is also chief or superior may stem from
the Confucian thought that the ideal or pristine lies in the primordial past.
This seeps through into present Japanese society; the *nempai* (predecessors)
are usually elected to office regardless of ability, a custom prevailing from
student clubs continuing right through business structures. The literal meaning
for teacher (*sensei*) is *one born before*. This same concept is found in the
cognates for *arche*, e.g., *archaios* is the ruler. Important divergent thought
is that the Bible rejects any cyclical view of time found in Gk. philosophy
(*apeiron*) or Buddhist transitory views (*mujō*). The Bible posits a historical
beginning in time of events and persons with God as the inaugurator. When
arche is applied to God or Christ, it loses its historical nuance but thrusts
origins and beginnings into supratemporal and qualitative concepts which transcend human thought.

END 終 OWARI

Japanese Concepts of End

Chinese character etymology

Owari is comprised of one character having two components: 糸 (thread), and 冬 (winter). *KGJ* sees the concept of bringing threads together, making them complete and full. *KGJ* quotes from *Shokyo*, "There is nothing that has no beginning but only a few things *end* well."[1] Hence emphasis is not on chronological ending but on completion. *KCJ* sees three ideas in the character: (1) making a knot on the end of a thread, (2) tying a knot and cutting the thread, (3) complete or bring to an end.

Semantic changes in Japan

Owari is found in classical literature in the sense of *to die*. The *Ujishui Monogatari* (A.D. 1213-1221) has the phrase, "He made a beautiful end" [to his life].[2]

Modern range of meaning

KCJ: (1) end, exhaust (*owaru, tsukiru*), (2) complete (*oeru*), (3) finally (*tsui ni*), (4) go to the extreme or limit (*kiwamaru*), (5) die (*shinu*), (6) become (*naru*), (7) get full (*michiru*).

DNKJ: (1) finish (*owaru koto*), (2) limit (*kagiri*), (3) die (*shinu koto*), (4) last period or stage (*makki*).

KJ: (1) finish (*owaru*), (2) limit (*hate*), (3) die (*shinu*), (4) end time (*makki*).

Buddhist concepts

Of significance to our study is the concept of the last age of Buddhist law, rendered in the word *mappō* (end law), tr. of the Sanskrit *saddharma-vipralopa*. This is the last of the three periods in Buddhist philosophy, the first being *shōbō*, "the period when Buddhist doctrines, practices, and enlightenment all exist."[3] Second period is called *zōbō*, the "period of imitative law... when both doctrine and practices still exist, but there is no longer any enlightenment.

---

1 *KGJ*, p. 179.

2 *DGK*, p. 2207.

3 *Japanese-English Buddhist Dictionary* (Tokyo: Daitō Shuppansha, 1965), p. 299. [Cited hereafter as *BD*.]

That is why it is called the imitation of the law."[4] *Mappō*, the third period, is the time when "doctrine alone is still alive, but there is neither practice nor enlightenment. After these periods, the doctrine itself vanishes."[5] *Mappō* is uniformly agreed upon as lasting 10,000 years, but there are four views of the duration of the first two periods, ranging from 500 to 1000 years each.[6] The word is found in Japanese literature, not so much denoting *last law period* but rather the end of the world, ushered in by national disasters. *DNKJ* quotes the phrase, "Certainly this is the sign that the end of the world has come."[7] Ōno stresses that this apprehension was common in the Heian period, especially when calamities struck the imperial court. It went hand in hand with the concept of the impermanence of all things (*shogyō mujō*), both terms appearing in the *Tale of Heike* (*Heike Monogatari*, 13th century).[8]

Biblical Concepts of End

Old Testament concepts

Key Hebrew words for *end* are *kes*, *ephes*, and *kalah*. Their emphasis is upon final object or purpose, but they are used to denote the following: (1) cessation, (2) final period, (3) outcome. But in all of these the emphasis is that God grants the end; it is His doing. Cessation may be of life (Psa. 39:4), of a people (Amos 8:2), or of the world (Gen. 6:13). But God effects or permits these ends. He is seen as the Lord of history, declaring the end from the beginning (Isa. 46:10).

New Testament concepts

Gk. symbol is *eschatos* denoting the last of something: (1) in order (Matt. 5:26, Luke 12:59), (2) in space (Acts 1:8, 13:47), or (3) time (Matt. 12:45, 20:8, II Pet. 2:20). It is used in I Cor. 15:8 to describe the *last* resurrection appearance to Paul. The "end times" concept, which was poured into the word giving it the "eschatalogical" nuance, grew from the OT teaching on the Day of Jehovah. NT writers, especially Paul, saw that the Messianic age had dawned, that upon the first century Christians the end of the ages had come (I Cor. 10:11). This *end* began when Jesus came (Heb. 1:2, I Pet. 2:20), and is characterized by hostility to God's revelation in Christ (II Tim. 3:1-4, James 5:3, II Pet. 3:3) and the work of the Spirit (Acts 2:17). Though participating in this obsolete age, Christians are equally citizens of the new era—the age to come (Matt. 13:39, 40, 49). They are forewarned about the last day of this *aion* as being marked by *last* plagues (Rev. 15:1, 21:9), the overthrow of the *last* enemy (I Cor. 15:26), and the sound of the *last* trumpet (I Cor. 15:52). Thus the NT

---

4 *Ibid.*

5 *Ibid.*

6 *Ibid.*

7 *DNKJ*, p. 2370.

8 *DNKJ*, p. 2370.

end is not merely the termination of a sequence of events but a grand finale towards which God shapes history. Its final aspects are those in which death, judgment, and victory are resolved by the appearing of Christ.

Encounter

The sense of completion in *owari* is akin to the Biblical concept of completion, but there is not a hint of external forces impinging upon history to effect this. Buddhist *mappō* and Biblical *eschatos* essentially have nothing in common, though usage during the Nara-Heian periods invested the concept of calamity into *mappō* which is contextually present in *eschatos*. However, the decisive difference lies in the contents of both these ends. *Mappō* is the time of pure law, without practice nor enlightenment; *eschatos* is the time of God's active intervention in history to effect His purposes for man. It is probable that this confusion of *mappō* with *eschatos* in Japan has vitiated thorough treatment of the subject by Japanese pastors, for the Biblical translation of *eschatos* into *yo no sue* (end of the world) employed the same character found in *mappō*. This would certainly conjure up Buddhist philosophical complexities and unhistoricity to the man on the street and not lend to the distinctiveness of the Christian message.[9]

---

9 Newer translations are correcting the problem by employing *owari* instead of *sue*.

ETERNITY 永 遠 *EIEN*

Japanese Concepts of Eternity

Chinese character etymology

Eien is comprised of two characters: 永 (long), and 遠 (far). *KGJ* finds in 永 (long) components of "water" and "river, "hence two rivers flowing into one another and getting increasingly wider. *Shikyo*: "The *length* of the river."[1]

Semantic changes in Japan

Indigenous Japanese word for "eternity" is *tokoshie*, having no equivalent Chinese characters for it. Ōno sees within the word two concepts: (1) "upon" (*no ue*), and (2) "river bed" (*toko*). A rock fixed in a river bed is permanent in contrast to the flowing stream. Hence the concept is not so much temporal but "changeless," "everlasting."

Modern range of meaning

DGK: without a change.
DNKJ: changeless.

English idiom parallels

Lasting peace (*eien no heiwa*). Eternal life (*eien no inochi*). Semi-permanent (*han'eikyūteki*). No end to (*kiri ga nai*). Infinity (*mugen*).

Buddhist concepts

The concept of "eternity" or "changelessness" runs counter to the key Buddhist concept of *mujō* (impermanence), tr. of the Sk. *anitya*. *BD*: "Everything in the world arises, changes, and perishes; nothing remains constant for even a single moment."[2] Supratemporal concepts are revealed in the phrase *"ichinen-mannen,"* which *BD* translates as "In one moment is an eternity.[3]

Biblical Concepts of Eternity

Old Testament concepts

Key Hebrew word for "eternity" is *olam*, used by the prophets to describe God as being above the limits of time. His love is everlasting (Jer. 31:3), as

---

1 *KGJ*, p. 416.
2 *BD*, p. 202.
3 *Ibid.*, p. 125.

are His covenant (Jer. 32:40), His righteousness (Isa. 51:6), His salvation (Isa. 45:17), and His word (Isa. 40:8). Mortality is the mark of man, everlasting-ness that of God (Zech. 1:5). The prophets metaphorically attempt to describe eternity of God with this as an adjective (Isa. 26:4, Psa. 90:2).

New Testament concepts

Gk. word is (*aion*), having the following range of meaning in the NT: (1) a long time, in the past or future (John 9:32, 6:51), (2) a segment of time, as (a) the present (Matt. 12:32), or (b) the future (Luke 20:35), (3) the world as a spatial concept (Heb. 1:2), (4) a person (Col. 1:26, Eph. 2:2, 3:9).[4] Aristotle held the view that the *aion* was "a relative period of time allotted to each specific thing."[5] The word had a cultic significance in the Hellenistic age by "virtue of the fact that *Aion* becomes the name of a god of eternity whose mysteries are known to have been celebrated in Alexandria from 200 B.C.[6] This personification of *Aion*, Sasse sees in Eph. 2:2. He also suggests that the concept of recurring aeons — the sense of transition from one aeon to the other, with the thought of eternal recurrence — was derived from Babylonian or Orien-tal astrology, and though it may have affected the Septuagint translators' use of plural *aiones* instead of singular *aion* for *olam*, it is a concept foreign to the Bible. He says:

> This understanding is contrary to the Biblical doctrine of time and eternity. The idea of eternal recurrence cannot be united with the understanding of the creation and end of the world as absolute beginning and absolute conclusion.[7]

This concept, says Sasse, comes from a "confusion of God and the world, of eternity and time."[8]

The NT consistently casts God and His revelation in a supratemporal mold, seeing beyond history a purpose transcending history but active and latent within it (Eph. 3:9, Col. 1:26, Rev. 13:8). Paul insists that Christian believers are sharers in the *aion* to come, which *aion* was inaugurated by the resurrection of Christ. Eternal life in the NT is one of quality, not quantity. Marsh ex-presses it: "So the eternal in the NT is not an uncharacterized duration; it is a filled magnitude."[9] Temporal boundaries of life do not cramp or curb it. Life in Christ brings with it an eternal dimension (John 4:14, 8:51, 10:28, 11:26, 17:3).

Encounter

Japanese concepts of eternity denote long duration and changelessness. Diametrically opposed to this is the Buddhist doctrine of *mujō* (impermanence

---

4 *A Greek-English Lexicon of the New Testament*, ed. William F. Arndt and F. Wilbur Gingrich (Chicago: The University of Chicago Press, 1957). [Cited hereafter as *Arnt*.]

5 Hermann Sasse, "*aion*," "*TDNT*, I, 198.

6 *Ibid.*

7 *Ibid.*, p. 205.

8 *Ibid.*

9 John Marsh, "Time," *TWBB*, p. 267.

or constant change). Sasse attributes this to an identification of the divine with nature. Here may be a clue to a basic difference in Japanese and English thinking. If the ultimate in Japanese thinking is trapped within the nexus of the microcosm, and by observation phenomena and nature appear to be in constant flux, then the Japanese absolute must be characterized by im-permanence. Eternity, then, at best is long, like the wide river seen in the Chinese ideograph. The Bible places God and those united to Him by faith in an eternal milieu, an eternity which more than duration or changelessness is a transcendent dimension, beyond the bounds of time.

REALITY 現 実 *GENJITSU*

Japanese Concepts of Reality

Chinese character etymology

Genjitsu is comprised of two characters: 現 (phenomena, that which appears), and 實 (full, fruit). *Gen* has two components: 見 (see), and 王 (jewel). *KGJ*: concept of light streaming from a jewel. Something hidden to assume form and appear before the eyes; a phenomenological appearing. *Jitsu* has three components: 宀 (house), 毋 (field), and 貝 (shell). *KGJ*: concept of storing possessions under one's roof, hence "full." The man who is "*jitsu*" is a person with much learning and culture. *KCJ* traces *jitsu* to the same concept of "abundant" or "full."

Semantic changes in Japan

DGK finds the word *jitsu* used in classical literature in the sense of "one's *true* parents," "one's *true* self" (in contrast to one's name), e.g., "Cast off your name and become the actual (*jitsu*) person."[1] Used also to designate the hero or good person in a play.

Modern range of meaning

DGK: (1) that which presently appears, (2) the actual facts or situation (in contrast with the ideal).

GS: (1) status quo (*genzai no mama naru koto*), (2) actual existence (*gen ni sonzai suru koto*), (3) real existence (*jitsuzai*), (4) that which appears, either fact or situation (as against theory).

KJ: (1) that which is truly existent, (2) the concrete or objective situation, (3) that which is practically effected.

English idiom parallels

Be in accordance with the facts (*jissai ni sokushite*), Down to earth (*jissaiteki*). Be unrealistic (*jitsugensei ni toboshii*). Existentialism (*jitsuzonshugi*). Objective (*kyakkanteki*).

Buddhist concepts

Buddhism does not use the term *genjitsu* as much as *yū* (to be). *Yū* is the tr. of the Sk *bhava*, and is not considered in its essential qualities but as the antonym of "non-existence" or "relativity" (*mu* and *kū*). Buddhism joins two mutually exclusive terms, existence and non-existence, into one word *umu*

---

[1] *DGK*, p. 904.

(being and non-being). The explanation: "A *dharma* which is produced by causation is thought to exist; yet because it is the product of causation, it is lacking a real permanent nature of its own; thus in the ultimate sense it is non-existent."[2] Non-reality is a pillar concept of Buddhism, as evidenced by the summary statement defining Buddhism found in the introduction to the *Japanese-English Buddhist Dictionary*:

> A fundamental expression of Buddhist thought is the concept of *sunyata* (*kū*; non-substantiality, relativity, voidness). This concept denies the validity of reality as normally experienced, including the self; negates both existence and non-existence as normally understood; and states that when all illusion is at last abandoned, then there will be found the absolute void which is wondrously real. The apprehension and formulation of this reality are achieved without the reference to the experience or concept of god, respectively.[3]

Sunyata is tr. *kū* in Japanese. But *kū* is literally "space" and has no religious significance in many compound words, e.g., *kūkō* is "airport." Thus Buddhist scholars have heralded Stcherbatsky's tr. of *sunyata* into the English word, "relativity":

> Although often translated as void or nothingness, the translation 'relativity', given by Stcherbatsky is preferable. *Sunyata* does not deny the concept of existence as such but holds that all existence and the constituent elements which make up existence are dependent upon causation. Since the causal factors are changing every moment, it follows that there can be no static existence. *Kū*, therefore, categorically denies the possibility of any form of phenomenal static existence. All phenomena are relative and dependent upon other phenomena.[4]

Another Buddhist term, *shōsōfuni*, which literally means "noumenon and phenomenon are not two"[5] reveals the lack of a dichotomy in Buddhist philosophy between thought and matter. Buddhism further denies past and future things as having real existence. The five things which have real existence, called *goun* (five aggregates) are: (1) a generic term for all forms of matter, (2) perception, (3) mental conception and ideas, (4) volition, (5) consciousness of the mind.[6] Hence four out of five of the general terms for reality are noumenal and one, matter, (which for man means his body) is phenomenal.

Biblical Concepts of Reality

The word "reality" does not occur in the Bible. Rather the Bible discusses or declares things in realistic language. Nature, the heavens, the stars appear to man in his walk through life. Biblical statements concerning these phenomena are not postulational nor philosophical but descriptive. The sun sets, there are four corners to the earth, etc. The Bible consistently refuses to embark on a

---

2 *BD*, p. 324.

3 *Ibid*., p. vii.

4 *BD*, p. 184.

5 *Ibid*., p. 298.

6 *Ibid*., p. 91.

speculative theory of primary and secondary causes. Phenomenal language is enduring, understandable in every age and culture. Ramm stresses this: "This attitude of non-committal as to the method of nature and secondary causes of phenomena is, as we shall see, eminently characteristic of the Bible."[7] Further, the Bible does not theorize as to the actual nature of things. In the words of the Biblical Commission of Leo XIII: "The Bible is silent as to the inmost constitution of visible things."[8] Putting it another way, the Biblical concept of reality is not found in some word or definition. Rather the Jew or Christian was taken up with the One who *is*, Jehovah, "I am that I am" (Ex. 3:14). Things which appear, the *blepomena* (II Cor. 4:17), are not eternal and hence are not the essence of reality. Biblical writers synthesized phenomena and matter not in natural law but in a Person: "all things are held together in him" (Col. 1:18).

Encounter

Biblical realistic dualism stands in sharp contradistinction to Buddhist idealistic monism. Buddhist emphasis upon voidness or relativity, the uniting of existence and non-existence into one monistic framework, not only is incompatible with Biblical premises, but such philosophic gyrations have made little *prima-facie* impact upon the Japanese lay viewpoint. Modern Japan was ideologically founded upon the utilitarian pragmatism of Fukuzawa and has maintained that same existential approach to life ever since. In fact the word "realist" is the summary word given to a description of the Japanese philosophy of life in the Asahi Broadcasting Corporation's work, *Here is Japan*.[9] However, if our linguistic analysis is valid, the *real* is that which appears; reality does not necessarily lie in principles nor the ideal.[10] Could this account for the dearth of scientific discovery of principle in comparison to the rapid progress in adapting Western technology to Japan's immediate needs? Of course Fukuzawa fulminated against this indiscriminate adapting of Western techniques to the neglect of thorough investigation into the nature of things, the *ri*. The glaring contradiction of modern Tokyo, with myriads of TV sets and private automobiles, while still lacking a modern sewage system, could possibly be traced to pragmatic stopping short at what *appears* workable rather than a pursuing through to basic principles of city planning, a setting up of basic priority values in establishing a home.

Hebrew-Christian concepts of reality find their nexus in a Person, who infuses nature and phenomena with immutable *laws and principles*, as trustworthy

---

7 Bernard Ramm, *The Christian View of Science and Scripture* (Grand Rapids: Wm. B. Eerdmans Publishing Company, 1955), p. 69.

8 *Ibid*.

9 *Here is Japan*, ed. Noriko Ikeda (Tokyo: Asahi Broadcasting Corp., 1964).

10 Hajime Nakamura arrives at the same conclusion, *viz*., "the theory that the phenomenal is actually the real"... "accept the phenomenal world as absolute" in his *Ways of Thinking....*, p. 351, through other avenues of analysis — literature, psychology.

as the One who vouchsafed them to man. The promise, "While the earth remaineth, seedtime and harvest, and cold and heat, and summer and winter, and day and night shall not cease" (Gen. 8:22) is founded upon His covenant. Hence there is incentive and assurance to the searcher for truth, for when he discovers basic principles inherent in phenomena he is encountering reality. That is, the foundation of natural law in the Biblical tradition rests in a Divine legislator. Having given natural law, God intended that man discover and understand His universe and its law. Thus there is no conflict with science and the Bible; to the contrary, the Bible by positing the foundation of natural law upon the immutability of God's promise, gave encouragement to the first Christian men of science, like Newton, to analyze and postulate natural law in mathematical equations. Japanese concepts of reality as being that which *appears* can be traced to a basic Oriental philosophy of the universe which sees nature in flux without order. Man is not to analytically understand and control nature but harmonize with it, observe it, appreciate it (as did Chu Hsi[11] in watching the bamboo shoot grow, without plucking it up by the roots and dissecting it).

---

[11] 12th century Chinese historian and philosopher of the Neo-Confucian school, who posited a unifying principle (*li*) of the universe to be discovered both in nature and in man by observation. His ideas were followed by Japan's Fukuzawa and served as basis for the new Japanese science of the Meiji era — the investigation of things.

CAUSE-EFFECT 原 因 結 果 GEN'IN-KEKKA

Japanese Concepts of Cause-Effect

Chinese character etymology

Gen'in-kekka is comprised of four characters which we must treat separately. *Gen* has two components: 厂 (cliff), and 泉 (spring). *KGJ*: water flowing from the side of a cliff, hence *source* or *origin*. *KCJ*: spring flowing from a cliff. *In* has two components: 大 (outstreched body), and 口 (open mouth). *KGJ*; man lying down on a pallet with arms oustretched and mouth open, hence reclining upon or trusting oneself to something. *KCJ*: make something suitable to rest upon, or something to which one can commit himself. Thus the sense of "through," "because of," "trust." *Ke* has two components: 糸 (thread) and 吉 (full). *KCJ*: the knot of a thread, hence bound together. *Ka* has two components: 田 (field), and 木 (tree). However *KCJ* maintains the earlier form was not a field but fruit with a mark across it. General concept, thus, is a sheaf of fruit, the result or fruit of labor.

Semantic changes in Japan

Japanese indigenous words are *yue* and *kara*. *Yue* originally was the root of a tree. *Kara* pointed to blood lineage. Japanese emphasis was upon the process in motion, not so much original causes. *Gen* appears in *Manyōshū* signifying a flat field,[1] but had already been used to denote source or origin. *In* retained its essential Buddhist sense in Japan. *In* is the tr. of the Sk. *betu*, denoting direct cause. In *Dentōroku*, the character appears alone as follows: "One should desire to ascertain the *in* of his previous life. Receiving life now is the result of the *in* of a previous life."[2]

Modern range of meaning

Gen

KCJ: (1) field (*hara*), (2) base (*moto*), (3) source or origin (*minamoto*), (4) establish (*motozuku*), (5) seek out (*tazuneru*), (6) second time (*futatabi*), (7) forgive (*yurusu*), (8) take care, be prudent (*tsutsushimu*).

GS: (1) source of a phenomenon (*koto no moto*), (2) source, origin (*okori*), (3) that which begins (*hajimari*), (4) foundation (*kiin*).

DNKJ: (1) field (*hara*), (2) source, base (*moto*), (3) root (*nemoto*), (4) base, source (*minamoto*), (5) foundation (*kompon*).

---

[1] *DGK*, p. 1632.

[2] *Ibid.*, p. 210.

In

   KCJ: (1) lean upon (*tayoru*), (2) through, because of, whereupon (*yotte*), (3) establish, make a foundation (*motozuku*), (4) happen (*chinamu*), (5) reason (*wake*), (6) source, origin (*moto*).

   KJ: (1) that which causes something to occur and continues to keep it in motion, (2) that which fixes a result and timewise causes it to diminish, (3) origin, source.

Kekka

   GS: (1) the last appearance or final appearance of an action; the net result of an action, (2) consequence.

   KJ: (1) bear fruit, (2) the visible, outward influence or effect produced by an inward thought or interior activity, (3) phenomenon produced by an act.

English idiom parallels

   Search for the cause(*gen'in o saguru*). Cause unknown (*gen'in fumei*). Where there's smoke there's fire (*Hi no nai tokoro ni kemuri wa tatanu*). Let nature take its course (*shizen no nariyuki ni makaseru*).

Buddhist concepts

   Buddhist aspect of *in* in *genin* is lost in common parlance. *Gen'in* simply conveys the concept of the root cause, e.g., of a sickness, of price fluctuations, etc. However when *in* occurs with the *ka* of *kekka*, the final word *inga* is strictly a Buddhist religious word. It is defined by *BD* as: "Every action which is cause (*in*) will have a result or an effect... the law of cause and effect is a fundamental concept within Buddhism governing all situations."[3] Related to *kekka* is the Buddhist word *engi*, tr. of the Sk. *pratitya samutpada*, defined by *BD* as: "arising from causation."[4] It is not the final result but an intermediate contributary cause. *BD* explains:

   A central concept in Buddhism [i.e., *engi*] that all phenomenon are produced by causation. It is a denial of spontaneity. Since all phenomena come into existence because of *engi*, they lack essential nature and are impermanent, hence *kū* [void or relative]. Colloquially *engi* often means fortune telling.[5]

The best explanation of this cause-effect relation is given by *GS*: "If one plants a kernel in the field, the result is rice; the kernel is the *in*, the field is the *engi*, and the rice is the *ka*.[6] However, this chain is pushed further back to the prime-causal factor *gō*, tr. of the Sk. *karma*, which is defined *BD* as: "A deed produced by the action of the mind.... *Gō*, when manifested, is produced either verbally or physically."[7]

These terms are essentially Buddhist in origin and thought, but they have slipped into everyday speech—not so much to convey the Buddhist ideas but rather as proverbial expressions to fit certain situations. The *BD* indicated that

---

3 *BD*, p. 129.

4 *BD*, p. 55.

5 *Ibid.*

6 *GS*, p. 1599.

7 *BD*, p. 77.

engi is used colloquially to mean "fortune telling." Actually it is used in the phrase, *engi o katsugu* (lit. "to carry about an intermediate cause") in the sense of "to be superstitious." *Inga o fukameru* (lit. to deepen the law of cause and effect) is in common use and means "to accept as inevitable."[8] *Inga o akirameru* is to resign to one's fate, that is, to the inexhorable course of cause and effect. The Buddhist phrase *innen shōmetsu no ri* has *in* within it and is defined by *BD* as: "The universe is produced as the result of our *karma* and evil passions. It is said that the universe will disappear and become void when these causes are removed."[9] *Innen sokkū no ri* is defined thus: "The theory of the voidness of the phenomenal world. Every being in the world is conditioned by the rule of cause and effect and appears to be born and die according to it. However in reality neither birth nor death exist as fixed concepts."[10]

Biblical Concepts of Cause and Effect

The Bible declares God as creator. He created the universe and man and sustains His creation by regulated natural law. The Hebrew word (*bara*) lit. meant to "cut out,"[11] hence to "form," "make," "create." Key Gk. word is *ginomai*, having the following range of meaning in the NT: (1) come to be, become, originate, as (a) being born, (Rom. 1:3); (b) occur, come about (Matt. 8:24), as events and phenomena of nature; (2) be made, be created (John 1:3); (3) happen, take place (Matt. 1:22). Rather than using the word "nature," the Bible uses the word (*ktisis*), "creature." Sasse declares:

> It [the creature] exists only by the will of the Creator and the Creative Word of Almighty God. Its existence is bordered by an absolute beginning and absolute end like that of the whole world of heaven and earth. The earth is God's possession.[12]

The sense of "becoming," latent in the word *geneseos*, cognate of *ginomai*, has raised the question whether James' use of the word in 3:6 is not a borrowing from Greek thought, which held that life was like a wheel, turning from top to bottom endlessly. Buchsel explains the Gk. idea:

> Behind this idea of the wheel stands the popular insight into the uncertainty of human circumstances rather than the Orphic theory of finitude as a recurrence of birth and death and what is enclosed by the two.[13]

The wheel of life in James 3:6 is afire; the Orphic wheel simply rolls on. Sasse traces the expression back to the popular Gk. sentiment that "The in-

---

8 E.g., a Buddhist priest will tell a bereaved parent to accept the death of a child using this expression.

9 *BD*, p. 130.

10 *Ibid*.

11 *Student's Hebrew and Chaldee Dictionary of the Testament*, ed. Alexander Harkavy (New York: Hebrew Publishing Co., 1914), p. 68.

12 Hermann Sasse, "ge," *TDNT*, I, 679.

13 Friedrich Buchsel, "genesis," *TDNT*, I, 683.

versions of life bring searing pain because of guilt."[14] He also divorces this symbol from Buddhist thought:

> In Buddhism there is much reference to the wheel, the wheel of rotation, becoming and time. The most striking feature is that this wheel is set on fire by self-consciousness. But the speculative nature of this view is too alien to justify any direct connection with James. There may be connections between Buddhism and Orphism, but they cannot be shown, and it is hardly likely that they will be.[15]

Buchsel mentions other contrasts in a footnote:

> The flaming of the tongue (*Mahavagga* I,21) can hardly be connected with Jm. 3:6. For the former reference is to the tongue as an organ of touch (i.e., taste), whereas in the latter it is an organ of speech... the wheel of (Buddhism) rolls through the world, whereas that of the Gk. and Jewish proverb rolls through our own lives.[16]

Encounter

The *in* of *gen'in* (cause) is a man outstretched on a pallet — man supported, undergirded. Phenomena are supported, borne along by some cause. This etymological sense is nearly lost in the modern usage of the word, but derivative phrases and meaning range point to a series or change of events called "cause and effect." Pushing this as far back as one is able in Buddhist thought we discover *gō* (*karma*). The flow of nature continues on; somehow man by his mind or activity inexplicably affects this series of events.

Is there a similar concept in the NT usage of the word *ginomai* (becoming)? Neither Sasse nor Buchsel trace NT usage to Orphic or Buddhist sources. But does the Bible hint at secondary causes? Ramm believes it does, but this secondary cause is not finally related to some impersonal law but to a personal Agent of natural law, the Holy Spirit. Ramm believes that fiat creationism alone or theistic evolution are equally unsatisfactory explanations of the Biblical record of creation and providence. He sees indirectly in Scripture the following order: (1) God the Creator fixes the means and ordained end of Creation, this fiat creationism fixing the void of Gen. 1:2, (2) the Holy Spirit as the effectual agent of providence infuses nature with power and processes, making nature a derivative creation. Ramm calls this *progressive creationism*, "the means whereby God as world ground and the Spirit of God as world Entelechy bring to pass the divine will in nature."[17] Ramm finds support in this theory with Mivert's view that (1) the movement in Nature comes from the law of cosmical evolution which is a principle of continuity, (2) the direction comes from the law of final causality.[18] We may say in conclusion that Japanese concepts

---

14 *Ibid.*
15 *Ibid.*, p. 684.
16 *Ibid.*, p. 684.
17 Ramm, p. 115-116.
18 *Ibid.*

of cause and effect are finally traced to some thought process (of man) as generator; Biblical progressive creationism is attributed to the secret workings of God's Spirit in nature, maintaining natural law and governing creation to the final goal predetermined by God the Creator.

CHANGE 変〔變〕化 *HENKA*

Japanese Concepts of Change

Chinese character etymology

Henka is comprised of two characters: 變 (change, rearrange), and 化 (change of posture). *Hen* has two components: 䜌 (disorder), and 攵 (strike). *KGJ*: putting one's hand to something in disarray to rearrange it. *KCJ*: strike something thereby effecting a change. *Ka* also has two components: 人 (man), and 匕 (man on his side). *KGJ*: man changing his shape or posture. *KCJ*: a man becoming changed.

Semantic changes in Japan

Japanese word is *kawaru*, from the root, *kau*, "to buy". Hence the concept was more of exchange than of turning into some thing new.

Hen alone appears in *Shiki*: "Go for the emperor to the far country and report the *change*"[1] (which probably meant a disturbance which occurred in a distant province). *KGJ* quotes the Taoist writing *Shushin*: "The shape *changes* (*ka*) but not the essence."[2] *DGK*: "What elevates and blesses a people is the *ethical change* (*ka*) wrought by humane government."[3] I have translated *ka* here into "ethical change," for contextually that is what is implied.

Modern range of meaning

Hen

KCJ: (1) change (*kawaru*), (2) a change (*kawari*), (3) disorder (*midare*), (4) disaster (*wazawai*), (5) strangeness (*fushigi*), (6) temporary expedient (*rinji no hakarigoto*), (7) move (*ugoku*).

GS: (1) something which is continually changing, (2) sudden occurrence, (3) something rare and unusual, (4) temporary expedient, (5) musical term.

The two characters conjoined together into the one word *henka* give the overall sense of changing from one state to another, or turning about.

English idiom parallels

Vicissitudes (*fuchin*). Full of variety (*henka no ōi*). Outward change (*mesaki no henka*). Change one's tune (*chōshi o kaeru*). Dyed in the wool (*aku made mo kawaranai*). Changes of the seasons (*kisetsu no utsurikawari*). Take turns (*kawarugawaru ni suru*).

---

[1] *DGK*, p. 1812.
[2] *KGJ*, p. 609.
[3] *DGK*, p. 566.

Buddhist concepts

Constant change or impermanence is a key Buddhist concept and is rendered by the word *mujō* (lit. "not constant"), tr. of the Sk. *anitya* and defined as follows: "Everything in the world arises, changes, and perishes; nothing remains constant for even a single moment."[4] This word is compounded with other words, such as *shogyō mujōge* to expand the above concept as: "All things are impermanent. They appear and disappear. When an end is put to this appearance and disappearance, then the bliss of nirvana is realized."[5]

Biblical Concepts of Change

Old Testament concepts

Nine Hebrew words convey this concept, ranging in meaning from change, exchange, turn, alter, make other than, etc. Key word is *chalaph*, having the etymological meaning of "passing over" (Isa. 10:3), later meaning simply "change," as grass changing (Psa. 90:5) or man's mood, e.g., "Then shall his spirit *change* and he shall pass over and offend"[6] (Hab. 1:11). When the negative form of the word *haphak* is used, it denotes the unchangeableness of Jehovah: "I Jehovah change not" (Mal. 3:6).

New Testament concepts

Gk. words for "change" in the NT "have mostly to do with spiritual realities."[7] *Metatithemi* is used to denote a change in the priesthood (Heb. 7:12); *metaschematidzo* to denote the bodily change at the resurrection (I Cor. 15:51, 52; Phil. 3:21); *metaballo* to denote the cataclysmical change in space in the great day of the Lord (II Pet. 3:10, 12). The prefix *meta* is in all these as in *metanoeo*, denoting "change of mind" or "change of heart."

Another basic word is *alasso*, stemming from *allos*, having the sense of "to make otherwise."[8] It is used in the sense of "alter" in Acts 6:14, and "exchange" (for the worse) in Rom. 1:23, 25, 26. Superficial change is contrasted with a deep abiding change in the NT by the use of *metaschematizo* for the former and *metamorphoo* for the latter.[9]

Encounter

Change is a fundamental concept of Japanese thinking. In a succinct two page summary of the Japanese philosophy of life found in *Here is Japan*, the following words appear once in almost every paragraph: "revolutionary changes

---

4 *BD*, p. 202.

5 *BD*, p. 294.

6 *HCD*, p. 173.

7 Dwight Pratt, "Change," *ISBE*, I, 593.

8 Friedrich Buchsel, "*alasso*," *TDNT*, I, 251.

9 Discussed more fully by Richard C. Trench, *Synonyms of the New Testament* (9th ed.; Grand Rapids: Wm. B. Eerdmans Publishing Co., 1948), pp. 261-266.

of time," "continuous," "vicissitudes of change," "embracing change," "universal human stream," "endless family cycle." It is not improbable that through simple observation of the Second law of Thermodynamics, called also the "law of entropy," which states simply that the universe is cooling off or running down, that ancient scholars came to the conclusion that this is a fundamental law of human life. Water flows downhill, the rising and falling of ripples and bubbles in the stream presented to them in minature this general law of change. This process of change seems to have been applied to outward forms, not essences. Man is inextricably involved in this process; he appears in the first character denoting change. *Nirvana* is the state where change ends.

The Bible recognizes change but does not lay great stress upon it as a blind force pulling everything with it in its path. Nature, flowers, grass, change; the world with its fleeting fashions is like the changing scenes of a theatre. But this calls not for apathetic resignation to blind forces of nature but for a fixing of one's hope upon the unchangeable realities of God Himself, His Word, and His promises. Biblical emphasis is not upon change itself but upon the one *changing*, such as *man*'s changing his thoughts, *God*'s changing of man's body, and the *Holy Spirit*'s effecting an inner moral change in man.

Two difficulties present themselves in making the *mujō* theory of constant change an absolute Weltanschauung. Change itself, or the law of entropy, mathematically cannot be pushed to the limits of infinity, for its very process indicates a starting point in time. Ramm stresses this:

> If the universe is infinitely old, the energy would have already been evenly distributed by now. The fact that there are still hot bodies in the universe means that the furnace was stoked, so to speak, at some measurable time in the past. This would be the moment of creation, or some creative activity.[10]

Second difficulty lies in its all-inclusiveness. Is *all* changing? If so, then men's theories are included and the *mujō* theory is in flux as well. Someday the theory might become, "All is changeless."

---

10 Ramm, pp. 153-154.

EDUCATION 教 育 KYŌIKU

Japanese Concepts of Education

Chinese character etymology

Kyōiku is comprised of two characters: 教 (teach), and 育 (grow). *Kyo* has two components: 孝 (adults and children), and 攵 (interaction). *KGJ*: the relationship between adults and children, or the interchange of ideas. *KCJ*: two components are "learn" and "whip," hence to whip a child and make him learn. *Iku* has two components: 去 (child upside down), and 月 (flesh). *KGJ*: hold a child upside down to lengthen his stature, hence to raise or rear. *KCJ*: components express a child being born, hence to raise up a child.

Semantic changes in Japan

Sodatsu is the indigenous Japanese word to which *iku* was affixed, and is traced to two words: *su* (nest) and *tatsu* (stand);[1] hence a bird leaving its nest and going on its own. *Kyō* is traced by *DGK* as having the sense of a signpost.[2] The Japanese word for teaching is *oshieru*, meaning literally to fix something upon an individual. Learning then is the receiving of external stimuli from another person.

Modern range of meaning

Kyō has the following range of meaning: (1) teach (*oshieru*), (2) learning (*gakumon*), (3) a particular teaching of a religion (*kyō*), (4) be influenced by (*shimu*).

Iku has the following range of meaning: (1) raise or rear (*sodateru*), (2) grow or cultivate (*yashinau*), (3) child (*osanai*), (4) give birth or to be born (*umu*).

Thus the two characters joined together combine the concepts of impartation of ideas and growth. *GS* defines *kyōiku* then as "the work which aims at improving and advancing the growth of body, mind, and spirit." *KJ*: (1) rear up and teach (*oshiesodateru*), (2) teach one so as to expand his knowledge, (3) a mature person attempts through fixed means and time to develop an immature person in mind and body.

---

1 *DGK*, p. 1154.
2 *Ibid.*, p. 220.

Biblical Concepts of Education

Old Testament concepts

Key Hebrew word is *chanakh*, meaning "train." In Gen. 14:14 it is used in the sense of "drill" or "train for war." As used in Prov. 22:6, the thought is more than "teach"; it "includes everything that pertains to the proper develop-ment of the child, especially in its moral and spiritual nature."[3] The primary responsibility for this spiritual training rested with the parents. They were specifically instructed by Scripture to be personally familiar with Scripture and to teach it in the home (Deut. 6:7-12).

New Testament concepts

Three key Gk. words for education or the impartation of knowledge in the NT are *euanggalidzomai*, *didache* and *kerugma*. The essence of *euanggelidzomai* was simply a proclamation that the reign of God was at hand. Christ first used the word in Luke 4:18, and the proclamation was tantamount to an announce-ment of deliverance from suffering and oppression. After Christ's death and resurrection the content of the Gospel was Christ Himself and His work. Paul insists that there is only one unique Gospel upon which the Church is built (Gal. 1:6,9). This Gospel must be received personally by faith or else it remains a mystery (II Cor. 4:3, Eph. 6:19). Essential to the idea of *euanggalidzo* is the concept of telling favorable news to those who have not heard it before. The word *didache* denotes ethical instruction, apologetics, doctrine. Paul's use of the words *tupon didache* (pattern of teaching) in Romans 6:17 indicates a catechism extant in his day. There were recognized *didaskoloi* (teachers) in the Church (I Cor. 12:28; Eph. 4:11), but they were merely assistants to the one Teacher, the Holy Spirit, whose office was to guide every believer into the truth (John 16:13). Hence the work of the *didaskolos* would be hampered unless this basic inner guidance and teaching were first given and received. Paul's wording is clear: "We are interpreting spiritul truths to those who have the Spirit" (I Cor. 2:13-16). *Kerugma* is literally "the thing preached" and is used in the *NT* as a summary term meaning the apostolic Gospel (I Cor. 1:21). "It may be summed up in the word as the message of the Cross and resurrection of Jesus Christ."[4] Dodd sums up the *kerugma* under six points:

1. The age of fulfillment has dawned (Acts 2:16; 3:18, 24).
2. This has taken place through the life, death, and resurrection of Jesus; the evi-dences of His messiahship are recounted, great emphasis being laid on the fulfill-ment of scriptural prophecy.
3. By virtue of the resurrection, Jesus has been exalted at the right hand of God as Messianic head of the new Israel (Acts 2:33-36; 3:13; 4:11).
4. The Holy Spirit in the church is the sign of Christ's present power and glory (Acts 2:33; 5:31-32).
5. The Messianic Age will shortly reach its consumation in the return of Christ (Acts 3:21).

---

3 *ISBE*, V, 3005.
4 Alan Richardson, "Preach, Teach," *TWBB*, pp. 172.

6. The *kerugma* always closes with an appeal for repentence, the offer of forgiveness and the gift of the Holy Spirit, and with the promise of salvation.[5]

Encounter

Japanese symbol for "education" embraces the concept of training mind and body through supervision of the educated. The Confucian ideal of the savant gathering around him promising youth, imparting wisdom in a personal way, has left its impress upon Japanese views of education. The concept of rigorous discipline manifests itself in what the Japanese call *suparuta kyōiku* (Spartan education), but this methodology has largely passed from the scene since the war. But the *sensei* (teacher) is still a *sine-qua-non* for education in Japan; homework for children must be supervised by *katei kyōshi* (home teachers), who are usually university students hired by parents to come regularly to their homes to supervise children in after-school hours. Homework, with research assignments on the personal level, is the rarity in Japan at the university level; the Westerner will be surprised to watch the thousands of students commuting to school with few if any books or notebooks. Libraries in the rural parts of Japan are usually empty, unheated, and with scant collections.

In the religious sphere, *kyō* is suffixed to Buddha and Christ to designate these religions. Buddhism then is Buk*kyō*; Christianity is Kirisuto*kyō*. Both religions thus are put in the same category; they are *teachings* imparted by religious founders to their followers. This no doubt accounts for the initial response to the Christian message being couched in terms of understanding or perception. Almost invariably the criterion of a Biblical message is its *understandableness*; seekers bend every effort to grasp the *teaching*. To the query, "What did you think of the morning worship service," the answer is rarely, "Inspiring," "Convicting," "Beautiful"; instead the pastor is complimented with the words, *"Yoku wakatta"* (I really understood it).

Against this, the Bible lays stress upon the contents of education rather than its methodology. The Biblical *kerugma* sums up in panoramic view what God has done by His saving acts; receiving or believing was the responsibility of the hearers. The preachers simply declared the facts as they knew them. More than on the visible teacher, the Bible lays stress upon the invisible teacher, the Holy Spirit who in His sovereign way guides the minds of men into the general truth of nature's secrets and the special truths of God's ways with men. Paul's highest appeal to the authority of His message was not to a scholastic tradition nor to personal instruction at the feet of a Christian teacher but to the special illumination vouchsafed him by the Holy Spirit on his way to Damascus (Gal. 1:12-24).

---

5 *Ibid.*

KNOWLEDGE 知 識 CHISHIKI

Japanese Concepts of Knowledge

Chinese character etymology

Chishiki is comprised of two characters: 知 (know), and 識 (flag, signboard). *Chi* has two components: 口 (mouth), and 矢 (arrow). *KGJ*: that which strikes the center of an issue, hence the truth. *KCJ*: breath or sound coming from the mouth. *Shiki* has the component 口 (mouth) within it. *KGJ*: ascribing names to things, e.g., A is A; B is B, etc. In *Raiki, shiki* appears alone in the sense of "remember."[1] *KCJ*: small placard standing upright and writing upon it, hence to make a sign or mark.

Semantic changes in Japan

The indigenous Japanese word to which the Chinese character 知 *chi* (know) was affixed is *shiru*. Ōno believes the word came from *senryō* (to occupy). Hence knowing a thing is to occupy every facet of its existence. Passive of *shiru* is found in *shiremono* (fool), for one dominated by someone else is a fool.

Modern range of meaning

Chi

KCJ: (1) know (*shiru*), (2) discriminate (*wakimaeru*), (3) remember (*oboeru*), (4) perceive (*satoru*), (5) settle (*osameru*), (6) acquaintance (*shiriai*), (7) let know (*shiraseru*), (8) lust of the body, desire (*me no yokubō*), (9) wisdom (*chie*).

Shiki

KCJ: (1) know (*shiru*), (2) distinguish (*miwakeru*), (3) recognize (*mitomeru*), (4) perception (*satori*), (5) thought (*kangae*), (6) acquaintance (*shiriai*), (7) that which is absoute and leads to an immortal life (Buddhism), (8) sign (*shirushi*), (9) remember (*oboeru*).

Chishiki

DNKJ: (1) intellectual capacity or ability (*chiryoku*), (2) wisdom (*chie*), (3) person of wisdom (4) taking money and rice to a temple for a wedding deposit.

KJ: (1) having a clear consciousness of facts and things, (2) knowledge of the contents of something, (3) that which is derived from consciousness, (4) acquaintance (*shiriai*), (5) knowlege of things (*monoshiri*). Summing up the

---

[1] *KGJ*, p. 84.

above usages we see that *chishiki* means "organized knowledge," acquired by learning.

English idiom parallels

Fuzzy knowledge (*ayafuya na chishiki*), Encyclopedic knowledge (*hyakka-zenshoteki chishiki*). Basic knowledge (*kiso chishiki*). Half-baked idea (*asahaka na kangae*). Stock of knowledge (*unchiku*).[2]

Buddhist concepts

Shiki is the tr. of the Sk. *vijnanan*, defined as: "An aspect of consciousness." "It is discriminating and dependent upon sense organs."[3] Buddhism typifies knowledge as in the word *sammyō*, the tr. of the Pali *tisso vijjā* which is defined: "Three types of knowledge: I. remembrance of former births, II. insight into the future destiny of all beings, and III. recognition of the origin of misery and of the way to its removal.[4]

Biblical Concepts of Knowledge

Old Testament concepts

Key Hebrew word for knowledge is *yadha*, which is translated into the Septuagint as *ginosko* and *eidos*. It is the act by which man comprehends the objects and phenomena of existence, the objects and circumstances of this worldly life. There is more emphasis upon feeling, learning by experience, knowing intimately in *yadha* than objective verification which is latent in the Gk. word *ginosko*. The OT maintains a difference between the subject and the object of knowledge. Reality in the OT does not lie in timeless and permanent forms, "which give shape to things" but in that "which constantly takes place in time."[5] Events are "not understood as the unfolding of a causal nexus of processes; they are the qualified action of God, or of men in relation to God."[6] Bultmann stresses this unique aspect of OT knowledge:

> The knowledge of God is not one of essences... it is knowledge of His claim... it is thus respectful and obedient acknowledgement of the power and grace and demand of God... Knowledge is possessed only in its exercise or actualization.[7]

Thus OT knowledge borders on acknowledgment. To know God is to confess or acknowledge Him, to give Him honour and obey His will (Deut. 11:2, Hos. 11:3, Isa. 41:20, Mic. 6:5, I Sam. 2:12, Psa. 9:10). Knowledge is a movement of the will, brought about by insight into the will of God. It is a submitting in grateful obedience to what is known.

---

2 No doubt some of these expressions have flowed into the language as direct translations of the English idiom.

3 *BD*, p. 278.

4 *BD*, p. 250.

5 Rudolph Bultmann, "*ginosko*" *TDNT*, I, 697.

6 *Ibid.*

7 *Ibid.*, p. 698.

New Testament concepts

Key Gk. word for knowledge is *gnosis*, with its verbal cognate *ginosko*. Bultmann defines it as "The intelligent comprehension of an object or matter, whether this comes for the first time or comes afresh, into the consideration of the one who grasps it."[8] Greek usage of the term makes it clear that this *gnosis* is from the *nous* or *logos*. *Dokein* (think, suppose) is to have an opinion; *ginosko* embraces things as they really are, the *aletheia* (truth). *Gnosis* is practical. It comes from close acquaintance with things in experience. It is achieved in seeing and hearing, in investating and reflecting. The empirical aspect of *ginosko* must be kept in mind, the nuance of visual verification. "The meaning and significance of the Greek ideal of knowledge are plain when we remember that knowing is understood as a kind of seeing."[9] *Gnosis* presses on to essences, to the Gk. concept of reality:

> Reality consists of forms and figures, or rather of the elements and principles which shape these forms and figures. Thus the *ginosko* of the investigator and philosopher has reference to these; the *eidos* is what makes possible the knowledge of things, as it also makes them what they are.[10]

We are approaching the quintessence of life for the Gk. philosopher. When his hand finally dipped down into the basic stuff of reality, pulled out the essences of phenomena, examined it, understood it, he had reached the last defile of his philosphic ascent. Bultmann expresses it: "The knowledge of what really is can be the supreme possibility of existence, for in it the one who knows encounters the eternal and participates in it."[11] Hence the *gnosis* approached divine illumination, and the goal of the gnostic was estatic mystical vision. It was esoteric knowledge, philosophical speculation. Rather than toward things or reality, the gnostic pressed on further toward the inner self:

> All knowledge serves the knowledge of self which is the condition of redemption and the vision of God. Self knowledge does not mean being perspicuous of oneself in the Gk. sense... It is knowledge of the tragic history of the soul, which coming from the world of light, is entangled in matter... *Gnosis* is a possession, though it is always in jeopardy and must be made secure by asceticism.[12]

In summary we note that the Gk. philosopher expresses in *ginosko* the deepest aspirations of his heart; through this medium he was approaching the ultimate as he knew it. And the gnostic, more than searching out reality or essences by thorough search of accidence, turned his inquiry inward. This was not to understand himself but to become aware of his plight — the plight of a soul enmeshed in matter.

Thus when turning to the NT usage of *ginosko* we are immediately driven back to the OT model of knowledge, not to the Gk. one. *Ginosko* to the Christian is primarily *acknowledgement and obedient submission* to what is known

---

8 *Ibid.*, p. 689.
9 *Ibid.*, p. 692.
10 *Ibid.*
11 *Ibid.*
12 *Ibid.*, p. 696.

(Rom. 3: 17, 10:19, Luke 19:42, Heb. 3:10, II Pet. 2:21). There is no speculative knowledge of God in the NT; such inquiry is beyond the limits imposed upon man as created being (Rom. 11:34, I Cor. 2:16). NT knowledge is intensely practical; in I Thess. 1:9 it is tantamount to serving God. Knowledge on God's part is revealed in acts of love and election (II Tim. 2:19, I Cor. 8:3, 13:12, Gal. 4:9). Of course there is theoretical knowledge gained by studying the Scriptures (II Tim 3:7), but decisive knowledge, *epignosis*, is that which results in conversion to the faith (I Tim. 2:4, II Tim. 2:25, Tit. 1:1). There is an apparent struggle in the NT against speculative knowledge, against its brand of wisdom (I Cor. 1:-17), against the special authority which the *gnosis* conferred to those of the inner circle (I Cor. 8:1ff.), and the pneumatic gifts it boasted of (II Cor. 10:13). The NT took to task this spurious *gnosis* for its asceticism and denial of the flesh and the resurrection of the body (I Cor. 7:15).

NT writers warned that genuine *gnosis* is accompanied by *agape* (love). And this *agape* is not mystical but finds expression in one's immediate home. Further true *gnosis* is not something springing up within man as a latent gift nor a reward for honest inquiry: it is a gift, flowing from a higher *gnosis* — God's knowledge of man (I Cor. 8:3). John employs *ginosko* to denote "the relationship to God and to Jesus as a personal fellowship in which each is decisively determined by the other in his own existence."[13] *Ginosko* is a high plane of living but not the highest: love supercedes and limits it (I John 4:8). "To be determined by love, then, is thus a criterion of the knowledge of God."[14] Hence knowledge in the NT as with the OT is an acknowledgment and submission in love to the revelation of God in His deeds and His commands. This knowledge increases and develops as obedience grows — a gift of grace to the obedient.

Encounter

Japanese knowledge approaches the Gk. concept of differentiating and naming phenomena. It is a virtue which in a Buddhist milieu opens the way to immortal life. It is the direction of inquiring man towards a target. Like the Gk. *gnosis* it can be in the religious realm highly speculative and its attainment is a high achievement tantamount to salvation.

Biblical knowledge is more a recognition of the Unseen fashioning the flower, the strong Arm shaping history. Knowledge begins in acknowledgment of God and His commands; beginning here the believer is taken to new thresholds of awareness and fellowship. Biblical knowledge carries with it an imperative to action — to confession of God as Lord and receiving forgiveness in the atonement. "It is acceptance of the divine act of love in Jesus and obedience to its commands."[15]

---

13 *Ibid.*, p. 711.
14 *Ibid.*
15 *Ibid.*, p. 712.

WISDOM 知 恵 CHIE

Japanese Concepts of Wisdom

Chinese character etymology

Chie is comprised of two characters; 知 (know), and 恵 (grace). *Chi* is identical to the first character of "knowledge": refer to this analysis for etymological treatment. *e* is the character for "grace" and is used only for its phonetic value in this word.

Semantic changes in Japan

DGK quotes an older definition: "The ability to perceive the essence of things (the *ri* 理) in one's heart and to discriminate in an issue."[1]

Modern range of meaning

KJ (1) perceive the essence (*ri*) of facts and things, (2) ability to ponder issues, formulate plans, and solve matters, (3) destroy illusions and attain enlightenment (Buddhist).

Chie does not always mean good wisdom. *Chie o tsukeru* (lit. "give wisdom") means actually "to give wrong ideas to."

English idiom paralells

A good head (*atama ga ii*).[2] Rack one's brains (*chie o shiboru*). Be short on grey matter (*nōmiso ga tarinai*). Shallow cunning (*sarujie* [lit., "monkey wisdom"]). Two heads are better than one (*Sannin yoreba, Monjū no chie*) [lit., "When three get together you have the wisdom of Monjū (boddhisattva of supreme wisdom). Wise men do not show their talents (*Nō aru taku wa tsume o kakusu* [lit., "The smart eagle hides his claws"]).

Buddhist concepts

Chie is a key symbol of Buddhist thought, the tr. of the Sk. *bodai* and defined as "the wisdom acquired through cutting of one's passions and illusory conceptions."[3] There are four types of Buddhist wisdom, called *shichi* and defined as: I. Mirror wisdom (*daienkyōchi*), which is free from all possible defilement, and is so called because it resembles a great mirror which reflects all things in their true state. II. Wisdom of equality (*byōdōshōchi*), seeing there is no separation between oneself and others. III. Wisdom of wondrous perception

---

1 *DGK*, p. 1256.

2 No doubt an import from English idiom.

3 *BD*, p. 18.

(*myōkanzachi*) when one has become free from taint, and so perceives all *dharma* forms in their true state. IV. Wisdom of accomplished metamorphoses (*jōshosachi*), to benefit unenlightened beings and lead them towad the truth of Buddhism.[4] But the general term *chie* is also used for tr. the Sk. *prajna* and is defined in its mental aspects as: "The mental function which enables one to perceive without error and to distinguish between what is true and what is false."[5] The *e* of Chie originally was a more complicated character and is defined as: "The function of the mind which makes decisions and eliminates doubts: it also enables the mind to gain understanding of phenomena."[6]

Biblical Concepts of Wisdom

Old Testament concepts

Key Hebrew word for wisdom is *hakham*, which with its cognates occurs over three hundred times in the OT. Smend's definition of the term is: "the art of reaching one's own end by the use of the right means."[7] Blackman defines it: "skill in making thought issue in appropriate action."[8] Such wisdom is gained through experience and comes with age (Job. 12:12, 15:10, Prov. 16:31). It is used of technical skill (Ex. 35:30,31), emphasizing its practical aspect. Those who are "wise" attain a special status, called "the wise" (Gen. 41:8, Ex. 7:11, Prov. 1:6). Solomon achieved the highest level in applying Biblical wisdom to the affairs of life (I Kings 4:30 ff.). There is a segment of Biblical writings termed "Wisdom Literature" in which are included Job, Proverbs, Ecclesiastes, and some Psalms. The OT prophets decried the wisdom of the heathen, for though their cultures were steadily advancing under this wisdom, it was basically man-centered, intellectual acumen without moral stopchecks. (Isa. 10:13, Ezek. 28:3-5, Jer. 49:7). For Biblical wisdom, in the words of Blackman, "includes the striving after the best ends as well as using of the best means — mental excellence in its highest and fullest sense. Wisdom is not separated from goodness or righteousness."[9]

The direction of OT wisdom was toward universals, derived from a study of natural phenomena, but resulting in a better knowledge of God (Psa. 19:1). But this wisdom is never absolute; to the contrary the man who rests in his own wisdom is actually a fool (Prov. 3:5-7; 19:21). True wisdom finds its locus in God Himself (Prov. 1:7, Psa. 111:10). The writer of Ecclesiastes is called by Blackman "a skeptical and very unorthodox wise man,"[10] whose worldly wisdom is shown to be an inadequate solution to life's central issues. In summary, the wise man of the OT is: (1) one who believes in God, (2) one who

---

4 *Ibid.*, p. 273.

5 *Ibid.*, p. 29.

6 *Ibid.*, p. 49.

7 Quoted by Burton Easton, "Wisdom," *ISBE*, V, 3089.

8 E. C. Blackman, "Wisdom," *TWBB*, p. 282.

9 *Ibid.*, p. 283.

10 *Ibid.*

endeavors to live by a prudence taught him by observing natural law, (3) one who is hard working, (4) one who rests not upon his own self-centered wisdom but upon a wisdom founded upon fear of God (Prov. 9:10).

New Testament concepts

Platonists made wisdom an ultimate. "Whithersoever reason (*logos*) leads, there we must go."[11] The *logos* and *sophos* became highest norms and guides for life. Into this Hellenistic setting, Christ came, employing the "wisdom method" — arriving at universal premises from observation of nature (John 12:24). His use of concise antithetical sayings stuck in the minds of his hearers. He was optimistic as Wisdom writers were. But he parted company with the "wise" because of their self-satisfaction (Luke 6:27-39). In fact, worldly wisdom made men impervious to His teaching. Wisdom from above, that is wisdom that is self-authenticating (Matt. 11:19), is received by a special group of divinely prepared men, called "wisdom's children" (Luke 7:35) as a divine bestowment (Eph. 1:17, Acts 7:10, Jas. 1:5; 3:17). Paul inveighed against the speculative wisdom of the Greeks. True wisdom is imparted by the Holy Spirit and unlocks spiritual realities for those who will be led by her (I Cor. 2: 6-13). This divine wisdom was supremely manifested in the Incarnation and the Cross (I Cor. 1:24-30, Col. 1:15-18; 2:3). Christ Himself becomes for Paul a reservoir of wisdom; the incarnation of the very wisdom of God (I Cor. 1:30).

Encounter

Japanese *chie* is the ability to discover basic principles, the essences of things, not dissimilar to the *sophos* of the Gk. philosopher. In Buddhist though it is the ability to destroy the illusion of opposites or entities. It is essentially a mental process by which knowledge is applied correctly to a situation yielding the right decision. It is almost synonymous with "intelligence" or "sharp thinking." For instance, the expression *chie ga tsuku* (lit., "wisdom comes upon one") is really the equivalent of "to show first signs of intelligence."

Biblical symbols convey a similar sense but their goals are not just wise decisions or the solving of difficulties. It has its locus in God, beginning from Him and effecting a clearer knowledge of His will. The wise man is taught by nature, but this knowledge leads him not to higher intellectual attainments but an understanding into the ways of God. Biblical wisdom, as anticipated by its personalization in Proverbs 8, is finally found in the person of Christ; hence the naivest of men, if united to Him as the source of wisdom, can walk circumspectly in the world.

---

[11] *Ibid.*

INSIGHT 洞 察 *DŌSATSU*

Japanese Concepts of Insight

Chinese character etymology

Dōsatsu is comprised of two characters: 洞 (cave), and 察 (look). *KGJ*: *Dō* is a cave or hole scooped out by flowing water. *Satsu* is a veil over the character for "look." Hence the concept of scrutinizing thoroughly an object, even though it be obscured by a veil. *KCJ*: to purify offerings and one's body in order to serve the gods. Hence the cultic sense of removing all impurities in order to clearly perceive an object.

Semantic changes in Japan

Japanese indigenous word is *minuku* which literally means to gaze and peer through a hole made by a nail or sharp object.

Modern range of meaning

Dō

KCJ (1) cave (*hora ana*), (2) flow rapidly (*hayaku nagareru*), (3) deep (*fukai*), (4) pass (*tōru*), (5) clear, bright (*horagaku*), (6) get through, pass through (*tsuranuku*).

Satsu

KCJ: (1) make clear (*akiraka ni suru*), (2) see (*miru*), (3) know (*shiru*), (4) weigh, consider (*kangaeru*).

Thus the two characters together convey the thought of looking deeply (as into a cave) and perceiving the reality of an object. Hence the range of meaning of *dōsatsu* is: DGK: (1) see through to the basic structure of things, (2) perceive the future. *DNKJ*: (1) look through (*minuku*), (2) peer through (*misukasu*). *KJ*: (1) surmise, infer (*sassuru*), (2) have pity on (*omoiyaru*).

English idiom parallels

Read between the lines (*gengai no imi o toru*). Determine what mood a person is in (*kaoiro o ukagau*). See right though a person (*kokoro o minuku*). Get to the bottom of (an issue) (*shinsō o kyūmei suru*).

Buddhist concepts

Buddhism does not use *dōsatsu* for insight; rather *fumbetsu*, tr. of the Sk. *vikalpa*, and is defined by *BD* as:

The process in which the mind and its components discern an object. There are three types of perception; direct perception, which is the action of the first five consciousnesses, perceiving their respective object realms; discriminating perception, which is the action of the consciousness perceiving various phenomena; and recollective discrimination, which is the action of the consciousness perceiving past events.[1]

Another Buddhist term conveying this concept is *genkan*, defined as immediate insight: "The insight of immediately perceiving the four noble truths by undefiled wisdom. In early Buddhism it means the enlightenment of the Buddha."[2]

Biblical Concepts of Insight

Key Gk. word for "insight" is *aisthanoma* ', denoting in secular usage, (1) sensual perception, (2) spiritual discernment, and (3) understanding. Delling says of the noun form: "*Aiothesis* is an organ of the *soma*, whereas *gnosis* is an organ of the *nous*."[3] In the LXX, the word is used to denote "judgment," either moral (Prov. 16:10) or religious (Isa. 49:26). In Prov. 1:7 it approaches the meaning of "wisdom": "the psychological point at which moral decision becomes actual."[4] In the NT it is used in three ways: (1) inner understanding (e.g., the disciples have no inner understanding of the Cross [Luke 9:45]), (2) power of moral discrimination (ethical judgment as distinct from religious [Phil. 1:9]), (3) capacity of moral decision (Heb. 5:14). It is to those who have trained this faculty that deeper spiritual truths can be preached.

Another word is *ereunao*. Delling traces it to the idea of horses sniffing with the nose. It means to investigate a matter. Used in the NT it signifies: (1) seeking the divine revelation in the Scriptures (John 7:52), (2) look into (I Pet. 1:11), (3) searching into innermost reality (Rom. 11:33). In the latter sense it is used negatively to stress that "God in His innermost reality is inaccessible to man; but while the non-biblical world relates this to God's essence the NT relates it to His action."[5] In Romans 11:33 it is clear that what is inaccessible to man is not God's attributes but His activity among men. Deeper understanding of the ways of God with men is given by the Holy Spirit (I Cor. 2:10). Biblical emphasis is not on speculative seeing but *responsible* seeing. "Man is responsible for making himself aware of what God is doing for his salvation."[6] Spiritual perception is the fruit of faith (John 20:29, I Pet. 1:8). But spiritual though it be, it is at best imperfect (I Cor. 13:12) and never transcends the bounds of seeing God (John 1:18, Deut. 4:12, I Tim. 6:16). Rather, vision of God is given to men in veiled form by the Incarnation (John 1:14). Full vision of the glory of God is reserved for man in the completely redeemed state (Matt. 5:8, I John 3:1-3).

---

[1] *BD*, p. 63.

[2] *BD*, p. 73.

[3] Gerhard Delling, "*aisthanomai*" *TDNT*, I, 187-188.

[4] *Ibid.*, p. 188.

[5] Gerhard Delling, "*ereunao*" *TDNT*, II, 657.

[6] E. C. Blackman, "See," *TWBB*, p. 223.

Encounter

Japanese *dōsatsu* and Biblical *aisthesis* both denote a seeing that is more than observation, a seeing that pierces accident and approaches essences. However, Buddhist concepts of illusion, the veil over one's heart, have focused attention on its achievement through clearing away of mental impairments and attitudes. Biblical insight is more in the moral and spiritual spheres, a seeing beyond the symbols of revelation the reality they portray. Such insight cannot be achieved unaided but must come through the assistance of God's Holy Spirit (I Cor. 2:9,10). More than on a speculative seeing into essences, the Biblical emphasis is upon responsible seeing of the spiritual truths behind the accidence of words and actions.

TRUTH 真〔眞〕実〔實〕 *SHINJITSU*

Japanese Concepts of Truth

Chinese character etymology

Shinjitsu is comprised of two characters: 真〔眞〕(straight, true), and 實 (full, fruit). *Jitsu* is treated under REALITY (GENJITSU), so will not be discussed here separately. *Shin* is the picture of a man upside down. *KGJ*: character was developed from the custom of burying a person upside down in the foundation of house. In human burial at the foundations of a Chinese house, the ground was packed full, hence the initial concept was "full."

Semantic changes in Japan

DGK quotes from *Kanshima*: "The gods and buddhas maintain the "*shin*" of life (i.e., its purity and genuineness)."[1] Japanese indigenous word for truth is *makoto*, the *ma* of which means "between". Truth lies in conformity, a matching of two things, word and action. Hence, the basis of truth lies in man and his integrity. Ōno points out the phonetic similarity of *koto* (fact, occurrence) and *kotoba* (word); this stemmed from the early belief in one's word's having *mana* in them, a spiritual force which would guarantee their realization and fulfillment. Both words and action summed up truth in primitive times.[2]

Modern range of meaning

Shin

KCJ: (1) truth (*makoto*), (2) truly, really (*hontō ni*), (3) natural (*shizen no mama*), (4) inner secret of a religious truth or teaching (*dokyō no okugi*).

KJ: (1) not false (*itsuwari de nai koto*), (2) true (*hontō*), (3) absolute truth (*zettai no shinri*).

DNKJ: (1) not false (*itsuwari de nai koto*), (2) true (*hontō*), (3) integrity (*seijitsu*).

The two characters together are compounded for emphasis and have the following range of meaning: (1) fullness, genuine, (3) inner part, (4) opposite of falsehood or illusion.[3]

English idiom parallels

Tell the plain truth (*ari no mama ni iu*). The proof of the pudding is in the eating (*Ron yori shōko*). Embellish the truth (*shinjitsu o mageru*). Ascertain the truth (*shinjitsu o tashikameru*). Flout the truth (*shinri ni hansuru*). Shoot wide of the truth (*shinri kara hazureru*).

---

1 *DGK*, p. 935.
2 Ōno, *Nihongo no...*, p. 223.
3 *KCJ*.

Buddhist concepts

Key word in Buddhism is not *shinjitsu* but *hō*, the tr. of the Sk. *dharma*, defined by *BD* as: "Something that mainains a certain character always and becomes a standard of things."[4] *Hō* has the following range of meaning: (1) law, truth, righteousness, (2) universal norms or laws which govern human existence, (3) The Buddha's teachings; the Buddhist canon, (4) Good deeds that have no defilement, (5) The consequences of action, or *karman*; the result of previous action which must work itself out, (6) The whole universe as the object of thought, (7) the predicate of a preposition in Indian logic, (8) Religious truth as opposed to secular truth.[5] Joined with this word *hō*, denoting truth or law, is the character for Buddha, giving the word *buppō*, defined as: "(1) the teachings of the Buddha. Traditionally there are said to be 84,000 types of doctrine, (2) the truth acquired by the Buddha, the truth of the universe."[6] *Tendai* Buddhism posits three kinds of truth, *viz.*, "(1) *kūtai*, All existence is non-substantial and void, (2) *ketai*, All existence is non-substantial, but nevertheless has a provisional reality, (3) *Chūtai*, All existence is neither void nor provisionally real, but there is a truth which transcends this dichotomy, which is none other than the middle way."[7]

Shin alone occurs in the Buddhist word, *sokujishin*, which is defined as: "All things or phenomena are identical with the truth. Phenomena which appear or disappear are nothing but the eternal truth itself."[8] It also occurs in the word *shintai*, tr. of the Sk. *paramartha*, which is equivalent for the "absolute truth."[9] In Buddhism there can be mutually exclusive doctrines or "truths," as expressed in the term *sozogusetsushu*, which *BD* defines as: "The truth is beyond form and perception, and inexplicable.[10] Thus there can be *hōben*, tr. of the Sk. *upaya*, meaning simply "convenience" in common parlance but defined by *BD* as: "The temporary or provisional teachings as a means to lead sentient beings to the final truth."[11] This explains how with no thought of contradiction, Buddhist priests who theoretically believe in the "no soul" doctrine of philosophical Buddhism can participate in requiem masses for the souls of the dead. This is "provisional truth" (*hōben*) which may lead the participant into deeper Buddhist truths, though the *hōben* be logically false. *Zen* carries this concept to the extreme by saying that the sayings of Buddha and his teachings are not *the* truth. The phrase used to convey this concept is *ichijifusetsu*, defined by *BD* as: "To say not one word. Buddha's enlightenment cannot be expressed by words and letters, and the truth was not indicated by the Buddha in the various teachings."[12]

---

4 *BD*, p. 107.

5 *BD*, p. 107.

6 *BD*, p. 23.

7 *BD*, p. 260.

8 *BD*, p. 307.

9 *BD*, p. 286.

10 *BD*, p. 308.

11 *BD*, p. 107.

12 *BD*, p. 123.

Biblical Concepts of Truth

Old Testament Concepts

Key Hebrew word for denoting truth is *amen*, occuring 126 times in the OT. It denotes a reality which is firm, solid, and therefore valid. The man whose conduct "falls under the norm of *amen* is a man of integrity."[13] *Amen* is sometimes synonymous with faith, and used to illucidate peace (*shalom*), lovingkindness (*hesed*), and righteousness (*sedeq*). It is used in a legal sense in Deut. 22:20 and Zech. 8:16: "if the matter rests on authentic facts."[14]

But *amen* is essentially a religious quality. It is the foundation of God's acts and word. Thus the man who is in fellowship with God must be a man of truth (Psa. 51:6, 15:2). Quell summarizes: "In every sphere of life, truthfulness grows out of unerring knowledge of God's will, and... such knowledge is for its part an actualization of truthfulness."[15] God is the final norm for truth and He becomes the guarantor of moral and legal standards. Thus His truth is embodied in His word to man (Psa. 19:9), and the laws promulgated at Sinai are truth and establish norms for truth (Neh. 9:13).

New Testament concepts

Key Gk. word denoting "truth" in the NT is *alētheia*, which etymologically is traced to the concept of "non-concealment." It is the state of affairs where the thing disclosed is really as it is — there is nothing truncated or hidden. It "denotes the full or real state of affairs."[16] Arnt finds three main usages of *alētheia* in the *NT*: (1) truthfulness, dependability, uprightness, (Rom. 3:7), (2) truth (Eph. 4:25), (3) reality as opposed to appearance (Phil. 1:18). Bultmann finds seven usages: (1) that which has certainty and force, like the OT *amen* (Eph. 4:21, Gal. 2:5), (2) that which is reliable (Rom. 3:3-7, 15:8), (3) sincerity (II Cor. 7:14), (4) the revealed reality of God (Rom. 1:18), (5) truth of statement (Acts 26:25), (6) true teaching or faith (II Cor. 13:8, I Pet. 1:22), (7) genuineness, divine reality, revelation, in the dualistic sense, contrasted with falsehood (John 8:40, 44, 45).[17] Biblical truth then is God-centered truth and its comprehension is not simply a matter of empirical research. Bultmann stresses this: "Its comprehension is not a free act of existence, but is grounded on the determination of existence by divine reality; everyone who is of the truth heareth my voice."[18] Thus the NT emphasis is not on speculative or ontological truth but upon truth as found in personality, the Personality of God and Jesus Christ. Carver says: "It must be kept in mind that only vaguely and indirectly does truth have abstract, metaphysical meaning to the Biblical writers. For John it approaches this but the primary interest is always concrete."[19] Thus Christ does not just declare truth to the human

---

13 Gottfried Quell, "alētheia," *TDNT*, I, 233.

14 *Ibid.*

15 *Ibid.*, p. 235.

16 Rudolph Bultmann, "alētheia," *TDNT*, I, 238.

17 *Ibid.*, pp. 245-246.

18 *Ibid.*, p. 246.

19 William O. Carver, "Truth," *ISBE*, V, 3025.

understanding; He comes as embodied truth (John 14:6). God's truth is reality
found in a Person (John 1:17).

> The fact that the Word of revelation is not a complex of statements or ideas, that it
> is not cosmological or soteriological speculation, but an address fulfilled in concrete
> encounter, is shown by the fact that it cannot be separated from the person of Jesus
> and the events fulfilled in His history (John 17:17-19).[20]

Thus *true* worship can only be accomplished through Christ, not through some
normative procedure or determined locale (John 4:24-25). After His departure
from this earth, the Spirit of Truth was sent to guide men into all truth (John
16:13). He not only reveals truth but *works truth in* the Christian community.
Hence the criterion for truth in the community becomes actual behavior; those
who are of the truth work out the truth in their lives (I John 4:6, III John 3).
When the Spirit of Truth has so inwrought truth into the character of the
believer, his actions can be characterized as "truth" (III John 8). In this way
man can approach the highest truth of God, for the Spirit of truth is at work
in his being. Carver stresses this: "Highest truth in correspondence to ideal is
possible only by the working of the God of truth in the spirit of man."[21]
For that reason, the Biblical test for truth is not left to the whim and mercy
of a select few richly endowed with intellectual acumen, who alone can com-
prehend essential truth by canons of logic; rather the truth is revealed to those
who submit in active obedience to the declared will of God (John 7:17).

Encounter

Japanese concepts of truth stemming from earliest meanings of "straight,"
"full" to the present usage as "genuine," "inner part" and idiomatic synonymous phrases lay stress upon the dualistic contrast with that which is false,
crooked, exterior. The word finds its standard in man; he is either "true" or
"false." Man has inherently within him the capacity for truth; he can be
"shinjitsu" if he speaks sincerely and in accordance with the facts as he knows
them. Buddhist philosophical notions concerning different realms and grades of
truth no doubt have escaped the thinking of the man on the street, except to
the point of making absolute truth seem only attainable to the few; it does
not lie close at hand. The word *dōri* (reason) which has within it the
character of "way," "road" can be traced to the Buddhist emphasis upon *Hō*,
(law),[22] but is equivalent to "common sense" in everyday speech. Departing
from *dōri* (e.g., *dōri ni kanawanai*) means really *acting in an unconventional
or unethical way.* This is a Buddhist word, yet very few Japanese have this
concept when using the word. The point is simply that originally it did have
a point of reference, the way of Buddha, but now it does not. Hence there are
ambiguous notions about absolute standards or tests for truth. Pressed farther

---

20 Rudolph Bultmann, *"alḗtheia,"* *TDNT*, I, 238.
21 Carver, *ISBE*, V, p. 3026.
22 Defined by *BD* as: "The laws or rules to be followed by all beings," p. 48.

"*shinjitsu*" means to the average man, "What I think and feel is right." *Truth* then is not sifted through the Western screen of (a) logical consistency, and (b) fitting with facts, but is sifted through Japanese sentiment and notions built in through tradition and custom.

The *mana* concept of words having their own power of authentication is observed in the Japanese occupation with the classical Chinese characters as being respositories of profound thought. The ubiquitous printed signs, name cards, titles after names, reveal an undue confidence in *words*. The slovenly, seedy-looking vender going through the trains sells his product, though it may run a high bacteria count, though no one purchasing his item has ever heard (or will again) of the company manufacturing it; his sales result from the simple cry "Ice Cream." Highest selling magazines are not the translated Reader's Digest, nor factual-type magazines but those which abound with short stories of samurai exploits having little or no historical value. The test for truth lies within the emotional framework of the reader.

Biblical truth finds its locus in the character of God. In the words of Carver:

> God's nature is all comprehensive of fact and goodness, and so is, all in all, the source, support, and objective of all concrete being. The will of God thus reveals, persuades to, and achieves the ideals and ends of complete existence. The term truth, therefore is sometimes nearly equivalent to the revealed will of God.[23]

Hence truth, as expressive of His will, qualifies His relations and activities. It is the guarantee of His constancy (Deut. 32:4, Psa. 100:5, Jas. 1:17), the ground for confidence in His promises (Ex. 34:6, Psa. 91:4). Men thus find the source and test for truth in God and His revelation, whether it be the inscripturated or the incarnate Word. Man himself has a proclivity to falsehood, hypocrisy, lying, and vanity. The Bible constantly warns men against men and suggests setting up criteria for truth, e.g., by their actions, by the actual fulfillment of their words, or by orthodox confession of Christ (I John 4:1-6). Men can only become "of the truth" by the supernatural work of the Spirit of Truth. Japanese "truth" finds its nexus in man; Biblical truth finds its nexus in the character of God.

---

23 Carver, *ISBE*, V, 3025.

THOUGHT 思 想 SHISŌ

Japanese Concepts of Thought

Chinese character etymology

Shisō is comprised of two characters: 思 (think), and 想 (idea). *Shi* has two components: 心 (heart), and 囟 (water of the ears). *KGJ*: thinking processes take place in the heart and in the water cavity near the ears; hence thinking. *KCJ*: locale of thinking processes is man's heart. *Sō* has two components: 心 (heart), and 相 (the other person or encounter). *KGJ*: being drawn or influenced by another. *KCJ*: pondering in one's heart. The two characters thus compound the idea of man mulling over ideas in his inner self.

Semantic changes in Japan

Ōno traces *omou*, the Japanese indigenous word to which *shi* was affixed, from the word "face"; hence "what one thinks in his heart is expressed on the face."[1]

Modern range of meaning

Shi

KCJ: (1) think (*omou*), (2) ask (*negau*), (3) long for (*shitau*), (4) worry (*shimpai*), (5) be sad (*kanashimu*).

Sō

KCJ: (1) think (*omou*), (2) idea (*kangae*), (3) contents of literature or art, i.e., ideals.

Shisō

KJ: (1) thought (*kangae*), (2) formation of a logical concept, (3) view (of life, society, etc.).

English idiom parallles

Take into consideration (*kangae ni ireru*). Think logically (*sujimichi tatete kangaeru*). Not go beyond the realm of conjecture (*okusoku no han'i o denai*). Make hay while the sun shines (*Omoitatta ga kichinichi*). Association of ideas (*rensō*).

Buddhist concepts

Shi of *Shisō* is a Buddhist term, tr. of the Sk. *cetana* and defined by *BD* as follows: "Volition. The name of a mental function... It is that type of mental

---

1 Ōno, *Nihongo no...*, p. 203.

activity which stimulates the mind to make *karman*."[2] But actually Buddhism de-emphasizes discriminatory thinking; this tendency is revealed by the use of many cognates of *Shi*, prefixed by the negative *mu* (not, negation). For example there is *musōten*, tr. of the Sk. *asamjni-sattvah*, which is defined by *BD* as: "The heaven without thought; beings in this heaven have no thought."[3] Another is *munen-musō* (without concepts or ideas), a Zen term. Zen uses the word *mushin* (without mind), defined by *BD* as: "Non-existence of the mind... in Zen it usually indicates naturalness of freedom from discriminating think- ing."[4] The *Sō* of *Shisō* is also defined by BD as: "A mental function in which an image of the object is drawn into one's mind and its conception is con- structed."[5] This is the tr. of the Sk. *samjna*. Another expression which in- herently de-emphasizes discriminative thinking is *ichinen fushō*, defined as: "Without one thought arising. It is said that if you do not cherish the notion of desire, the state of your mind is the same as that of the Buddha."[6]

Biblical Concepts of Thought

Old Testament concepts

Most frequently used Hebrew symbol is *mahashebheth*, which like its cognates *damah* and *zamman* signify "thought with a view to action... disinterested academic reflection is not a mark of the Hebrew mind but is characteristic of the Greek."[7]

New Testament concepts

Gk. words such as *dialogismos*, *enthumesis*, and *epinoia*, though intrinsically having a philosophic flavor from Gk. culture, are used in the NT more with the OT sense of "practical devising" or "fixing a purpose." Hence when the query is raised, "What do you think?" (Acts 28:22), the speaker is not asking about one's casual off-hand ideas but about one's whole attitude. To be *mindful* of the flesh (Rom. 8:5ff), is not just thinking about carnal things but to have one's whole course of action, one's direction of daily life bent on their pursuit. The Gk. word *hegeomai* is a near approach to the philosophical aspects of making a logical deduction from premises, as employed in Acts 26:2, Phil. 2:6. *Enthumoumai* as used in Matt. 1:20 and Acts 10:19 "refers to the mental process itself, the thinking out of a project, the concentration of the faculties upon the formulation of a plan."[8]

---

2 *BD*, p. 272.

3 *BD*, p. 205.

4 *BD*, p. 204.

5 *BD*, p. 305.

6 *BD*, p. 125.

7 E. C. Blackman, "Thought," *TWBB*, p. 257.

8 H. E. Jacobs, "Think," *ISBE*, V, 2973.

Encounter

From its earliest etymology to the modern range of meaning the Japanese ideas for "thought" converge on the concept of *thought processes* rather than the Western concept of logical deduction from discriminative thinking. It is the idea of mulling over ideas that have entered the mind with the self as reference point, not some abstract frame of reference like the law of contradiction. The Bible also mentions this deliberating with oneself, but usually such thinking issues in undue worry, anxiety, or in many cases clever schemes against one's fellow man. Thus the Biblical verdict is "every imagination of the thoughts of his heart is only evil continually" (Gen. 6:5), "man's thoughts are not God's thoughts" (Isa. 55:7-9), "take no thought" (occuring seven times in Matt.). That is, the Bible places little credibility upon man left to his own thoughts. Buddhism is largely a religion of thought, an attempt to correct man's inherent proclivity toward discriminative thinking. Hence "non-thought" does not mean an obliteration of thought processes but an attempt to take man to higher thought processes, those which transcend logical and deductive barriers. The Bible attempts to take man in his thought processes to the plateau of thinking God's thoughts after Him.

Excursus

At this point we should attempt to give a linguistic hint toward solving the historical enigma that Japan has had a dearth of original philosophic or scientific thought emerge from her culture. Many books treating Japanese sentiment and emotions flow out each year to the bookstands, but a coordinated philosophic system of thought that is essentially Japanese can hardly be found. Hajime Nakamura suggests that the riddle is solved in the language itself: "The expressive forms of Japanese sentences put more emphasis upon emotive factors than on cognitive."[9] This has handicapped original scientific thinking as well, he asserts:

> Its illogical, unscientific character naturally handicaps the development of ability in logical, scientific thinking among the Japanese people, and has actually brought about grave inconveniences to their practical lives... although it is unsuitable for logically precise expression, it is well adapted to the expression of intuition and of individual emotion.[10]

Basil H. Chamberlain found very few if any abstract words in Japanese poetry; he says:

> Abstract words are comparatively few and it does not occur to the Japanese poet to represent Truth, Justice, and Faith as comely damsels... Graces, Virtues, Furies, in short the host of personifications, without which Western poetry would only be a shadow of itself, have little counterpart in Japanese literature.[11]

---

9 Hajime Nakamura, p. 462.

10 *Ibid.*, pp. 465, 486.

11 Quoted in *A History of Japanese Literature with Notes* (Tōkyō: Gansuido, 1936), p. 27.

Of course, with the importation of Buddhism in the Nara-Heian periods, the Japanese literati began to sense the relation of the macrocosm to their personal lives. The fleeting course of nature was vivid expression of the transitoriness of court life, with its tragic vicissitudes — exiled from Kyoto, in favor, out of favor, etc. But beyond this sense of transitoriness there is little philosophical thought. Chamberlain observes:

> There are no soundings of the depths of the human heart; that would be philosophy and not poetry; and for philosophy there was no need in the land of the gods where all men were naturally perfect. There were no invectives against rulers or aspirations after liberty: that would be not poetry but politics, or rather treason against the heaven-born Mikado... There are for similar reasons but few prayers to the upper powers; neither are there in a country possessing indeed a mythology, but no religion properly so-called, any yearnings after a life beyond the grave. What we find is the expression in natural language of the simple feelings common to all mankind; love, regret, loyalty, attachment to old traditions, and in the place of religion and moralizing, nothing but that hopeless sense of the transitoriness of life, which precedes as it survives, all culture and philosophy.[12]

The modern authority on Japanese court poetry, Brower of Stanford, makes a similar observation: "The personified abstraction of a moral or ethical quality we owe to Hebrew, late Latin and medieval literature simply is not a part of Japanese poetry."[13] Ōno has sought in vain to find the word for "nature" in Japanese classical literature. This he attributes to the peculiar Japanese sentiment that no boundary exists between man and nature. He says: "The Japanese considered themselves as integral parts of nature. She did not stand apart from man as an object to overcome; man and nature were one."[14]

Hence in summary of the different views as to why there is an absence of philosophical thinking in Japan, Chamberlain traces the phenomenon to a cultural insistence upon submissiveness, the lack of enquiry or questioning in a "divinely constituted" society. Nakamura traces it to the emotive characteristic of the language itself. As against Nakamura's view, it would be linguistically difficult to maintain that a symbol system *per se* is inadequate to express phenomena or ideas. To the contrary, upon the introduction of Western technology into Japan during the Meiji era, Yukichi Fukuzawa, the foremost introducer of Western ideas at that time, was able to quickly assign time-worn Chinese symbols to modern inventions.

I would like to suggest another explanation. New ideas which produced inventions in America developed from necessity. American farm machinery, for example, was developed in the tool shed of the frustrated American farmer, perplexed at the growing higher costs of labor (as the exodus to the cities produced a shortage of farm labor) and the vast unplowed fields lying before him. As he bent and shaped old plows, he noticed new workable ways of rigging them up. He had no preconceived ideas about the theoretical reasons for plowing

---

12 B. H. Chamberlain, *The Classical Poetry of the Japanese* (London: Trubner and Co., 1880), p. 19.

13 Brower and Miner, *Japanese Court Poetry* (Stanford: Stanford University Press, 1961), p. 6.

14 Ōno, *Nihongo no...*, p. 11.

(he might have thought it was to let the rain percolate through the soil, when actually it has been demonstrated that its basic function is weed control). He did not wade through laborious tomes on soil types, laws of motion, stress of steel. Ford developed the internal combustion engine by dropping gasoline into a rudely constructed pipe in his home shop after working hours.

In the East, and especially in Japan, ideas flow into the mind initially not as meaningless units of sound (phonemes), but as morphemic units of meaning. Hence to develop a new idea, these characters have to be reorganized in a new pattern first. This is going against tradition and a sublimating of the notion that perhaps such ideas had already been well thought out in the past (for the characters are *idea* graphs). Summing up can we hint that *the morphemic structure of the Japanese language has inhibited original thought*? If there were an abandoning of the pictorial system of writing, the Japanese searcher for new ideas could turn his attention away from the concepts *in language* to language as a tool and to the phenomena of life itself. Here grappling with steel, mud, wood, he will discover by trial and error new ways to shape nature to his liking.[15]

---

15 Dr. Cyrus Peake pointed out to me a social factor in this heretofore lag in Japanese original thinking. He points out that the Oriental artisan was like the ingenious and inventive Westerner
   but his aristocracy, bureaucracy and priestly class disdained him and his works, providing no
   cumulative principle or basis for his "science." In the West, not so; learned men work with
   artisans or were themselves mechanics who made telescopes and other things. They felt they were
   working with God in so doing. The individualistic, democratic essence of Christianity is that
   God through Christ enters men and elevates them to a moral par. Hence humility and submissiveness to a bureaucratic society is not so dominant in the West as in the Orient. In the West
   thus, there is social mobility for the individual—no castes, classes. There are of course, minority
   barriers for Negroes, Jews, etc., but this is not like a barrier *built on kinds of work done*. Also
   in the Orient, guilds and families cherished secrets of their skills for economic reasons, not
   sharing their findings with philosophers who might go on to discover nature's laws.

ILLUSION 迷 MAYOI

Japanese Concepts of Illusion

Chinese character etymology

Mayoi is one character with two components: 辶 (road), and 米 (rice). *KGJ* gives two explanations: (1) rice spilled out on a road cannot be counted, hence "perplexity," (2) be perplexed at a crossroads. *KCJ*: development from the character for "eye"; one's eye is not clear or to lose one's way on the road.

Semantic changes in Japan

Actually the word *mayoi* stems from the Japanese silkworm, *mayu*. When silk threads get entangled you have *mayoi*.

DGK quotes from *Shin Gosenshū* (A.D. 1303): "On a dark night when the cloud covered (*madoi*) moon suddenly cleared up, I could clearly see the moon."[1] Hence bound up with the word and its cognates is the concept of a "veil" or "fog." Ōno mentions the concept of "inability to discern a boundary."

Modern range of meaning

KCJ: (1) go off the right road onto a wrong one (*mayou*), (2) delude, deceive (*madowaseru*), (3) perplexity arising from inability to decide (*mayoi*), (4) be vague (*bonyari suru*).

DNKJ: (1) get lost (*mayou koto*), (2) be confused (*magireru*), (3) be in confusion (*midareru*).

KJ: (1) wander (*mayou koto*), (2) get confused (*magireru*), (3) have an evil attachment preventing the attainment of Buddhahood. The evil attachment is from the dead, (4) inability to achieve enlightenment.

English idiom parallels

Fumble around in the dark (*tomadou*). Be in the dark (*gōri muchū*). Come under a delusion (*mayoi ga deru*; lit., "a delusion comes out"). Get lost (*michi ni mayou*). Turn from the path of duty (*michi o fumihazusu*). Be bewildered (*tōhō ni kureru*).

Buddhist concepts

Key Buddhist words are *waku*, *mayoi*, and *bonnō*. *Waku* is the tr. of the Sk. *kleśa*, defined by *BD* as: "A term denoting defilement which causes us to become bewildered in perceiving objects and confused in understanding the reality of things."[2] There are three kinds of *waku*, called *sanwaku*, and defined

---

[1] *DGK*, p. 1907.
[2] *BD*, p. 328.

as, "I. Illusions of Hinayana Buddhism. II. Illusions preventing *bodhisattvas* from saving others. III. Illusions preventing *bodhisattvas* from attaining the middle way."[3] *Bonnō* is the tr. of *klesa* also, defined as: "Those mental functions which disturb the mind."[4] The fundamental illusions are (1) covetousness, (2) anger, (3) ignorance, (4) arrogance, (5) doubt, (6) false views.[5] Enlightenment (*kaigo*) is "the state wherein one overcomes illusion and desire and thereby is enabled to apprehend the truth of the universe."[6] The *bhagavat* (*bagaba*) then is the one who has got rid of these illusions. Man's mind in Buddhism is essentially pure; like the moon it has clouds over it — illusions. Thus, "when the illusion is removed, the pure mind shines forth and perfect enlightenment is achieved."[7]

Biblical Concepts of Illusion

Key Hebrew word is *ta'ah*, used to denote a moral wandering into paths of sin (Isa. 53:6). This wandering is not the root of sin but its fruit. "The wicked are estranged from the womb; they go *astray* as soon as they be born, speaking lies" (Psa. 58:3). False shepherds lead people astray (Jer. 50:6). Key Gk. word in the NT is *plane*, more fully discussed under *ERROR*, but in general it signifies a wandering or roaming from paths of righteousness (II Thess. 2:11, I Pet. 2:25). Christ comes to seek and to save the sheep who have *wandered* from the fold (Matt. 18:12,13).

Encounter

The concept of illusion as a veil over the human heart, keeping man from clear perception of the basic truths of Buddhism, has seeped into everyday Japanese thinking. Evil is not inherent wickedness but mental obscurantism. A cloud comes over one's thinking processes preventing clear intellectual perception. Of course, in modern speech, this cloud (*mayoi*) has lost the sense of eclipsing the Buddha-nature within and simply means, "wandering off from accepted patterns of conduct." Biblical "illusion" is more literal — actually walking away from paths of worship, Christian duty, paths clearly outlined in Scripture. Sin — rebellion against the known will of God — becomes the cause of this activity. That is, Buddhism sees illusion as shutting man out from himself; the Bible posits sin as shutting men out from God and causing him to wander from His known will. Illusion, and salvation from it, in Buddhism is basically mental. In the words of Takenaka, "In Buddhism, if a man by contemplation is able to perceive a god-like nature (*hotoke-gokoro*) within himself, he attains the enlightenment; in Christianity, when one perceives the basic sinfulness of his nature, he becomes a seeker after God."[8]

---

3 *BD*, p. 260.

4 *BD*, p. 20.

5 *BD*, p. 178.

6 *BD*, p. 156.

7 *BD*, p. 225.

8 *Encyclopaedia of Buddhism*, unpublished manuscript in the files of Tōyō University, Tokyo. (Cited hereafter as *EBu.*)

ERROR 誤 *AYAMARI*

Japanese Concepts of Error

Chinese character etymology

Ayamari is one character with two components: 言 (word), and 呉 (arrow and mouth). *KGJ* gives two interpretations: (1) picture of a person wagging his head, speaking many things; such a person makes mistakes, (2) the arrow runs counter to the word, hence fabrication of the truth. *KCJ*: from another character meaning "big talk," hence to enlarge things and talk irresponsibly; later comes to mean simply the opposite of truth.

Semantic changes in Japan

The Japanese indigenous word to which this character was affixed is from the word *"aya,"* meaning "a knot"[1] — something that was hard to untie, fathom, understand. Thus the expression *"ayashi to omou"* has within it the same phonetic sounds and means "difficult to understand." To make an *ayamari* was to injure someone without intention. When questioned about a mistake or such an accident the reply would be, "Oh, that was an *ayamari*." Thus *ayamari* is *unintentional error*. For example in the *Man'yōshū*, there is the phrase, "Even a serene, well-meaning person sometimes makes *mistakes (ayamari)*."[2] Thus the word was tantamount to apologizing for mistakes committed and has that nuance in its modern range of meaning.

Modern range of meaning

KCJ: (1) make a mistake (*ayamaru*), (2) get wrong (*machigaeru*), (3) bungle (*ayamachi*), (4) delude, mislead (*madowasu*).

GS: (1) make a mistake (*ayamaru koto*), (2) get wrong (*machigaeru*), (3) error (*ayamachi*), (4) bungle, miss (*gobyō*), (5) apology (*wabi*).

DNKJ: (1) make a mistake (*ayamaru koto*), (2) mistake (*ayamachi*), (3) do wrong (*shisokonai*), (4) bungle (*shikujiri*), (5) apologize (*shazai*).

KJ: (1) make a mistake (*ayamaru koto*), (2) mistake, get wrong (*machigae*), (3) go amiss (*shisokonai*).

English idiom parallels

Trip a person up (*ageashi o toru*). To err is human (*Hito tare ka ayama-chi nakaran*). Nobody is perfect (*Kōbō mo fude no ayamari*; lit., Even Kōbō

---

[1] Mentioned in an interview with Prof. Ōno, Peers University, Feb. 12, 1966.
[2] *DGK*, p. 101.

[A master of Chinese calligraphy] makes a mistake with his brush). Get off on the wrong foot (*michi o ayamaru*). Barking up the wrong tree (*okado chigae*). Upset the applecart (*hema o yaru*). Even the best make mistakes (*Saru mo ki kara ochiru*; lit., Even a monkey falls from a tree). We learn by trial and error (*Shippai wa seikō no moto*).

Buddhist concepts

Error in Buddhism is *gedō*, lit., "outside the way," defined as: "Non-buddhist religions or philosophies... Confucianism and Taoism in China. Heresy in general."[3] This concept of being off the right path — the Buddhist path — has percolated down to common parlance in just the word "path" or "way." Error or going astray is wandering from this. Thus "error" is intrinsically departure from accepted norms or patterns of conduct. It originates in wrong views. The way to right these wrong views is through meditation, *viz.*, meditating upon the concepts that (1) the body is impure, (2) perception leads to suffering, (3) the mind is impermanent, (4) *dharmas* are non-substantial.[4]

Biblical Concepts of Error

Old Testament concepts

This concept is rendered by various words, such as *shaghah* which, like *ta'ah* (illusion) denotes "wandering" as in I Sam. 26:21, "I have played the fool and have *erred*.", or in Amos 2:4, "Their lies (idols, or false deities) have caused them to *err*." Other words are *kazabh* and *sheker*, both denoting "deceit." The opposite of truth is emptiness or vanity, for truth in the OT is that which is firm or reliable. In the words of Blackman: "As Truth is that which is the normal, permanent characteristic of the good man, so it is that lying and cognate words mean by contrast what is abnormal, empty, lacking stability and permanence, disturbing of trust and harmony."[5] Another word is *hebel*, referring to that which is impermanent and unsubstantial, like breath. In Psa. 62:9 it is used to convey the thought that all men are unreliable. It is used in reference to idols in Jer. 8:19.

New Testament concepts

Error in the NT is considered under the two aspects of "wandering" and "ignorance." The Gk. word for "wandering" is *plane*, but it denotes "getting something wrong" (Mk. 12:24) and "deceit" (I Thess. 2:3). The "wandering" aspect shades into the sense of "unnatural" in Rom. 1:27, "sinning against the truth" in James 5:20, and "unorthodoxy" in I John 4:6. The absolute standard of truth from which men wander, then, is either natural law or special revelation. Another term *agnoema* which lit., is "not to know" denotes "being

---

3 *BD*, p. 71.
4 *BD*, p. 281.
5 Blackman, "Lie," *TWBB*, p. 127.

mistaken," or "in error," as the character of an action. And it is culpable ignorance. Bultmann stresses this:

> The Biblical concept is not so much a lack of understanding or lack of information, but a misunderstanding which stands under the wrath of God and needs forgiveness (I Tim. 1:13)... Accordingly, the knowledge by which *agnoema* is removed does not derive from human reflection or enquiry, but from the proclamation which demands faith.[6]

Cognate with *agnoema* is *agnosia* which denotes the lack of knowledge essential to Biblical salvation—the lack of a knowledge of God (Acts 17:30, I Pet. 1:14, Eph. 4:18). "It expresses the destiny of the world's alienation from God, its fallen state, and its dependence upon revelation."[7] The term *agnostos theos* (the unknown God), found in Acts 17:23 is not traced to the idea that God is unknowable but simply to the idea that the heathen do not know God as the Christians do. Bultmann challenges Norden's view that this phrase denotes the irrationality of God. The Gnostic idea that God is irrational cannot be traced to Oriental influences, he affirms, and had nothing to do with the dialogue on Mars Hill.

Encounter

Japanese concept of error lays stress on one's mental frame of reference. The character for "word" appearing in it naturally lends to this development. Error in Buddhism is wandering into non-Buddhist systems of thought; reshuffling of thought patterns can correct error. This religious color to the idea is preserved in the modern use of the word *ayamari*; error is unintentional; it can be corrected with apology. In fact the apology (*ayamari*) is simply just stating that the deed committed was an error, an *ayamari*. This phenomenon is observed by the host of words used in daily life that come with the bumps of social intercourse. Grossest mistakes can be readily smoothed over with the proper *word*. If error is essentially in the realm of thought and words (not action), it is corrected through this medium. For the Westerner to expect restitution in the form of payment or replacement, after his Chinaware cups slip from the hands of the maid and lie shattered on the floor — such expectation is running head-on against this concept of error. For full apology has been made in such terms as "Sumimasen" (Lit., "it will never end," "it" meaning "my indebtedness to you"). Dr. Peake points out at this point that the prevailing concern in the Orient over mistakes committed is with the *disharmony* they cause, either in the family or in the community. Hence the offended one is reticent to go hastily to law courts (as in the West), for thereby the disharmony is perpetuated. Rather he looks for a *sense of shame* in the offender for having caused

---

6 Rudolph Bultmann, "*agnoema*" *TDNT*, I, 116.

7 *Ibid.*, p. 119.

the disharmony.[8] But this creates problems in a transcultural context. Japanese diplomats travelling in Southeast Asia after the war, offering "apologies" for Japan's wartime activities in those countries, began creating serious problems for the Japanese government. Heretofore unthought-of demands for reparations began pouring into the Foreign Affairs office. Finally the word was passed to visiting dignitaries to avoid indiscriminate use of the word "apologize" for in other countries it had the nuance of restitution in the form of concrete action.

Biblical error is that which is culpable action against known truth, either natural law or spiritual revelation. It is not excused by better thinking nor apology but by repentence, seeking for forgiveness from God and followed by practical steps of restitution aimed at correcting the error.

8 Interview, April, 1966.

CHAPTER II
CONCEPTS OF EMOTIONAL EXPERIENCE

LOVE 愛 AI

Japanese Concepts of Love

Chinese character etymology

Ai is one character having two components: 愛 (heart) and 夂 (footstep).
KGJ: previous character from which this was derived had two components;
"heart" and "full." "Full" stemmed from the concept of a man who had eaten
to the full and fallen asleep. Hence one's heart is full. It also connoted pain;
hence the nuance of regret (*oshimu*) in the word. Present character is that of a
person in motion striking an object; hence one is feeling miserable and cannot
move ahead. *KCJ*: two interpretations: (a) concept of bestowing something
or having pity upon another, (b) component of "foot" implies slowly seeking
something one desires.[1]

Semantic changes in Japan

There is the sense of regret, compassion and condescension found in the
usage of the word in classical Japanese literature. From *Shoin*, Confucius is
quoted: "Love is the beginning of '*jin*'; it is compassion and grace."[2] Love is
to grudge or be remorseful. For example, in the *Eiga Monogatari*: "When a
man dies, he *loves* (or regrets leaving) three things: rice wine, poems, and
the Japanese *koto*."[3] *Ai* had this interplay of affection and sadness for the
cherished one or thing was usually taken away.

Ōno points out that this word *ai* in its verb form is not used by people over
fifty in Japan today. This stems from the fact that gradations in society and
the inferiority of women are still lingering concepts in modern Japan. Instead
of "love," words denoting "pity" or "feeling sorry for" were used in previous
generations. Ōno continues:

> In the late Meiji period, as revealed in the literature, women were seen as having a
> distinct personality and being on equal par with men. Hence "*ai*" was used as the
> translation of the German *lieben* or English "love." Before this, in the Heian period,
> for instance, the word was used in the sense of being fond of insects, but never in
> relation to the sexes. When the Catholics came to Japan, they thus avoided *ai* for
> expressing Biblical love and used instead *taisetsu ni suru* (to treat carefully).[4]

---

1 *KCJ*, p. 393.
2 *DGK*, p. 1.
3 *GS*, p. 2.
4 Ōno, *Nihongo no...*, p. 100.

But in translating the European concept of love on the basis of mutual respect, *ai* gradually came to be used. Ōno wonders if the European concept of love has truly found its way into the word. He continues:

> The God of the Christians is the witness of this love in equality. And the God of Christianity has had an entirely different effect upon the lives of the people of Europe than the eight million gods had upon the people of Japan. The God of Christianity is only One. Such a concept has not been in Japan from of old. So the Japanese people may adopt the outward forms of European civilization and become civilized, but unless with this they assimilate the concept of the God of Christianity, it is an open question whether they can fathom the European concept of love.[5]

Modern range of meaning

KCJ: (1) love (*aisuru*), (2) to feel compassion for (*itsukushimu*), (3) like (*konomu*), (4) to begrudge, or feel remorse (*oshimu*), (5) in Christianity, it is the blessing God bestows on man.[6]

KJ: (1) show compassion for, (2) feeling a man and woman have for each other, (4) to be drawn by something, (5) to be fond of (pets, etc.) (*aigan suru*), (6) caress, (7) in Christianity, the blessing God bestows on humanity, (8) to consider others as brothers and so be fond of them.

DNKJ: (1) to be fond of (*kawaigaru koto*), (2) to feel regret over (*oshimu koto*), (3) to have compassion on (*awaremu koto*), (4) love between man and woman, (5) in a religious sense, the nature of God which protects and loves humanity.

English idiom parallels

Overflow with love (*ai ni afureru*). Be infatuated with (*aijō ni oboreru*). Be full of compassionate love (*jiai ni tomu*). Fall in love with at first sight (*hitomebore suru*). Be the apple of one's eye (*me ni irete mo itakunai*). One-sided love (*kata omoi*).

Buddhist concepts

Buddhism makes a dichotomy between defiled and undefiled love. Defiled love (*zemma ai*) "stems from attachment to self and includes desire for fame, wealth and carnal pleasure."[7] It is used to denote that lust for life "which arises at the point of death and serves as a contributory cause leading to rebirth."[8] The other love, called *fuzemma ai*, is "characterized by selfless compassion for all sentient beings."[9] However, in actual usage the word *ai* has the sense of craving and lust and thus is deprecated in Buddhist thought. Ichikawa lists it with the catalogue of Buddhist sins.[10] Joined with "opinion" (*aiken*) it

---

5 *Ibid.*, p. 102.

6 This is not the Biblical sense of love, but it shows how difficult it is for Japanese scholars to express the Biblical concept of love.

7 *BD*, p. 4.

8 *Ibid.*

9 *Ibid.*

10 The other sins listed are covetousness, anger, doubt, indolence, self-indulgence, ignorance, ambition. Found in *EBu*.

means "love and opinions in a false sense. Thirst or craving, and delusion."[11] With the character for "joining" it becomes *aiketsu* meaning "the bondage of craving... it binds all human beings making emancipation from transmigration impossible."[12] Since this word *ai* has the sense of passion in it, the word *jihi* (compassion) is used instead. And this is an attitude of sympathy for all sentient beings. *BD* defines *jihi*: "The mind or mental condition of being compassionate or sympathetic toward sentient beings."[13]

Biblical Concepts of Love

Old Testament concepts

Key Hebrew word in the secular sphere is *ahebh*, which with its cognates is used for persons and things. It is a spontaneous human emotion impelling one to grasp after the desired object. It can be used in the sexual sphere (Hos. 3:1), but it has an ethical content as well. Thus it becomes the norm for social relationships. However this norm of love cannot be legally enforced for "the command to love, wearing the clothes of the law reduces the law itself to absurdity, since it shows the boundary beyond which there can be no legislation, human or divine, and establishes the claim of a way of life that is above law."[14] Quell feels that such OT commands to love (as in Zech. 8:17) were to awaken Israel to the goal of all social legislation, *viz.*, "brotherhood; its protection, cultivation, and sometimes also its creation."[15] But Cranfield feels Quell has missed the point; this *ahebh* is theological; it is man's response to God's love, a response expressed toward one's neighbor and stranger and even enemy. "It starts at home but works outward, and it is to be shown by deeds, though it is a matter of the heart."[16] It is to be demonstrated to anyone in need of help (Exod. 23:4, Deut. 22:1-4). The word is avoided when referring to God's love for man, perhaps, as Cranfield suggests, because it suggests a very creaturely feeling in the Divine nature, or perhaps because of its associations on a lower plain with the fertility cults of pagan religion.

Key Hebrew word in the religious sphere is *chesed*, variously translated in different versions as "mercy" or "lovingkindness." The word is a technical word used in relation to the covenant of God with Israel. Snaith says, "Without the prior existence of a covenant, there could never be any *chesed* at all."[17] It has the etymological meaning of "keenness," "eagerness." Used secularly it denoted the loyalty and faithfulness two parties were to maintain toward each

---

11 *BD*, p. 4.

12 *Ibid.*

13 *BD*, p. 137.

14 Gottfied Quell and Ethelbert Stauffer, "Love," *Bible Key Words*, ed. Gerhard Kittel, trans. J.R. Coates (New York: Harper and Row, 1951), I, 8.

15 *Ibid.*

16 C.E.B. Cranfield, "Love," *TWBB*, p. 133.

17 Norman Snaith, *The Distinctive Ideas of the Old Testament* (London: The Epworth Press, 1944), p. 95.

other. But when used by Biblical writers it was filled with a one-sided love nuance—the unchanging, unfading love of Jehovah directed towards the keeping of His covenant pledge, however much unfaithfulness on Israel's part threatened it. As Snaith says, "It was realized by the prophets that such a covenant could be maintained only by that persistent, determined, steadfast love of God, which transcends every other love by its nature and depth."[18] Snaith demonstrates that in forty-three cases *chesed* is joined by a copula to such nouns as *emeth* (faithfulness, firmness), *berith* (covenant), *tsedek* (righteousness), and *rachamim* (compassion), making it almost synonymous with these words. In a word, *chesed* is the covenant love of God, his "determined faithfulness to a covenant."[19] And this makes OT love supremely distinctive: "The most important of all the distinctive ideas of the OT is God's steady and extraordinary persistence in continuing to love wayward Israel in spite of Israel's insistent waywardness."[20] An example of *chesed* in action is seen in the covenant relation between Jonathan and David, (I Sam. 20:14-16) and was literally portrayed in Hosea's experience with an unfaithful wife. "Because of his own attitude to his wayward wife, he came to know that the *chesed* of God meant God's steadfast determination to be true to His share of the covenant obligation whatever Israel did on her part."[21]

But *ahebh* is also used in the religious sphere as well, denoting both God's love for man (thirty-two times) and man's love for God (twenty-two times). It is that spontaneous love that initiated the covenant. And it has the sense of condescension from a superior to an inferior. It expresses the election love of God; it initiates the covenant, *chesed* maintains it. The word sometimes is set in apposition to hatred as in Gen. 29:31, "Leah is hated." This hatred is not a virulent hatred but in contrast with electing love it simply means "rejected." God's love for Israel is preferential love; thus His attitude to other peoples can be expressed in terms of rejection. Jehovah's love for Israel then is an unconditional love. He knows Israel in a personal, intimate way (Amos 3:2). Deuteronomy continually reiterates that God's elective love for Israel cannot be traced to any ethical superiority on Israel's part. "Only the Lord had a delight in their fathers to love them and He chose their seed after them, yea even among you above all peoples" (Deut. 10:15). Such love is not fathomed by the human mind, for human love is never wholly disinterested love. Such love may appear irrational, arbitrary, and exclusive. But we are invading Divine counsels when we push the "why" of electing love any further. To this electing love man's response is to be in the form of humble, obedient love to His commands. Yet this obedient love does not spring from Israel's heart; it is Jehovah's action upon her heart of flesh, circumcising it that it might love Him wholly (Deut. 30:6, Jer. 4:4). In the words of Snaith:

> He will never let Israel go, but always the conditions of the Covenant must be fulfilled. Israel must serve Him in humble, dutiful love, with true piety, though as

18 *Ibid.*, p. 99.
19 *Ibid.*, p. 100.
20 *Ibid.*, p. 102.
21 *Ibid.*, p. 111.

experience has proved this is achieved only by that new heart and spirit which God Himself implants in Israel's heart, and by that new strength which God Himself alone can give.[22]

New Testament concepts

Cranfield gives summary definitions of the different words for "love" which appeared in Gk. classical literature: (1) *eros* is sexual love, "but also spiritualized... of the upward striving and quest of the human soul toward the suprasensual and divine... it is a love called forth by the worth or attractiveness of the object and wishes to possess its object."[23] It is intrinsically selfish love reaching out to possess an object for its own satisfaction and self enhancement; (2) *philia* is affection among friends. But as Trench observes, it has a warmth to it, making it suitable (over *eros*) for depicting man's love for God; (3) *stergo* is family affection; (4) *philadelphia*, love between brothers and sisters; (5) *philanthropia*, love for humanity; (6) *agape*, a love of the will rather than the emotions, which expresses itself in action. The last word, though it is seldom used in pre-Biblical Gk. literature, was the very word "born within the bosom of revealed religion."[24] *Philadelphia or philanthropia* was about the highest pinnacle reached by the Gk. classicists; *agape* of its own etymology merely had the sense of "be content with," or "like," and was in Cranfield's word, "colorless." LXX translators preferred the word for rendering *ahebh* (over against *eros*), "because it (*agape*) was free from erotic associations and conveyed the idea of a love that showed itself by helping its object rather than by desiring to possess and enjoy it,"[25] says Cranfield. But Trench points out a subtler and more valid reason. *Eros* had been spiritualized in a gnostic sense, as the word conveying the upward striving of the soul. But it fared poorly because of its nuance of "unattainment," not because of its warmth from sensuous association; *eros* never quite possessed. Trench says:

> *Eros* might have fared as so many other words have fared, might have been consecrated anew, despite the deep degradations of its past history; and there were tendencies already working for this in the Platonist use of it, namely as the longing and yearning desire after that unseen but eternal beauty,... The mere longing and yearning, and *eros* at the best is no more, has given place, since the incarnation, to the love which is not in desire only, but also in possession.[26]

Now just how did the NT baptize and give birth to a concept of love hitherto inconceivable to the best of the Platonists? Jesus Christ came and qualified all religious and secular duty with this word "*agape*." Righteousness, He declared, must be expressed in love (Mark 12:28 ff., Matt. 22:39). Loving God is total commitment to Him, like a slave to his master (Luke 17:7 ff.). This love to God is so all-embracing that it undercuts any other support in life but God Himself.

---

22 *Ibid.*, p. 142.
23 Cranfield, *TWBB*, p. 133.
24 William Evans, "Love," *ISBE*, III, 1933.
25 Cranfield, *TWBB*, p. 134.
26 Trench, p. 44.

Love of things is an interloper (Matt. 6:24, 30ff.); prestige vitiates it (Luke 11:43); persecution cools it off (Matt. 24:10, 12). Christ brought a new order, a manifesto of love. He not only declared that this was the supreme criterion in life but by His life and death showed that this love is intrinsic to the very nature of God. This is the endearing, sacrificial, pardoning love of God which moves out to embrace sinful men. That *agape* is not used in the Synoptists for expressing God's love to men does not militate against this contention. For *agape* acts, and the incarnate *agape* of God, Jesus Christ, filled this word with its divine content by His acts of mercy, love for the unlovely, forgiveness of sinners, sacrificial death.' 'Greater love hath no man than this" can be the summary of His life.

Those who are to follow Him must carry with them the *agape* credentials—burning love for God coupled with unshakeable love for fellow men. There is no graded love here as in the Confucian tradition; this love must be excercised to the nearest person needing help and succour. It is not calculating. In the words of Quell:

> They must practice love without expecting any return, lend where there is no hope of repayment, give away with boundless generosity. They must willingly accept the world's hostility in a sacrificial spirit of non-resistance (Luke 6:28), even doing good to those who hate them, countering curses with blessings and praying for their persecutors (Luke 6:27 ff., Matt. 5:44).[27]

Paul in retrospect sees this Divine love supremely manifested in the Incarnation and the Cross. It particularized upon those whom God has chosen as His own; they are "the beloved," or the "ones being loved" (Rom. 1:7). Those who have been immersed in this *agape* are called upon to water the thirsty deserts of a hate-prone world with this overflowing supply gushing up from within (Rom. 5:5-8). Paul sees this Divine *agape* at work in God's electing, calling, justifying, sanctifying, and glorifying acts (Rom. 8:28-30). Such love is infused into the believer and makes him an instrument of love, the creator of a new dimension in society (Rom. 13:10, Gal. 6:10). *Agape* then is the one force in society which transcends human legislation (Gal. 5:22), and is the abiding characteristic of all those participating in the new *aion*.

To James, love is the royal law (James 2:8). To John, this divine love flows down through the Son to the world; those who participate in this love make it the principle of their new society. Love flowing as in a circle back to God is not completed unless this love is practically demonstrated in the Christian community (I John 4:9-21). In the words of Quell:

> In brotherly love the circle which consists of the Father and the Son and those who belong to Him becomes a fellowship which is not of this world. God's love is life's ultimate reality for this fellowship, and to abide in His love is the law of its life.[28]

---

27 Quell, *Bible Key Words*, I, 48.
28 *Ibid.*, p. 62.

Encounter

So many varied concepts of Japanese affection are conveyed by the word *ai* — compassion, desire, *eros*, regret — that it has become unwieldy for the average Japanese. The Japanese language up until the Edo period developed through court literature. In such surroundings the slightest expression of innuendo, the mere glance of the eye, the wave of the hand in guarded moments were keys unlocking unseen vaults of human emotion. And Buddhist frowning upon any human endeavor which released craving, desire, passion furthered this sublimating of affections. Thus even today the word *ai*, the forthright expression "I love you" is too outright, too naive. Rather the young suitor will tell his lover "I am fond of you" (*anata ga suki desu*); this is all she needs to know; he has told all. The character of "heart" in the word fixes it in the mind's eye as a human emotion springing from man towards a desired object. It expresses desire for possession and at the same time a regretting, since failure to possess or parting is man's common experience.

Nearest equivalent to Japanese *ai* is the Gk. *eros*, for *eros* can express desire to possess in both physical and spiritual senses. The Bible does not use *eros*, but implicitly acknowledges this human emotion, as it does brotherly love and philanthropic love. What sets Biblical love off from Japanese *ai* are the contextual uses of the Hebrew *chesed* and the Gk. *agape*; both words express a Divine love that soars above the human plane, a love which manifests itself in determined, one-sided condescending acts of salvation, pardon, adoption, faithfulness toward the unlovely, undeserving and unfaithful. Japanese *ai* is reaching out to possess; Biblical *agape* is God's reaching out to pardon.

COMPASSION 憐 AWAREMI

Japanese Concepts of Compassion

Chinese character etymology

Awaremi has three components: 米 (rice), and 舛 (dance), and 忄 (heart). *KGJ*: Original rice component was not rice but flame, which was later simplified to the rice component. Dance symbol is conveyed by the right and left knees spread apart and person leaning forward, in an intoxicated condition. Components also showed beads on a string. Thus with the component of heart it symbolized the connection or concantenation of thoughts; a continuing thought process. Hence the idea of empathy or one's emotion going out. *KCJ*: Components give the sound only.

Semantic changes in Japan

Japanese indigenous word to which the above character was affixed stemmed from the word *aware*. *Aware* is further broken down into two words: (1) *Aa!* an exclamatory expression similar to the English "Ah!", an expression of bewilderment; (2) *hare* means lit., "to clear up," as clouds clear up.[1] *Mono no aware* has been rendered "the sadness of things," but Ōno believes this is too strong, for *aware* can be used of joy and sadness alike.[2] Rather it has the meaning of "sentimentality," or "out going emotion," like empathy. Nature, life with its vicissitudes, its joys and sorrows and change draw out emotional feelings. In the *Gyokuyōshū* (A.D. 1312) we find the line, "One's heart becomes full of *sympathy* towards the poor, but when it comes to actually extending a hand with its gift, one discovers the sleeve of his kimono too tight for the hand to reach out."[3]

Modern range of meaning

DGK: (1) feel sorry for (*fubin ni omou*), (2) love condescendingly (*itsukushimu*).

KCJ: (1) feel sorry for (*kinodoku ni omou*), (2) to love condescendingly (*itsukushimu*), (3) be saddened (*kanashimu*).

---

[1] Pointed out by Norinaga and cited by Kamei Katsuichiro, "*Nihon no Chie to Seiyō no Chie*" (Wisdom of Japan and Wisdom of the West) (Tokyo: Mikasa Shobō, 1965), p. 106.

[2] Interview, March 1966.

[3] *DGK*, p. 85.

Buddhist concepts

Since the word *ai* (love) has the nuance of passion in it, Buddhism has favored compassion as a word to convey the mercy of Buddha to all sentient beings. The key word is *jihi* and is defined as "The mind or mental condition of being compassionate or sympathetic toward sentient beings."[4] The word for the compassion of the Buddha for sentient beings is *kaji*, tr. of the Sk. *adhisthana*.

English idiom parallels

Beg for mercy (*awaremi o kou*). Misery loves company (*dōbyō aiawaremu*). Extremely pitiable (*yo ni mo aware na*). Philanthropic spirit (*hakuai no sei-shin*).

Biblical Concepts of Mercy

Old Testament concepts

Key Hebrew words for conveying mercy are *chesed*, *racham*, and *chanan*. *Chesed* has been discussed under LOVE but in brief it signifies the continued forbearance of God towards Israel in the keeping of the covenant (Deut. 7:9). It rests upon the *berith*, (covenant) by which Jehovah has freely bound Himself to His people. Hence Israel could appeal to God's *chesed*. It is rendered "mercy" in 148 instances in the AV. *Chesed* takes on the form of pardoning grace, which of necessity must be brought into play if the covenant were to continue, since Israel had forfeited all claims to it through sinful rebellion. Finally *chesed* is developed into the concept of redemption—"definitive redemption from every need. *Chesed* thus becomes an eschatalogical term in salvation history."[5] *Chesed* is not a disposition but "the act or demonstration of assisting faithfulness."[6] *Racham* denotes an emotion—"the seat of a feeling which is felt physically."[7] Girdlestone defines the word as "a deep and tender feeling of compassion, such is aroused by the sight of weakness or suffering in those that are dear to us or need our help" (Psa. 103:13; 106:46, Exod. 33:19; 34:6).[8] *Chanan* is gracious, or generous, used in its adjectival form only in reference to Jehovah (II Kings 13:23, II Sam. 12:22). Snaith emphasizes that these words do not primarily concern the forgiveness of sin. In Deut. 21:8 and 32:43, another word is used — *kipper*, which is moving in the area of forgiveness of sin. Its cognate, *kapporeth* is translated "mercy-seat" in the AV and is "the place of covering, the pro-pitiatory, with reference to the space just above the Ark in the Holy of Holies, between the over-arching cherubim where the Presence of God was supposed to be most intensely located. The word 'Mercy-seat' is from Tindale, who got it as a rendering of Luther's *Gnadenstuhl*."[9]

---

4 *BD*, p. 135.

5 Rudolph Bultmann, "*eleos, TDNT*, II, 480.

6 *Ibid.*

7 *Ibid.*

8 Girdlestone, p. 108.

9 Snaith, "Mercy," *TWBB*, p. 144.

New Testament concepts

In Gk. thought "*eleos* is a pathos, the emotion roused by contact with an affliction which comes undeservedly on someone else."[10] Bultmann says there is an element of fear or awe in it. The word was used in the context of justice; the accused must seek the *eleos* of the judge. Stoicism had little use for *eleos* —it was a "sickness of the soul."[11] In the NT it sums up the divine require-ment of man in his social relationships. "I will have mercy and not sacrifice" (Matt. 9:13, 12:7) harked back to the OT concept (Hos. 6:6), and was a shocking reminder that the primary interests of the divine economy were not cultic but ethical. It is employed in the Good Samaritan story and elsewhere to denote the showing of love or acts of mercy to men in need (Matt. 18:33, Luke 10:37, James 3:17). It is commiseration in the face of a practical need. Paul uses the word in a theological, technical sense in Rom. 9:11-15, bringing out the long history of God's saving acts toward undeserving and rebellious men. The same thought is taken up in Rom. 15:9 and I Pet. 2:10. God's mercy can be mentioned just in general terms (Gal. 6:16) or mentioned in reference to the Incarnation (Tit. 3:5).

More specifically the Gk. word *charis* is the NT counterpart of the *chesed* of the OT. It not only signifies God's redemptive love towards undeserving sinful men but His sustained determination to maintain His relationship to them. Paul selected this word over *eleos* (in spite of the precedent set by the LXX to render *chesed* as *eleos*), for it had within it the added aspect of longsuffering and patience with recalcitrant sinners. Trench traces the development of the word *charis* as it is taken up and invested with new content. He says: "There has often been occasion to observe the manner in which Greek words taken up into Christian use are glorified and transformed, seeming to have awaited for this adoption of them, to come to their full rights, and to reveal all the depth and the riches of meaning which they contained, or might be made to contain."[12] *Charis*, he says, originally signified that property in something which elicited joy in the hearers or viewers of it. Later in Gk. usage, it denoted the gracious aspect of beauty—"the gracious or beautiful thing, act, thought, speech, or person it might be, itself—the grace embodying and uttering itself."[13] Then it signified "a favour freely done, without claim or expectation of return."[14] This word then is taken up into the NT and used to denote the freeness of the gift and the unworthiness of the recipient. *Eleos* (mercy) had to do with misery, pitying the miserable. Hence the nuance: "We may say that the *charis* of God, his free grace and gift, displayed in the forgiveness of sins, is extended to men as they are guilty; his *eleos* as they are miserable."[15] In the NT, "it is the grace of the OT formerly manifest in God's dealings with His covenant people, but now made manifest in the life and work of

---

10 Rudolph Bultmann, "*eleos*, *TDNT*, II, 477.
11 *Ibid.*, p. 478.
12 Trench, p. 166.
13 *Ibid.*, p. 167.
14 *Ibid.*, p. 168.
15 *Ibid.*, p. 170.

Jesus Christ."[16] For grace appears in the NT in the person of Christ. His character, life and work can all be summed up as a *parousia* of grace (John 1:14, Titus 2:11); the resurrected and exalted Christ is considered a repository of grace for those united to Him by faith. Thus Paul employs the term "grace which is *in* Christ Jesus" (Rom. 3:21-24). Arndt's definition succinctly expresses this concept of NT grace: "The context will show whether the emphasis is upon the *possession of divine grace* as a source of blessings for the believer, or upon a *store of grace* that is dispensed, or a *state of grace* (standing in God's favor), that is brought about, or a *deed of grace* wrought by God in Christ, or a *work of grace* that grows from more to more." Those who tap this reservoir of grace not only remain in a state of forgiveness for daily sins, but this grace actively produces in them the stamina, powers and capability for active mission (Rom. 1:5, I Cor. 3:10, II Cor. 8:1: 12:9). Hence peculiar gifts of preaching, teaching, leadership are called *charisma* — grace gifts (I Pet. 4:10, I Tim. 4:14, II Tim. 1:6). From start to finish, the NT economy is one of grace (Rom. 6:14). Faith (Eph. 1:19, Phil 1:29), repentance (Acts 5:31; 2:38, Heb. 6:6), sanctification (I Thess. 5:23), service — these visible responses of man to divine acts of grace on his behalf are not traced to some spark which kindles attitudes and actions befitting God's condescending acts; rather the responses themselves are traced to a secret inner working of God, vouchsafed in grace.

Encounter

Japanese concepts of compassion find their roots in two Buddhist thoughts — thoughts which made a profound impression upon Japanese classical literature during the Nara-Heian periods. One strand of thought is that of *mono no aware* — it is emotional outgo — towards that which is either sad or joyful. It is empathy. It is a sentimental *feeling*. But this does not necessarily result in *action* toward the miserable. That explains the fixed usage of words and phrases in the face of another person's calamity. When a person announces a sickness, a bereavement, an unfortunate turn of events, he receives invariably the immediate commiseration of one of three expressions, *viz.*, "*kawai sō*" (that's too bad; I feel for you), "*kinodoku*" (I feel sorry for you), "*sore wa ikemasen*" (that's too bad). These are *expressions* of sympathy and in these expressions the sorrowful or unfortunate one must find satisfaction. If a foreigner learning Japanese did not know the literal meaning of *kinodoku* (lit., this is poison to my spirit) but phenomenologically observed its usage in such social interactions of sadness — sympathy, misery — compassion, he would probably define the term as "I'm sorry but I can't help you" or more colloquially, "I feel for you but I can't reach you."

The second concept which has been woven into Japanese "compassion" is the Buddhist *jihi* which has been defined as a mental condition of compassion. Again, this "mental" aspect of compassion may solve the paradox of Buddhist compas-

---

16 Snaith, "Grace," *TWBB*, p. 101.

sion for all sentient beings and Buddhism's negligible efforts at social reform in Japan.

It is significant that the Bible avoided much use of the emotional aspect of compassion, as the Heb. word *racham* conveys, but employed a word conveying the practical aspect of compassion, *chesed*, which portrayed Jehovah's acts of faithfulness to His covenant. The NT as well purposely avoids the pathos and sentiment bound up in *eleos* but chose the word *charis* to convey the acts of forgiveness demonstrated through Christ to an undeserving world. Compasion or grace thus are not sentiments but decisive acts in history—the Incarnation and the Cross. These acts form the legal basis whereby God may freely save unworthy sinners.

BEAUTY 美 *BI*

Japanese Concepts of Beauty

Chinese character etymology

Bi has two components: 羊 (sheep), and 大 (big). *KGJ*: Sheep's meat was considered a delicacy. Same character is found in good (善), and righteousness (義), emphasizing the superlative aspect of the character. Later the character became applied to shapes and forms, hence, beautiful. *KCJ*: a large sheep was considered beautiful.

Semantic changes in Japan

The Japanese word *utsukushii* to which this character was affixed "did not describe beauty as much as affection between children and parents."[1] It is defined in dictionaries of that early period as *jin* (grace, gentleness) and compassion (*awaremi*). But Ōno points out, *utsukushii* did not mean beautiful. In the Heian period the word was used to denote affection for small things or a child. In the Muromachi period, the word came to mean "perfectly" or "completely." Thus one concept of Japanese beauty emerges here; it is the beauty of *smallness* and *definiteness*. Another word for conveying the concept of beauty was the word *kiyoshi*, which has a cultic significance (See PURITY-KIYOSA) but literally meant "clear." Nature as it is — water, landscape, trees — presented in an unadulterated simplicity and purity is another Japanese concept of beauty. The word *kuwashii* in the Nara period was another synonym for the beautiful. *Kuwashii* is literally "detailed." The branch pictured in detail, the flower portrayed in its detailed intricacy give another concept of beauty. The beauty of *indefiniteness*, however, presents another aspect of Japanese beauty. The flowers may be depicted in detail, but there will be also a mist in the distance, a mountain fading out in the clouds. The word which renders this idea is *kokoronikui*. It is the aggravating aspect of beauty. A person may have superior ability than yourself; you admire him, but underneath is the feeling of resentment—*kokoronikui*, which literally means "hateful in the heart." It is the beauty of vagueness. The word *sabishii*, which means simply "lonely," was used during the Heian period to describe desolate or waste places in winter. Later it was used of human experience; the nobility were losing their place in society due to the vicissitudes of internecine war at the capital. Thus the *sabi* were the ones who accepted their plight in life and accepted banishment or loneliness. It is the beauty of *loneliness* or *simplicity*. These different concepts

---

1 Ōno, *Nihongo no...*, p. 21.

were further developed and given expression by Zen artists. Zen art aimed at simplicity, sincerity, and frankness. Noma says:

> By restricting themselves to the simplest and most elemental of materials, the paint-ers reflected the manner by which the philosophic tradition in Zen Buddhism saw a fundamental, unifying core of reality, eternal and incorruptable within the com-plexity of the phenomenal, everyday world.[2]

These Zen artists gave birth to the famous *chunzō* art. Noma says:

> They were imbued with a frankness which was almost remorseless. The sitters and artists of the *chunzō*... disclaimed all forms of flattery, and the portraits showed the monks with all their blemishes and signs of age and illness, with no attempt to improve or idealize their appearances.[3]

Modern range of meaning

KCJ: (1) beautiful (*utsukushii*), (2) good (*zen*), (3) sweet (*amai*), (4) splendid (*migoto*), (5) praise (*homeru*), (6) beautify (*utsukushiku suru*).

DNKJ: (1) beautiful (*utsukushii*), (2) admirable (*uruwashii*), (3) good taste (*aji no yoi*), (4) right (*tadashii*), (5) praiseworthy thing (*homubeki koto*).

KJ: (1) beautiful (*utsukushii*), (2) good tasting (*aji no yoi*), (3) praiseworthy thing (*homubeki koto*), (4) righteous thing (*tadashii koto*), (5) that which produces a pure feeling toward that which is unified and harmonious.

English idiom parallels

Spread one's charm around (*aikyō o furimaku*). An eye for the beautiful (*bi o miru me*). Good looking (*kiryō ga yoi*).

Biblical Concepts of Beauty

There is an intermingling of aesthetics and ethics in Scripture. Righteousness and salvation are core issues, but these concepts are clothed in the garments of aesthetics. Humanity's first pair begin history in a pleasant garden (Gen. 2:9); man's final scene in heaven is also beautiful. This beauty is never an end in itself but has the purpose of conveying the good and the holy. David could see within the tabernacle precincts a picture of the beauty of Jehovah (Psa. 27:4). Yet the psalmists confess that Jehovah Himself is the source and standard of true beauty (Psa. 96:5, 6). Caverno expresses it: "Beauty becomes a messenger of and from God... beauty of form and color and harmony of sound were... integrated... with worship in holiness."[4] Thus beauty becomes a mode of revela-tion, through variegated colors as in nature herself, the rainbow (Eccl. 3:11), or the tapestry of the tabernacle (Exod. 25 ff.); the intricate woodwork of the

---

[2] Noma Seiroku, *The Arts of Japan, Ancient and Medieval*, tr. John Rosenfied (Tokyo: Kōdansha International, 1966), p. 189.

[3] *Ibid.*, p. 190.

[4] C. Caverno, "Beauty," *ISBE*, I, 420.

temple (I Kings 6 ff., II Chron. 3); manner of speech, as in poetry (Psalms) or metaphors of nature (Matt. 13:3-23). The NT has different words for rendering the concept of beauty. One word is *asteios*, meaning "proper," or "fair" (Acts 7:20, Heb. 11: 23). *Asteios* has a certain ethical nuance, being contrasted in Gk. literature with the "villain" or "boor."[5] Another word, *horaios*, found in Rom. 10:15, Acts 3:2,10, Matt. 23:27, has the concept of *time* in it. Trench relates the concept of time to beauty:

> All which in this world lives submitted to the laws of growth and decay, has its 'hour', the period, that is, when it makes fairest show of whatever of grace or beauty it may own. This *hora*, being thus the turning point of its existence, the time when it is at its loveliest and best, yields *horaios* with the first sense of timely;....[6]

Another word, *kalos* is used interchangeably for the concepts of either "good" or "beautiful," for its root meaning is "whole" or "harmonious." "It is harmonious completeness, the balance, proportion and measure of all parts with another."[7]

Encounter

Japanese concepts of beauty find their roots in observation of the phenomenal world. Smallness, definiteness, simplicity, naturalness all speak to the Japanese of beauty. Buddhist influences have brought concepts of indefiniteness, vagueness, loneliness into overall thought patterns on beauty. But the dominating theme of man being one with nature has shaped all these views into a consistent philosophical view of Japanese art and poetry. Man is not an observer of nature but a participator in nature. Hence, the artist's object in Japanese art is to involve the viewer in some aspect of nature and stimulate his thinking so that he completes the picture himself. The really good Japanese poem is the one which must be completed by the reader—the poet merely hints at alternatives.

The Bible places man in the garden, in nature as an observer. The intricate design, the beauty of the rose point to an unseen Fashioner. Nature is an imperfect picture of the beauty of the Lord. Natural beauty is accidence, pointing man to His Creator. Japanese concepts of beauty would lead man to the discovering of an ultimate in nature herself; Biblical concepts would employ natural beauty to lead man to a supernatural Creator.

---

[5] Trench, p. 387.

[6] *Ibid.*, p. 388.

[7] *Ibid*, p. 389.

HOPE 希 望 *KIBŌ*

Japanese Concepts of Hope

Chinese character etymology

Kibo is comprised of two characters: 希 (rare), and 望 (want, request). *Ki* has two components: 爻 (threads wrapped together), and 巾 (woven textile). *KCJ*: something rare or something one desires. *Bō* has three components: 月 (moon), 臣(亡) (person looking afar off), and 王 (to stand). *KGJ*: Person standing, waiting patiently for the moon to rise; hence expectation, looking far ahead. *KCJ*: person with open eyes scanning the distance, hence looking forward to; looking far ahead.

Semantic changes in Japan

Ki was affixed to the Japanese indigenous word *negau* (ask). *Negau* is traced to the word *nega*, meaning to pray. *Negai* appears in the *Shinkokinshū*: "The wind bears along the *wishes* of the people as a rope twisting on the closing gate."[1] In the *Manyōshū*: "Our lives are like a bubble in the stream, but we live in *hopes* of living as long as a long rope."[2] The Japanese word to which *bō* was affixed is *nozomi*, which originally meant "to glance at," "to survey." Hence in the *Manyōshū*, "Because of the waves, we lost *sight* of.."[3] It also was used in the sense of request, e.g., in the *Genji Monogatari*, "He heard her *request*, and laughed."[4] Similar to the word *nozomi* is the word *akogare*; it conveys the emotional aspect of hope. *Ako* is *place*; *gare* is to be removed to a distant place. So it is longing for something which is beyond one's capability of obtaining; it is longing for something that is nearly hopeless.

Modern range of meaning

Ki

KCJ: (1) rare (*mare*), (2) ask, hope for (*negau*), (3) scarce item (*mabara*), (4) stop (*todomaru*).

Bō

KCJ: (1) look far ahead (*tōku miwatasu*), (2) request, desire (*nozomi*), (3) expect (*machinozomu*), (4) popularity (*ninki*), (5) grudge (*urami*), (6) worship festival (*matsuri*).

---

1 *DGK.*, p. 1518.
2 *Ibid.*
3 *Ibid.*, p. 1536.
4 *Ibid.*

KJ: (1) look out for, stare (*nagame*), (2) request (*negai*), (3) popularity (*jinbō*).

Kibō

KJ: (1) to long to draw near something one doesn't possess, (2) the feeling one has while expecting something.

DNKJ: (1) wish for something (*nozomu koto*), (2) what one wants (*negau tokoro no mono*), (3) popularity (*jinbō*).

English idiom parallels

Crush one's hopes (*kibō o kujiku*). Did not come up to expectations (*kibō dōri ni ikanai*). Cherish a desire (*nozomi o idaku*). Ray of hope (*ichiri no nozomi*). Clutch at straws (*Oboreru mono wa wara o mo tsukamu*).

Buddhist concepts

The *Bō* of *Kibō* is also found in the word *yokubō* (craving), which is the root cause of man's suffering in Buddhist thought. The five desires (*goyoku*) are: desires for property, sexual love, eating and drinking, fame, and sleep.[5]

Biblical Concepts of Hope

Old Testament concepts

Key Heb. words are *betach*, *qu'ah*, and *kesah*. In the OT there is no neutral concept of expectation. An expectation is either good or bad, hope or fear. "Trust and certainty are always a hope that the present state will so persist that the factors on which one counts will not change. But where this is not hope in God, such confidence is irresponsible security which God will suddenly overthrow and change into fear and anxiety."[6] Thus trust in things or situations is perilous. One's riches (Psa. 52:7); righteousness (Ezek. 33:13); friends (Jer. 17:5); religious inheritance; whether the temple (Jer. 7:4), Bethel (Jer. 48:13), or idols (Hab. 2:18), are all inadequate grounds for confident hope. Hence OT hope is fixed upon God Himself (Psa. 62:4; 71:5). The believer is called upon not to fix his hope on controllable factors but on God who is uncontrollable (Isa. 12:2, Psa. 46:1, 2). In a word, the life of the righteous is grounded in hope. Thus Israel maintained vital hope through all her changing fortunes and even in the midst of seeming disaster. She belongs to Jehovah; this relationship gives birth to hope. Robinson says: "This hope... becomes the chief instrument in the maintenance of the national existence."[7] And such hope was not founded upon a nebulous presumption of Israel but found its ground in the immutable covenant (Jer. 33:20, 21). One great event to which Israel's hope was directed was the "day of Jehovah," that period of history when God will intervene to judge wickedness and purge out the dross from Israel (Zeph. 2, Amos 7:10 ff., Isa. 2:12, 17). This is the OT concept of the kingdom of God on earth, the

---

[5] *BD*, p. 91.

[6] Rudolph Bultmann, "elpis, *TDNT*, II, 523.

[7] H. Wheeler Robinson, p. 186.

time when, "Israel shall be wholly righteous, the earth shall be full of the knowledge of Yahweh, as the waters cover the sea, and that the light of the moon shall be as the light of the sun, the light of the sun sevenfold (Isa. 11:9; 30:26; 60:21).[8] Another focus of Israel's hope was upon the Messiah, the anointed deliverer (II Sam 7:12, Isa. 9:6, Zech. 9:9). Through this deliverer and Jehovah's eschatological acts in history, Israel would finally be restored, and through her other nations finally brought to Jerusalem to hear the law of the Lord. Incipient ideas of the universal reign of Jehovah are given in the Jonah and Ruth narratives. Isaiah also hints that finally Egypt and Assyria are to share the blessing of Jehovah (Isa. 19:24,25). In the words of Robinson, "Yahweh is pictured as removing the veil of mourning, and wiping the tears from the eyes, not of the Jews alone, but of all humanity."[9] In conclusion, however, the specific hope of Israel is not spelled out in concrete material blessings or historical unfoldings, though these are mentioned vaguely, but rather this hope fixed itself upon Jehovah Himself. Thus we may say that the principal OT usage in the theological sense is that Jehovah is the hope of Israel and of the pious Israelite (Psa. 130:5,7; Jer. 14:8).

New Testament concepts

Key Gk. words for rendering the concept of hope are *elpis*, and *apokaradokia*. The latter word is less frequent than *elpis*, but is significant in that it has the same etymological meaning as the Japanese *kibō*. It stems from head and stretch; hence to stretch the head forward or wait tensely for something to appear. Linked with *elpis* in Phil. 1:20, *apokaradokia* expresses confident expectation; the *elpis* denotes "well-founded hope," the *apokaradokia* "unreserved waiting." Paul uses *elpis* to distinguish Christian hope from the anxiety of creation (*apokaradokia*) in Rom. 8:24 and 8:19. Delling points out this contrast:

> It may be that Paul is here conscious of the anxious waiting of creation under the stress of the inner and reciprocal conflict of creatures and elements. Or it may be that he is simply drawing a theological conclusion from the dominion of anti-godly power over this aeon in consequence of the fall.[10]

The word *elpis* in Gk. thought was an important concept. Man's existence was not only determined by his understanding of the present and remembrance of the past, but also by his hope in the future. "Man's own being thus determines what he hopes and how he hopes."[11] But mere hope is easily deceived. Thus hope of the wise is no longer *elpis*, but is based on the *phusis* (natural order, or inner nature of things) "which can be scientifically investigated.[12] Here is a typical expression of the distinctive Gk. tendency to insure against the future by a conscious integration into the order of the cosmos."[13]

---

8 Robinson, p. 198.

9 *Ibid.*, p. 210.

10 Gerhard Delling, "*apokaradokia*" *TDNT*, I, 393.

11 Rudolph Bultmamm, *TDNT*, II, 518.

12 A view similar to Fukuzawa's who attempted to find ethics and solutions for the future in the scientific investigation of the "*ri*" of nature. Cf. Carmen Blacker, *The Japanese Enlightenment*, (Cambridge: University Press, 1964) *passim*.

13 Bultmann, *TDNT*, II, 520.

The NT does not use *elpis* in its philosophic Gk. setting of vague, utopia-type thinking. Rather it finds its root concepts in the OT, where hope was fixed upon the unchangeable God and His covenant. It means expectation but with a strong nuance of *counting upon* (Luke 6:34, I Cor. 9:10, II Cor. 8:5, I Tim. 3:14, Acts 16:19). Hope may be in men, "though for Paul this attitude rests on the corresponding relationship to God, as shown by the natural transition from the one to the other."[14] Bultmann's point is well taken; hope in men may be dangerous unless trusting men have a transcendent hope in God.

There are three aspects to NT hope; (1) *trust*—as is brought out in its use for defining faith in Heb. 11:1: "faith is the substance of things hoped for," (2) *expectation of the future*—as is stressed in Rom. 8:24. Paul appeals to formal logic, namely, that "hope is the only possible attitude to the future if the object is not yet present."[15] *Elpis* cannot be directed at the present situation, the *prokaira* (II Cor. 4:18), for everything "visible belongs to the sphere of the *sarx* on which no hope can be founded,"[16] and (3) *patient waiting*— the Christian cannot depend on controllable factors and thus must trust in divine providence for the future (Rom. 8:24, 4:18).

What are the grounds for Christian hope? The noun form of *elpis* does not appear in the Gospels; rather we discover an anxiety and questioning over the future in the minds of the disciples. This is because true Christian hope is grounded on the historical fact of Christ's resurrection (I Pet. 1:3), as Richardson asserts: "The Resurrection of Christ is God's mightiest act; it has created our faith; and it is, as it were, an eschatological symbol in history of our ultimate salvation and therefore the ground of our hope (Rom. 5:1-5)."[17] Or in Bultmann's words, "The Christian hope rests on the divine act of salvation accomplished in Christ."[18] Paul says the non-Christian has no hope, not in the sense that he has no concept of a future beyond this life, but rather such hope has no well-founded basis for trust (I Thess. 4:13). This hope in the future, founded upon the resurrection of Christ, is likened to an anchor of the soul; it keeps the ship of the soul steady during the immediate storm and crisis, though the anchor itself is hung upon a rock beyond human sight (Heb. 6:18). Faith is perhaps the historical aspect of trust—looking back in personal trust upon God's historical acts in the Incarnation and the Cross and appropriating the blessings which flow from these acts to oneself in the historical present. Hope also looks back for its roots in the historical act of the Resurrection, but since this Resurrection carries with it an eschatalogical significance — personal resurrection and the final triumph of Christ over all hostile forces, — it predominantly directs the believer's attention to the future. In the words of Richardson:

> It has nothing to do with an earthly utopia or any secular optimism. It is through and through eschatological, always bearing reference to the return of the Lord Jesus at the end of the age.[19]

---

14 *Ibid.*, p. 530.
15 *Ibid.*, p. 531.
16 *Ibid.*
17 Richardson, *TWBB*, p. 109.
18 Bultmann, *TDNT*, II, 533.
19 Richardson, *TWBB*, p. 109.

Encounter

The concept of hope in Japanese thinking has been impinged upon by various factors and ideas which make it at best something similar to the original Gk. concept; it is easily and thus most often deceived or disappointed. Hence the wise man[20] will pin his hopes on that which can be detected by visible means. From the Nara-Heian periods, hope became more like wishful thinking — the *akogare* — longing for something that is nearly hopeless of attaining. The Japanese word for "hope" (*nozomi*) stems from looking afar off in the distance. *Negai* also is a wish, a faint prayer. Modern range of meaning for different components of hope, such as "rare," "look ahead," "stare," "popularity," again point to a hope concept that does not go far beyond the human horizon. The *Bō* of *Kibō* connected with the focal point of Buddhist attention—*yokubō* (craving)—has given a somewhat pejorative sense to the word.

Biblical hope pierces beyond present situations, either of blessing or misfortune, to the person of God in the OT and Christ's saving acts in the NT. The Gk. word *apokaradokia* (anxious waiting), is used to denote the tense waiting of creation. Lost in the cosmos, this is no doubt the common experience of man, as expressed by Greek sentiment and also by the Japanese *akogare*. But the one who has fixed his hope upon Christ and His saving acts as revealed in Scripture is given a hope which engenders trust, expectation, and patience towards the future. Yet this hope is not an emotion stirred up within man by his own wishful thinking or even his erratic strivings of faith. Rather it is a divine gift, implanted in his heart by the God of hope, that is, the God who bestows hope to those united to Him (Rom. 15:13).

---

[20] It is significant that the word for resignation—*akirame*, means lit. "the clear eye." The truly wise man in Japanese life is not one who entertains vague visions of some castle in the sky, but who resigns himself to his life situation, whether good or ill.

JOY 喜 *YOROKOBI*

Japanese Concepts of Joy

Chinese character etymology

Yorokobi is one character having two components: 壴 (drum), and 口 (mouth). *KGJ*: (1) hear music and open one's mouth in laughter, (2) mouth and a feast, hence eating a good feast. Joy then is that emotion which springs from eating a feast or listening to music. *KCJ*: Offering food to the gods; eating with the gods was considered the supreme happiness.

Semantic changes in Japan

Yorokobi is used in the *Utsubo monogatari* (10th century A.D.) in the sense of a celebration, "The celebration which we held."[1] In the *Genpei Seisuiki* (A.D. 1313), it has a cultic significance, "Joy that one experiences on the way home from the shrines."[2]

Modern range of meaning

KJ: (1) rejoice (*yorokobu koto*), (2) celebrate (*iwau koto*), (3) to express one's appreciation (*rei o noberu koto*), (4) to be thankful for (*shasuru*).

DNKJ: (1) rejoice (*yorokobu koto*), (2) celebrate (*iwau koto*), (3) to express appreciation (*shasuru*).

KCJ: (1) to rejoice, enjoy (*yorokobu, tanoshimu*), (2) like (*konomu*).

English idiom parallels

Feel as if one were in his seventh heaven (*ten ni mo noboru kokochi*). One's heart dances for joy (*kokoro ga odoru yōni*). Jump for joy (*koodori shite yorokobu*).

Biblical Concepts of Joy

Old Testament concepts

Key Hebrew word is *shimhah*, variously tr. "joy," "gladness," "mirth." It means literally to be bright, to shine, and is so connected with light in Prov. 13:9, "The light of the righteous *rejoiceth*." Other Hebrew words such as *masos* and *sason*, bring out the exuberant aspect of joy and mean "to spring," "leap";

---

[1] *DGK*, p. 2102.

[2] *Ibid*.

hence "exult, rejoice, shout." In secular life "joy" is "the response of the mind to any pleasurable event or state."[3] The words are given a theological dimension in the OT in consequence of the Israelite's relation to Jehovah. Such joy is not sporadic but is an all-pervading attitude, as Smith asserts: "Joy is not an isolated or occasional consequence of faith but is an integral part of the whole relation to God."[4] Such joy is a natural outcome of intimate fellowship with God; He is not only the object but also the source of joy (Psa. 16:11, 4:7, 35:9, Isa. 29:19). The believer thus rejoices in Jehovah's loving kindness (Psa. 21:6, 7); His salvation (Psa. 21:1); His law (Psa. 1:2); His judgments (Psa. 48:11); His comfort (Jer. 15:15, 16); and His providential reign over creation, thus calling nature to join in chorus to sing and shout (Psa. 96:11, 13). Of course, God rejoices in His works (Psa. 104:31) and His people (Deut. 30:9, Zeph. 3:17). Joy is the fundamental trait of those who minister and serve Jehovah. Such serving is joy (Psa. 27:6), for thereby man achieves the highest goal and direction of created selfhood—self-fulfillment in the purposes and fellowship of God.

New Testament concepts

Three Gk. words in the NT for joy bring out important aspects of Christian joy. First, *agalliaomai* meant in Gk. poetry "to make resplendent or adorn," "to preen oneself," "to be proud." The term denotes "not so much a mood of satisfied joy as a consciousness of joyful pride expressed in the whole attitude."[5] It was employed in the LXX to render the Heb. *gil* and *halel*, which cluster of words celebrated the help and acts of God on behalf of Israel. It borders on pride in God or like David, dancing for joy before Him. NT usage preserves this exulting and jubilant character of the word (I Pet. 1:6, Acts 2:26). Another Gk. word is *kaukaomai* sometimes translated "boast" (Rom. 2:17, II Cor. 10:16), but in the sense of joy it means "to pride oneself in." Arndt gives the range of meaning as (1) boast, glory, pride oneself in, and (2) boast about.[6] The Christian is called upon to pride himself in afflictions and adverse circumstances (Rom. 5:3, II Cor. 12:9), not so much as a "superficial gaity which refuses to face or admit adverse circumstances but as the fruit of faith which sees beyond the immediate difficulties the final triumph of God."[7] The Gk. word *chairo* is the word denoting the joyful response of the believer who is participating in God's saving acts. The Songs of the Nativity demonstrate this expectant joy (Luke 1:14). "It is indeed the eschatological act of divine salvation which is supremely the theme of rejoicing, as is seen most clearly in the song of Revelation (Rev. 19:7)."[8] Christ's *parousia* will consumate the joy of believers, though at present they rejoice in anticipation of final triumph (I Pet. 1:8, 4:13). Jesus Christ came drinking and eating with the common man and talked to him about "His joy" (John 15:11, 16:24).

---

[3] D. Miall Edwards, "Joy," *ISBE*, III, 1755,

[4] R. Gregor Smith, "Joy," *TWBB*, p. 117.

[5] Bultmann, "*agalliamai*" *TDNT*, I, 19.

[6] Arndt, p. 426.

[7] Edwards, *ISBE*, III, 1755.

[8] Bultmann, *TDNT*, I, 20.

He commanded his followers to rejoice and be exceedingly glad (Matt. 5:12). But this joy does not find its source in man but in divine innerworking — it is one of the gifts of the Holy Spirit (Rom. 14:17, Gal. 5:22). Hence, the NT enjoins the Christian to continually exhibit this confident joy, this inner pride in God and His work of salvation (Phil. 4:4, Rom. 5:11).

Encounter

Japanese concepts of joy stem from the emotional response to a pleasant situation. From the earliest etymological meanings of joy derived from sensual delights to the modern usage, there has crept into the word the sense of "celebration," "gratitude," and "enjoy." The word could not be found in the Buddhist dictionary. The over-concern with sufferings and man's escape from the hopeless cycle of existence has made joy a concept not associated with Buddhism. Rather the gay Shrines and festivals of Shinto have monopolized this aspect of Japanese emotional experience. Reischauer says, "Shinto, lacking any moral sense of guilt or sin, is an essentially cheerful, sunny religion."[9] Aston called Shinto "a religion of gratitude and love."[10] Nitobe sees this optimism as stemming from a thoroughgoing "this worldly" philosophy of Shinto:

> The awful sense of condemnation which torments Bunyan's Christian and all other seekers with the soul-rending cry, "How can I flee from the wrath to come?" assumes with the Shintoist a far lighter strain, "Is this good to be preferred to that good?" The dilemna in the one case lies between eternal salvation and eternal damnation, between heaven and hell; whereas in the other it is a choice between two benefactions of different degrees, between this and that sunny spot in the groves of paradise.[11]

The Japanese are walking between two poles, Buddhist pessimism and Shinto optimism. It is an open question which has had greater impact upon the Japanese psyche.

A check of the frequency list of the National Language Research Institute[12] reveals that the word *dame* (no good; it won't do) and the word *yorokobi* (joy) have the frequency ratings of .203 and .089 respectively. The frequency thus is about two and one-half times greater for *dame*. This proves little, but it lends weight to the conviction that words conveying pessimism or negation are heard much more than words expressing optimism and positiveness in Japan today. The *mono no aware* (sadness of things) from the Nara-Heian periods and classical literature has made profound influence upon Japanese thinking in this area of human emotions. One seldom sees smiling faces on trains, nor are

---

9 Edwin Reishcauer and John Fairbank, *East Asia, The Great Tradition* (Boston: Houghton Mifflin Co., 1958), p. 473.

10 Cited by Inazo Nitobe, *The Japanese Nation*, (New York: G. P. Putman's Sons, 1912), p. 133.

11 *Ibid.*, p. 136.

12 The National Language Research Institute, *Vocabulary and Chinese Characters in Ninety Magazines of Today*, General Description and Vocabulary Frequency Tables (Tokyo: National Language Research Institute, 1962) I, pp. 119, 179.

portrait pictures often taken with the subject smiling. Joyful expression is seen to be a Western innovation or a mark of superficiality.

Biblical emphasis is upon joy rooted in confidence in one's relationship with the Creator and sustainer of life. Being thus related to Jehovah, one may receive from His hand the pleasing and painful alike, confident that both are purposeful. Such purpose the believer knows is the final triumph of God and Christ over every force dimming the glory of God. The immediate purpose may not be apparent, but he knows it is hidden in the secret counsels of God. Such joy and confidence must spring from another source—God's Spirit at work in his innermost being.

HAPPINESS 幸 福 *KŌFUKU*

Japanese Concepts of Happiness

Chinese character etymology

Kōfuku is comprised of two characters: 幸 (happiness, lucky) and 福 (blessing, fortunate). *Kō* has two components: 土 (to die young) and 平 (opposite). Hence *KCJ*: escape an untimely death. Later it came to mean request help or be happy, good fortune, or be helped. *KGJ*: originally had the concept of a hand-cuff; hence the milieu of escaping from danger. Later it came to mean "bless-ed" or "happy." (*Fuku* has two components: 衤 (a divinity), and 畐 (wine in a container). *KGJ*: hence the meaning is full or wealth, and this comes about through the goodness of the gods. *KGJ*: the *sake* wine one receives at the festival. Later the *sake* wine idea dropped out and it came to mean the favor bestowed upon men by the gods.

Semantic changes in Japan

Ōno says the Japanese word to which the *Kō* of *kōfuku* was affixed, i.e., *sachi* originally designated the arrow of the hunters. If one's arrow hit the mark, he "brought home the bacon." Thus in the *Kojiki* (712 A.D.) we have the words, *yama no sachi* (the prey taken in the mountains), *umi no sachi* (the catch of the sea). The word occurs in the *Manyōshū*, "How *happy* it would be if I could live until we are old together."[1] The word is traced by *DGK* to *sakitori*, which also means, "prize" or "catch." *Shokyō* mentions five blessings: (1) long life, (2) wealth, (3) health, (4) yearning for virtue, (5) be able to think as long as one can live. The word for "celebrate" — *iwau* — is synonymous with *yorokobi* in the *Manyōshū* and was used in the sense of performing a divination. To insure something good happening, a person would perform such a rite. Thus *saiwai* today has kept some of this cultic significance and speaks often in terms of a disaster just missed through divine intervention; e.g., "It was a dangerous situation, but *saiwai*, I escaped injury."

Modern range of meaning

Kō

KCJ: (1) happy, fortunate (*saiwai*), (2) fortunately (*unyoku*), (3) good (*yoi*), (4) request (*negau*).

KJ: good fortune (*kōun*), (2) blessed (*saiwai*).

---

[1] *DGK*, p. 810.

Fuku

    KCJ: (1) happy (*saiwai*), (2) help from the gods, (3) to bestow blessings, (4) good, (5) meat offered at the festival.

    KJ: (1) happy (*saiwai*), (2) good fortune (*shiawase*).

Kōfuku

    KJ: (1) have things turn out well (*meguriawase no yoi koto*), (2) to be in a full condition (*michitarita jōtai ni aru koto*).

English idiom parallels

    Be full of happiness (*kōfuku ni afureru*). Hit a streak of luck (*un ga muku*). Luck is picking up (*me o fuku*). One good thing about the disaster (*fukōchū no saiwai*).

Biblical Concepts of Happiness

Old Testament concepts

    That the English word "happiness" does not occur in the noun form in the Bible can perhaps be traced to its etymological nuance of "chance" from "hap." Biblical translators chose rather the word "blessed" and "blest" to indicate the purposeful activity of God in bestowing blessings upon man and to underscore the fact that man comes into happiness not by chance but by Divine help. OT happiness and prosperity may be simply the increase of material goods, like family, crops, wealth, peace, etc. (Gen. 1:22, Deut. 33:11). Or it may take the religious sense of "setting apart," as in blessing the seventh day (Gen. 2:3). The chief Heb. word is *barak*; it signifies either material or spiritual blessings. It sometimes is used in the sense of "praise," as men blessing Jehovah (Gen. 24:48). Men bless men in the OT, and such blessing is usually irrevocable, as in the case of Jacob's deception of Isaac (Gen. 27:1 ff.). But this blessing is usually in the form of a prayer—May He bless thee with the blessings of heaven (Gen. 49:25)—thus acknowledging the conviction that ultimately all blessings flow from one divine source. Beyer elaborates on this aspect of OT blessing:

> Blessing does not work in the form of a magical power overflowing man. It is not a psychical power which makes its possessor a "lucky fellow" and endows him with special ability. The blessing of Yahweh is the gracious divine gift which He dispenses in sovereign freedom, granting His favour to individuals or to a people and causing the work of their hands to succeed (Deut. 28:12).[2]

"The Israelite who knows that his whole life is in the hands of the Creator cannot find any better expression for his faith and gratitude and hope than by giving God the glory,"[3] and so "blesses" God.

New Testament concepts

    Key Gk. words are *makarios* and its cognates, and *eulogia* which is a tr. of the Heb. *barak*. Arndt gives the range of meaning as: (1) blessed, (2) fortunate,

---

2 Hermann Beyer, "*eulogia*" *TDNT*, II, 756.

3 *Ibid*., p. 758.

(3) happy. It is the word of the Beatitudes of Matt. 5, tr. by Zahn *et. al.*, "O the happiness of" or "Hail to those."[4] There seems to be a twofold direction of such blessing: (1) the persons possessing such ideal character are indeed blest by the very fact of the possession of such qualities as purity, peacemaking, humility, etc., and (2) the possessing of such Christian character carries with it the promise of eschatalogical rewards from Christ, the judge of men's actions. Lambert sums up the twofold blessedness: "The declaration of blessedness, therefore, is based not only on the possession of the quality or experience described, but on the present or future rewards in which it issues."[5] The Beatitudes appear on the surface as a paradox; for *renouncing* the very things men seek for and require for happiness (wealth, power, joy) could only appear to the most idealistic as a state of blessedness. Thus the blessing bestowed upon self-emptying and sacrifice of one's natural desires is cast in an eschatological mold. In the words of Lambert:

> Christ does demand of His followers a renunciation of many things that seem desirable to the natural heart, and a readiness to endure many other things from which men naturally shrink. But just as in His own case the great self-emptying was followed by the glorious exaltation (Phil. 2:6), so in the case of His disciples spiritual poverty and the bearing of the cross carry with them the inheritance of the earth and a great reward in heaven.[6]

Encounter

Japanese concepts of happiness have a cultic significance, as derived from earliest uses of the word and also from the association of *kōfuku* with festivals and shrine activities. It is strictly a happiness which consists of material benefits, fullness, wealth, a happy turn of events. It speaks of a mystical play of events turning out in one's favor, either positively in material favor or negatively in the avoidance of an impending disaster. Shrine worship is directed towards this end; New Year's pilgrimages to the shrines, the receiving of white-feather arrows, *sachi* (looking back to the original sense of hitting one's prey on the hunt), good luck rice cakes are all directed towards the ends of securing material blessings. Business officials' standing before the great white canvas at Ise, clapping their hands; politicians' reporting to the shrines before making visits abroad are acts directed towards this one supreme end—fortune, success, blessing.

This concept of happiness is so fixed in Japanese thinking that its importance is raised almost to the ultimate in values—the measure of all things. Japanese Christian pastors eventually fall into the pattern of declaring the blessings which accrue to those believing the Christian message rather than simply stating the contents of the *kerugma*. It is significant that the promise of earthly felicity is not one of the essential points of the Biblical *kerugma*.

---

4 Cited by Arndt, p. 487.

5 J. C. Lambert, "Beatitudes," *ISBE*, I, 420.

6 *Ibid.*

Biblical concepts of blessing have developed from OT ideas of earthly felicity and long life to that of receiving spiritual qualities of character, such as righteousness, peace, humility, purity. This latter becomes the NT emphasis, and the possessing of such blessings may yield the opposite of what men call happiness, i.e., poverty, sadness, persecution. The paradox is resolved in the ultimate bestowing of blessings and honor in the last judgment. The Bible presents a circle of blessing: blessing flowing down from God the Provider to men—men in turn blessing God by giving Him due thanks and worship—the circle finally being completed in an eschatological framework of eternal rewards.

PLEASURE 楽 TANOSHIMI

Japanese Concepts of Pleasure

Chinese character etymolngy

Tanoshimi 楽 is comprised of two components: 糸 (stringed instrument), and 木 (wood). *KGJ*: signified musical instrument, later the sounds of people and instruments, hence that which is pleasant. *KCJ*: two components are "string" and "wood," hence a stringed instrument.

Semantic changes in Japan

DGK: Japanese indigenous word is *tanoshimi* to which the Chinese character was affixed. Derived from field (*ta*) and fruit (*mi*).[1]

Modern range of meaning

KCJ: (1) music (*ongaku*), (2) pleasureful, enjoyable (*tanoshii*), (3) like (*konomu*), (4) easy (*raku*), (5) love, like (*aisuru*).

DNKJ: (1) enjoy something (*tanoshimu koto*), (2) amusement, enjoyment (*nagusami*), (3) interest (*omoshiromi*), (4) interest (*kyō*), (5) pleasure (*kairaku*), (6) elegant (*fuga*).

KJ: (1) enjoy something (*tanoshimu*), (2) pleasantness (*yukai*), (3) pleasure (*kairaku*).

English idiom parallels

Be in rapture (*etsu ni iru*). Have the world by the tail on a downhill pull (*oni no kubi demo totta yōni*, lit. act as if one had just taken the head off a demon). Libertine (*dōrakumono*). Addicted to wine and women (*yūkyō ni fukeru*).

Buddhist concepts

Raku is the tr. of Sk. *sukha*, defined as: "the sensation which arises when one comes into contact with that which pleases one."[2] When conjoined with the character meaning "extreme" (*goku*) the word is the Buddhist symbol for heaven or paradise, *gokuraku*, tr. of Sk. *sukhavati*, meaning "highest joy, the name of the pure land of Amitabha."[3]

Biblical Concepts of Pleasure

Old Testament concepts

Heb. words tr. into English pleasure are *hephec*, and *rason*. But the Hebrew sense is more of "inclination" or "good pleasure" or "care." *Hephec* is found

---

[1] *DGK*, p. 1222.

[2] *BD*, p. 231.

[3] *BD*, p. 84.

in Job. 21:21, "What *pleasure* hath He in this house?". So other usages bring out the sense of will or purpose (Isa. 44:28, 46:10, 48:14). The Heb. word *tosam* is rendered by the Gk. word *hedone* in the LXX (Nu. 11:8, Prov. 17:1), where it simply means "sense of taste."

New Testament concepts

Gk. equivalent to the OT sense of "good will" is rendered by *eudokia*, which Arndt tr. as (1) good will (Phil. 1:15, 2:13), (2) favor (Matt. 11:26), and (3) wish, desire (Rom. 10:1). Pleasure *per se* is not presented in a favorable light in the NT. Rather the emphasis is upon (a) *joy*, as springing from an inner source and rooted in one's relation to God; and (b) *blessing*, as vouch-safed by God to obedient men, and these blessings may take the form of experience exactly opposite to what men call pleasure. Key Gk. word for pleasure is *hedone*, derived from the root *adous*, meaning "sweet, pleasant, delightful." Hence *hedone* is something which is pleasant to the physical senses. In Gk. literature the word meant "sensual pleasure" or "enjoyment." Later development of the word increased its range to mean something ethically pleasurable, hence something which enriched life. Whether *hedone* is intrinsically good or evil was determined by its relation to that which is "comfortable to nature, to reason, and to virtue."[4] There are higher and lower *hedone*. Thus the hedonistic philosophy of life developed—the "noble view of *hedone* and, with greater or lesser reservations, ascribed to it great significance for the ideal of human life."[5] However such a philosophy was antithetic to the Christian ideal of finding true happiness and self-fulfillment through fellowship with Christ, serving God and men with one's body as a weapon of righteousness. In short, as Stahlin says, *hedone* "represents one of the many forces which belong to the world of unsanctified carnality, which strive against the work of God and his spirit and which drag man back again into the kingdom of evil."[6] *Hedone* is of this aion, this life (Luke 8:14). Our bodily members are the seat where *hedone* freely works (James 4:1). *Hedone* is a force directed against the purposes of God in the world, for it (a) opposes the will of God (I Pet. 4:2), (b) stifles the Biblical word from achieving full growth in men's hearts (Mark 4:19), (c) stands between men and God in the fellowship of prayer (James 4:3). James 4:2 brings in sharp contrast the conflict between seeking God's will through prayer and the greedy lust to possess, which finds its locus in the *hedone* (lust for pleasure).

> The *bios hedokikos* (life of pleasure) is a vicious circle in the literal sense. Its starting point is *hedone* and its goals are *hedone* (James 4:3) which simply give rise to new desire. It never reaches its goal and ends only in death.[7]

Hedone is seen as a self-destrutive force in man. It produces conflict and bondage to self:

---

4 Gustav Stahlin, "*hēdonē*" *TDNT*, II, 914.

5 *Ibid.*, p. 916.

6 *Ibid.*, p. 909.

7 *Ibid.*, p. 992.

Hedone are masters which rule men instead of God the Lord. In the pre-Christian and non-Christian life, the service of *hedone* takes the place of service to God.[8]

The NT sees three classes of men who are following *hedone* as the main direction of their lives: (1) non-Christians (Tit. 3:3), (2) unstable or doubleminded Christians (James 4:8), and (3) false teachers (II Tim. 3:4). Loving *hedone* is a mark of the age prior to the end of this age. The Bible does not deny that happiness and enjoyment are instinctive goals of human endeavor. But it directs the believer towards goals in God and sharing with Christ His passion for a lost world. Trials, hardships, suffering must be crossed and experienced enroute to this goal. But in their very seeking, the inner joy and pleasure which the hedonist goal promises but never achieves becomes the present possession and foretaste of eternal joys in heaven (James 1:4).

Encounter

Japanese concepts of pleasure have developed from that which is pleasing to the senses to that which is ethically pleasant and enjoyable. The Buddhist de-emphasis upon seeking pleasure has made little impact upon normal Japanese thinking; the word "*tanoshii*" falls from the lips of highest politicians as their goal for the people of the electorate. Seeking a pleasant, enjoyable time is as natural as seeking food, clothing, and education. One of the chief epithets hurled against the Christian community is that they are ascetic and disapproving of one of the most normal pursuits in Japanese life—pleasure. And it is a truism that few Christian communities have been able to resolve a happy balance between enjoying the things freely given to them to enjoy and shouldering their Cross in meaningful discipleship.

Biblical emphasis is upon *pleasure discovered in goals*. Hence the word *hedone* is presented in critical light, for it fixes the drives of human affections upon *objects* that promise to satisfy. Rather the Bible would have man fix his goals on God and His purposes in Christ, assured that the pleasures and joys of life will be given by a loving Father who gives His creatures all things freely to enjoy. One of the strange paradoxes of Japanese life is that though much effort and expense are thrown into the pursuit of pleasure, few there be who find it. The press of humanity converging on the limited sources of pleasure —parks, music halls, beaches— and pandemonium prevailing when the pursuer arrives have made this one of the most elusive of Japanese goals. But the problem runs deeper. The nature of *hedone* is that it leads the seeker upon a treadmill of unsatisfied desire, and such frustration becomes the impelling drive to intensify the search.[9]

---

8 *Ibid.*, p. 923.

9 Economic factors alone do not account for the continuing exodus of Japan's youth from the open fields of the country to the cramped quarters of the cities. The cultural lag in rural Japan has aggravated the problem. If a generation would step off the *hedone* treadmill and pioneer to make rural Japan more enjoyable, perhaps this trend could be reversed. Yet, as Niebuhr hints, little cultural progress has ever been made without transcendent faith.

HARDSHIP, DIFFICULTY 困難 KONNAN

Japanese Concepts of Hardship

Chinese character etymology

Konnan 困難 is comprised of two characters; 困 (plight, pain) and 難 (firm, hard, difficult). *Kon* consists of two components: 口 (box), and 木 (tree). *KGJ*: figure of a tree cramped in a box, unable to grow; hence, be troubled, be put in a difficult situation. *KCJ*: tree inside a house, hence a bother. *Nan* consists of two components: 薁 (fat), and 隹 (name of a bird). *KGJ*: bird roasting in fat; hence a disaster. *KCJ*: name of a bird.

Semantic change in Japan

DGK: Used in the sense of being shortened or reduced in size. Also in the sense of being poor or reduced to poverty. Japanese indigenous word is *katashi*, "hard". It speaks of restricted movement.

Modern range of meaning

Kon

KCJ: (1) to be troubled or put in a plight (*komaru*), (2) to be in pain (*kurushimu*), (3) to be in anguish (*nayamu*), (4) be tired (*tsukareru*), (5) be in disarray (*midareru*), (6) poor (*mazushii*), (7) be at a limit (*kiwameru*).

Nan

KCJ: (1) firm (*katai*), (2) difficult (*muzukashii*), (3) be in anguish (*nayamu*), (4) worry (*shinpai*), (5) be in pain (*kurushimu*), (6) be fearful (*osoreru*), (7) enemy (*teki*), (8) be at odds with (*tagai ni tekishi suru*), (9) press upon (*semeru*), (10) suppress (*kobamu*), (11) be in disarray (*midare*).

Konnan

DNKJ: (1) be in pain and distress (*kurushiminayamu koto*), (2) be in perplexity, be troubled, be restricted, (3) difficulties (*nangi*).

English idiom parallels

Run into trouble (*konnan ni au*). Adversity makes the man wise (*Konnan nanji o tamanisu*). Fight a losing battle (*akusen kutō suru*). There's always a way out (*Kyūsureba tsūzu*).

Buddhist concepts

Ku is the tr. of the Sk. *dukha* and is defined by *BD* as: "I. Suffering pain. The first of the four noble truths. II. Another name for *asrava-dharma* (*urobo*), because these are the cause of all suffering."[1] Buddhism posits three kinds of sufferings, called *sanku*; the *ku-ku* "suffering which results from torment; *e-ku*, suffering which results from the prevention of pleasure; and *gyō-ku*, or suffering which results from the impermanence of phenomena."[2] There also the "four sufferings" (*shiku*) viz., of birth, old age, sickness, death.[3] *Shiku-haku* is a term which lit. means, "the four sufferings, the eight sufferings," but is used in common parlance without any religious significance to mean simply "great hardship" or "mental anguish." Suffering is central in the teachings of Gautama. It actually became the springboard for developing his metaphysical system—a system directed towards the escape from suffering. Cause of suffering he put as the tenacious refusal of man to resign himself to his situation in life. Suffering then is inherent in the life situation in which man finds himself.

Biblical Concepts of Hardship

Old Testament Concepts

Key Hebrew word is *sar* meaning "narrow," "pent-up," as streams pent up (Isa. 59:9), or seals closely pressed (Job 41:15). Hence it is used to mean "straitened circumstances" (Deut. 4:30, Psa. 4:1). Through the entrance of sin hardships, suffering, and sorrow are part of the human lot. Hardships and suffering thus conceived in a punitive or probationary light underscore the fact that history is ruled by God. God's judgments are in history but also consumated beyond history in the final day of Jehovah. The Eastern concept that "outward circumstances of life are an index of character"[4] is logically presented by Elihu in Job's case (Job 36:8, 9). But the Biblical position clearly refutes this: "The denouement of the poem suggests that the events of life are subject to the control of divine intelligence, which man with his natural limitations is not always able to perceive."[5] Rankin puts the whole issue in broader perspective: "A man's good and evil deeds might not be observed to bear appropriate fruit in his lifetime, but Javhe would bring them to light in his descendants with whom his personal life was bound up."[6] Hammer lists various aspects of the Biblical view: (1) suffering is probationary (Judges 2:22-3:6). (2) prosperity of the wicked is only apparent or at best short lived (Psa. 73:

---

1 *BD*, p. 184.

2 *BD*. p. 256.

3 *BD*, p. 279.

4 O. S. Rankin, *Israel's Wisdom Literature*, p. 79, cited by R. J. Hammer, "Suffer," *TWBB*, p. 249.

5 Hammer, *TWBB*, p. 249.

6 Rankin, p. 81.

49:15-20), (3) suffering is disciplinary (Psa. 119:67, Mal. 3:2), (4) suffering leads to a yearning for deliverance and God's intervention (Isa. 30:20, Psa. 88:1), (5) suffering can be vicarious and redemptive (Isa. 53).

Synonymous term conveying this concept or that of "oppression" is *lahac*. It was used to denote the general sense of wrong done to others through violence, as, e.g., the acts of the Egyptian taskmasters (Exod. 3:9, Deut. 26:7). The word is used also of social oppression within Israel's community; the Psalms abound with plaints against unjust oppressors (Psa. 12:1-4, 42:9, 43:2, 44:24).

New Testament concepts

The Gk. word *stenochoria* tr. "anguish" in Rom 2:9 and "necessities" in II Cor. 6:4, stems from the same concept as in Japanese; lit. it means "to be shut up in a cage," hence "driven in," "oppressed." Most frequent word is *thlipsis*, used to denote (1) distress brought about by outward circumstances (Acts 11:19, Rom. 5:3, II Cor. 1:8, Rev. 1:9) and (2) mental distress (II Cor. 2:4, Phil. 1:16). The word is used concerning the eschatalogical calamities of the end times (Matt. 24:21, Mark 13:19, 24). Another word *pathema* is used in the sense of "suffering affliction" (II Cor. 6:4, Col. 1:24, I Pet. 5:9, Heb. 2:10), and is the technical NT term used of Christ's passion (I Pet. 4:13; 5:1). However, it can simply mean physical passion (Rom. 7:5). The root idea as Trench asserts is that of "pressure," "hemming in." The same motifs for suffering can be found in the NT as were in the OT; suffering "is the essence of the mission of the Messiah."[7] Hardships and suffering can be retributive (Gal. 6:7), probationary (James 1:3, 12, I Pet. 4:17, II Cor. 12:10), but the essence of vicarious suffering is fully developed in the passion of Christ (I Pet. 2:19-23). There is the inexplicable aspect of suffering. But Jesus refuted the theory that suffering is directly related to personal sin (John 9:2 ff.). The NT also employs *anagke*, a term which suggests a cosmic principle which restricts and inhibits normal growth. To Aristotle it was "all that which is apart from the true fashioning of life and which constricts and opposes it."[8] It is a means of compulsion and oppression, conditioning reality and resisting the spirit. Used in the NT it signified a "situation of need" (Luke 21:23), the "afflictions which derive from the tension between the new creation in Christ and the old cosmos (II Cor. 12:10, I Th. 3:7, I Cor. 7:26)."[9] Outright persecution is conveyed by the word *diogmos* and is part of the lot of the follower of Christ as He foretold (Matt. 16:24). Persecution becomes in the providence of God a test of discipleship (Mark 4:17) and means of blessing (Matt. 5:10, 11). Finally hardship is narrowed down to actual *bonds*. Paul was imprisoned for Christ's sake, he was the ambassador in bonds (II Tim. 1:8, Eph. 4:1, Phlm. 13, Phil. 1:13). This *desmos*, as with all hardship, suffering, bondage, and oppression, is seen in a theological dimension by the NT writers and as such is not to be cause for terror or consternation.

---

7 Hammer, *TWBB*, p. 252.

8 Walter Grundmunn, "*anagkadzo*" *TDNT*, I, 344.

9 *Ibid.*, p. 346.

But this real imprisonment is set in relation to Christ and the Gospel. Christ is its author. He is the One for whose sake it is fulfilled and also the One to whom human self-will should be offered in sacrifice.[10]

Encounter

There is marked similarity to the etymological meanings of hardship in Japanese and Biblical words. These words speak of something pressing upon man; something oppressing, restricting, stifling, inhibiting his free course of action. In the Japanese tradition, then, all hardships are seen in a negative light for they stand pitted against the epitome of values—a happy and pleasant life upon earth. Biblical "hardship" is seen under varying aspects—man's common lot as the fruit of his sin, discipline, a means of turning man's attention to God, a vicarious effect bringing good to others—all which underscore one point: hardships and suffering do not happen but are under the providence of a wise Heavenly Father. And lest men despair amidst hardships, they are given an unforgettable picture of God's own Son plunging to the depths of suffering, tracing out an unmistakeable path—"the sufferings of Christ and the glory that should follow" (I Pet. 1:11).

---

10 G. Kittel, "*desmos*" *TDNT*, II, 43.

SORROW 悲 KANASHIMI

Japanese Concepts of Sorrow

Chinese character etymology

Kanashimi is one character with two components, 非 (divided), and 心 (heart). *KGJ*: (1) one's heart is divided, or (2) something in the heart that seeks for release. *KCJ*: one's heart is torn and a feeling of sorrow comes to the surface.

Semantic changes in Japan

Kanashimi is an indigenous Japanese word, the above character just being affixed to it. Ōno traces the word back to the concept of "difficult" (*kane*), used in earlier periods to denote the "grief of parting." Also the word was used to express love for another person; one's heart becomes full when he thinks of that person.

Modern range of meaning

KCJ: (1) sorrow, sadness (*kanashii*), (2) Buddhist compassion and kindness. *KJ*: (1) be sad (*kanashimu koto*), (2) sadness (*kanashimi*), (3) pathos (*hiai*). *DNKJ*: (1) sadness (*kanashisa*), (2) be sad (*kanashimu koto*).

English idiom parallels

Be overwhelmed with sorrow (*kanashimi ni shizumu*). Be overcome with grief (*hitan ni kureru*). Cry inside (*kokoro no naka de naku*). Heart-rending sorrow (*mune o harisakeru yōna omoi*). Eating one's heart out (*setsunai omoi o suru*).

Buddhist concepts

Sadness stems from suffering and suffering is produced by impermanence. *Gyōku* is the tr. of the Sk. *samskara-duhkhata* and literally means, "going-suffering," that is the suffering which develops from life in motion. *BD* defines it as "the suffering that is felt when one sees the transciency of all phenomenal elements in this world."[1] Classical writers of the Nara period were optimistic. It was good to be alive. Nature is throbbing with life, alive with color, beckoning man to harmonize with it. Emperor Jomei (593-641 A.D.) climbed Kagu-yama and described his realm thus:

---

[1] *BD*, p. 94.

> Countless are the mountains in Yamato,
> But perfect is the heavenly hill of Kagu;
> When I climb it and survey my realm,
> Over the wide plain the smoke wreaths rise and rise,
> Over the wide lake the gulls are on the wing;
> A beautiful land it is, the Land of Yamato![2]

But the shift from optimism to pessimism is noted in the Heian period. Sincerity, expressing things as they are, which so marked Nara literature gave way to emotionalism and sentimentality, summed up in the words, *mono no aware* (the sadness of things). The priest Mansei depicts poignantly the ephemeral world:

> To what shall I compare
> This world?
> To the white wake behind
> A ship that has rowed away
> At dawn![3]

Shiranami (white wave) which occurs in the poem is a *kake-kotoba* (pivot word), which was a technical device employed by the poets for conveying two ideas with one word (similar to our pun). It could mean to the reader *shiranu* (unknown), or *namida* (tears). Poetry of this period was characterized by the use of such words so that even beautiful scenes of a forest were given the tinge of pathos by the implied secondary meaning. The "sadness of things" conceived by the Japanese at that time has characterized their views of life and nature; impermance, vicissitudes, change, and separation cast a hue of sadness over every earthly joy.

Biblical Concepts of Sorrow

Old Testament concepts

Hebrew words are *hebhel, yaghon,* and *makhobh. Hebhel* approaches the meaning of pain, as birthpains of a woman (Hos. 13:13), but also used of the sorrow of death (Job 39:3). *Makhobh* is mental suffering or grief (Lam. 1:12, Eccl. 1:18). Sorrow is seen as one of the immediate effects of the Fall (Gen. 3:16). The writer in Eccl. 7:3 says that *sorrow* is better than laughter for by it the heart is made better. That is, sorrow is considered to have its probationary effects upon man. But the Ecclesiastes writer becomes over-occupied with this negative emotional experience in man; and says, "all his days are sorrows" (Eccl. 2:23). More generally, in the OT sorrow, physical and mental, is seen as the consequence of sin, perhaps as its proleptic punishment; "God distributeth sorrows in his anger" (Job 21:17). Such being the life course of man, it is not surprising that the Suffering Servant of Jehovah came not as the apochryphal

---

2 Cited by Donald Keene, *Anthology of Japanese Literature* (New York: Groves Press, 1955), p. 34.
3 *Ibid.,* p. 93.

writers portrayed Him, *viz.*, the conqueror coming to put down all of Israel's
foes, but as a man of sorrows, acquainted with grief (Isa. 53:3).

New Testament concepts

Gk. words are *lupe*, which is "grief," "sorrow," "pain of mind or spirit"
(Luke 22:45, John 16:6, II Cor. 2:3);[4] another is *penthes*, which is more
"mourning" (James 4:9, Rev. 18:8). *Odune* is of more cosmic significance, used
in an eschatological framework of final tribulation (Matt. 24:8), but it can be
simply "mental anguish" (Rom. 9:2). Trench distinguishes *lupe* and *penthes*:
Lupe can be experienced in the heart alone; *penthes* is grief which cannot be
hid. Paul distinguishes godly sorrow from worldly sorrow in II Cor. 7:9-11.
The former awakens the person to the real situation he is in and leads him to
repentence; the latter simply closes the man in upon himself in sorrow upon
sorrow—it works death. That is, sorrow comes to man unqualified; what he
does with it qualifies it as either worldly or godly. Heaven is portrayed as the
place where all sorrow is banished from man's life (Rev. 21:4).

Encounter

Japanese concepts of sorrow do not appreciably differ from Biblical concepts
except in the philosophical context of source and purpose. Japanese see sorrow
as bound up with their lives which are integral with nature's change and
ephemerity. All human relationships are finally to be severed, as green leaves
finally fall from the tree during the cold blasts of winter. The Japanese proverb,
"to meet someone is just the beginning of saying 'Goodbye' " (*Ai wa wakare
no hajimari*), brings out this concept. Even the expression for "Goodbye"—
"*Sayonara*"—is not the idea of "May blessings be upon you while we are
apart," but signifies a final severance.

Biblical sorrow traces its source to the Fall and the situation of man's being
estranged from God, the source of joy and true life. But to those who will be
trained by it, sorrow can bring men back to God. Thus they will see in its
purpose a final goodness. Hence the Christian can be "sorrowful, yet always
rejoicing" (II Cor. 6:10).

---

4 Arndt, p. 483.

ENDURANCE 忍 耐 NINTAI

Japanese Concepts of Endurance

Chinese character etymology

Nintai is comprised of two characters: 忍 (endure, bear), and 耐 (support, endure). *Nin* has two components: 刃 (sword), and 心 (heart). It is thus commonly held that this stemmed from the idea of a sword piercing one's heart. But *KCJ*: Sword radical is for phonetic usage only. Components convey (a) enduring in one's heart, or (b) twisting one's heart in an excruciating manner. *Tai* has two components: 而 (beard or jaw) and 寸 (hand). It came to mean "patience" because it had the same phonetic character as *Nin*; hence compounded with it to emphasize patience.

Semantic changes in Japan

Japanese word to which this character was affixed is *shinobu*, used, for instance, in the sense of enduring the wrath of (or putting up with) another (*ikari o shinobu*).[1] In *Shuishū* (1000 A.D.): "If I *bear up* (*shinobu*) under the sadness of this love disappointment, everyone will think I have no feelings."[2] Its literal meaning is *hide*; hence to endure is to hide one's feelings.

Modern range of meaning

Nin

    KCJ: (1) bear up, endure (*shinobu*), (2) forgive (*yurusu*), (3) hide (*kakushimotsu*), (4) avoid people (*hitome o shinobu*).

    KJ: (1) bear (*koraeru koto*), (2) not to become angry at another person.

Tai

    KCJ: (1) endure, accomplish (*taeru*), (2) put up with (*gaman suru*) (3) support, undergird (*sasaeru*).

Nintai

    KCJ: (1) endure and bear up under (*taeshinobu*), (2) be patient (*shinbō suru*).

    DNKJ: (1) endure and bear up under (*taeshinobu*), (2) suffer, bear (*koraeru koto*), (3) be patient (*shinbō suru*).

---

[1] *DGK*. p. 916.
[2] *Ibid.*

Biblical Concepts of Endurance

Old Testament concepts

The word "patience" does not occur in the OT, though the adverb "patiently" appears in Psa. 40:1, used in the sense of waiting patiently for God's intervention. More germane to the concept are the Hebrew words *erekj appayim*, meaning lit., "long of nose." As anger is indicated by quick and violent breathing, so the opposite would be long breathing, hence "long of anger." The English rendering in the AV is "longsuffering." It is used in Exod. 34:6 and Num. 14:18 concerning Jehovah to illustrate that He is plenteous in mercy. In short, it

> describes that attitude of God whereby strict justice would long ago have swept Israel away in penalty for her sin and rebellion, if it had not been that God is slow to anger and of great mercy. This struggle between strict justice and mercy is admirably portrayed in Hos. 11:8.[3]

Patience then is intrinsically part of God's nature, and this patience as declared by the prophets was to engender patience in men towards one another.

New Testament concepts

Three Gk. words are used specifically to render this concept of patience in the NT; *viz.*, *makrothumia, upomone*, and *anoche*. Arndt defines *makrothumia* as (1) patience, steadfastness, endurance (II Tim. 3:10, Heb. 6:12, James 5:10); (2) forbearance towards others (a) by men (Eph. 4:2, II Cor. 6:6), (b) by God towards men (Rom. 2:4; 9:22), (c) by Christ in His passion towards an unbelieving world (II Pet. 3:15). Trench gives this definition: "A patient holding out under trial, rather than a long-suffering under provocation. It is the long holding out of the mind before it gives room to action or passion."[4]

Upomone has two meanings: (1) patience, endurance, fortitude (Rom. 5:3 ff., Rev. 13:10); and (2) patient expectation (Rev. 1:9). Trench defines it: "The brave patience with which the Christian contends against the various hindrances, persecutions and temptations that befall him in his conflict with the inward and outward world."[5] Thus *makrothumia* is in respect to persons, *upomone* to things. Hence the man who has *makrothumia* does not easily get provoked at people who injure or displease him (II Tim. 4:2); the man who has *upomone* does not lose heart because of the many trials and difficulties under which he is laboring (Rom. 5:3 ff.). These difficulties may assume the form of physical trials, delayed promises, or actual temptations. This endurance has its grounds in faith, trusting in His goodness, wisdom, and faithfulness, though they may seem hid by the clouds of trial. In the face of temporary reverse or even permanent separation, it does not question but looks beyond to the faithfulness of God, taking the good and bad as from His Hand. For this reason true patience is not just quiet resignation in the face of life's reverses but a "lively

---

3 Snaith, "Long-suffering," *TWBB*, p. 130.

4 Trench, p. 196.

5 *Ibid.*, p. 197.

outgoing power of faith, an active energy rather than a passive resignation. For it is an expectation which has been fulfilled in Christ, and is thus perfected and also continually merging into hope and faith in the coming of Christ."[6] Paul mentions patience in Rom. 5:2-5 as one link in the chain from hope to hope, leading those who will be trained by it to new heights of confident expectation. Thus this virtue, like most of those enumerated in the NT, cannot be conjured up from man's inner being; it has a divine dimension.

The patience of Christ (II Thess. 3:5) is no doubt subjective genetive, stressing the patience which Christ bestows to those in union with Him. Similarly, the term "God of patience" (Rom. 15:5) is referring to God's gift of patience to men.

The last Gk. word, *anoche* has the nuance of "taking up," "bearing and enduring." It is restraining oneself or tolerating others.[7] Trench defines it: "It is temporary, transient; we may say that, like our 'truce', it asserts its own temporary, transient character; that after a certain lapse of time, and unless other conditions intervene, it will pass away."[8] Thus Jesus is described as putting up with the unfaithful generation of His day (Mark 9:19). In Eph. 4:2 and Col. 3:13, the Christian community is encouraged to put up with one another. It is used in reference to persecution, not so much in the sense of standing under a trial and enduring it (this would be *upomone*), but it "implies the constant acceptance of the claims of others as shown by the parallel *eulogein* and *parakalein*."[9] Thus *anoche* has time limits, used in the sense of withholding immediate deserved judgment in hopes that repentence will bring the offender to his senses. Such is God's patience with unbelieving men. He does not forgive them; He tolerates them (Rom. 2:4, 3:26). This tolerance calls in question the absolute justice of God; thus Paul's argument presents the necessity of the Cross to declare openly the internal justice of God (Rom. 3:26). In the words of Trench: "It is that forebearance or suspense of wrath, that truce with the sinner, which by no means implies that the wrath will not be executed at the last; nay it involves that it certainly will, unless he be found under new conditions of repentence and obedience (Luke 13:9, Rom. 2:3-6)."[10]

Encounter

Endurance is one of the Spartan virtues developed in the Samurai tradition of Japan. The language abounds with proverbial sayings extolling this very important ingredient in Japanese life. For example, "The Samurai glories in honorable poverty" (*Bushi wa kuwanedo, takayōji*, which lit. means, "Even though the samurai has been without food, he puts a toothpick in his mouth

---

6 R. Gregor Smith, "Patience," *TWBB*, 165.

7 Heinrich Schlier, "*anecho*" *TDNT*, I, 359.

8 Trench, p. 199.

9 Schlier, *TDNT*, I, 359.

10 Trench, p. 200.

as if he had just finished eating."), "Patience will wear out a stone"(*Ishi no ue ni mo sannen*), Rome wasn't built in a day (*Itchō isseki de wa dekinai*), Enduring the unendurable is true endurance (*Naranu kannin suru ga kannin*).

The writer Watsuji Tetsurō in his *Fūdo* (Climate) attributes this characteristic to the centuries of Japanese bending and adapting to adverse weather conditions. One wonders how such a cultural characteristic could be directly attributed to weather. It rather might be demonstrated that in a feudalistic stratified society, buttressed by Buddhist emphasis upon resignation, the Japanese found no outlet for outright rebellion or independent expression. Also n a land too little for too many, where the press of humanity is felt in every phase of life, some means of quelling desires and actions destructive to one's niche had to be developed. This is endurance.

Biblical patience finds its roots in God's longsuffering and forebearance towards obstinate and recalcitrant men. This is an aspect of His steadfast love. Men are called upon to evidence this patience with each other, forebearing one another in Christian love. They are also called upon to remain steadfast under trial and temptation—not in the spartan "grin and bear it" spirit—but in faith, active faith which sees beyond the immediate trial the purpose of God.

ANGER 怒 IKARI

Japanese Concepts of Anger

Chinese character etymology

Ikari is comprised of one character with two components: 奴 (slave), and 心 (heart). *KCJ*: Suppress an outburst of feeling from the heart. *KCJ*: A slave gets angry.

Semantic changes in Japan

Ikari stems from the idea of being big, enlarged, great. Ōno points out that the original Japanese word stems from the oblique or pointed shape of the fish called *"ika."* When a person is angry he reveals it by his pointed eyes or raised eyebrows which reminded the Japanese of the *ika* fish; hence *ikari*. In the *Genji Monogatari* the word appears in the sentence, "If the emperor *is out of sorts with you*, you cannot move freely around the palace."[1] *Ikari*, then is *visible anger*.

Modern range of meaning

KCJ: (1) become angry (*okoru*), (2) to be full of enthusiasm and tremble, (3) make angry, encourage (*okoraseru, hagemasu*).

KJ: (1) get angry (*ikaru koto*), (2) fit of anger (*haradachi*), (3) anger (*rippuku*).

DNKJ: (1) become angry (*ikaru koto*), (2) fit of anger (*haradachi*).

English idiom parallels

Turn purple with rage (*aosuji o tateru*). Burst into anger (*bakuhatsu suru*). Fly into a rage (*mukappara o tateru*). Be raked over the coals (*medama no tobideru hodo okorareru*). Touch one's sore spot (*kan ni sawaru*). One's patience runs out (*Kannin bukuro no o ga kireru*). Get peeved at (*shaku ni sawaru*). Let off steam (*uppun o harasu*).

Biblical Concepts of Anger

Old Testament concepts

Most frequent Hebrew word is *'ap*, etymologically stemming from the idea of "snort"; fierce breathing from the nostrils indicates a feeling of anger. This

---

[1] *DGK*, p. 190.

term is used for expressing both human and divine anger. Other words similarly convey the physical manifestation of anger, such as *hemath* from the idea of "hot"; hence the expression "one's anger is kindled." *Ebrah* means to flow over. Evans finds no legitimate reason for men showing anger in the OT. Human anger is "the exhibition of an enraged sinful nature and is therefore always inexcusable (Gen. 4:5,6).[2] However Biblical uses of these words do not always cast human anger in such negative light. Moses (Ex. 16:20), David (II Sam. 12:5), and Nehemiah (Neh. 5:6), for example, seemed to have valid reasons for their indignation, as Kleinknecht says, "Human wrath is just and godly whenever it is aroused not merely in order to preserve individual rights."[3] However, in general, as the Wisdom writers assert, anger is dangerous and those who suppress it act wisely (Prov. 14:29; 15:18).

Divine wrath against men and nations is portrayed in vivid symbols, such as fire (Jer. 15:14, Isa. 65:5), water (Hos. 5:10, Ezek. 7:8), and a rod (Isa. 10:5). Oftentimes those in closest relation to Jehovah become objects of His wrath; *viz.*, Moses (Exod. 4:14), Aaron (Deut. 9:20), and the nation Israel (Exod. 19). This wrath takes the form of sickness, oppression from enemies, and even death (Lev. 19). God is the One true God; violations of this express fact necessarily incur divine disapproval. That Israel's surrounding nations and their rulers will be visited by the wrath of God is the subject of many of the prophets. Sometimes the direct cause of suffering under the wrath of God is not apparent to the sufferers and we read of their complaints to Jehovah in the Psalms (Psa. 102:7-11; 88:16). But, in general, it is obvious: if God is holy and faithful, violations of His holiness and unfaithfulness to His covenant must evoke some other response besides indifference. And this arousing of wrath is not simply a temporary passion or vindictive action but has as its goal the purifying of the impure and regeneration of the wayward. As Kleinknecht says, "it is Yehovah's wounded, holy love which arouses His wrath."[4]

New Testament concepts

Key Gk. word for expressing wrath in the NT is *orge*. In Gk. literature *orge* implied the impulsive behavior of man and beast. But also *orge* of the gods is an accepted fact of pre-Homeric religion. Plato speaks of unusually serious illnesses and sufferings which befell this or that family as a result of resentment from the gods. Storms, illnesses can be traced to the *orge* of the gods. Roman concepts were similar; the *ira deum* acts against men, as in bringing the Roman legions down to defeat. And this wrath of the gods was incurred when there was improper observance of ritual and ceremony. The word is used of human wrath in the NT in the sense of "hating what God hates."[5] But such wrath was properly demonstrated only by the Son of Man against the sin and rebellion of man (Mark 3:5, Matt. 12:34; 23:33, John 8:44). There appears to be an advance over the concept of human wrath in the OT, for not much

---

2 William Evans, "Wrath," *ISBE*, V, 3113.

3 Hermann Kleinknecht, J. Fichtner, and G. Stahlin, "Wrath," *BKW*, IV, 19.

4 *Ibid.*, p. 39.

5 *Ibid.*, p. 76.

encouragement is given even to the use of wrath by man in achieving divine purposes. When a man is angry, sin is close at hand. It is the "first step to murder."[6] Thus provoking others to wrath is sin because it opens the sluice-gate of more serious sin. Giving vent to anger is giving opportunity for satanic forces to be unleashed (Eph. 4:26-31; 6:4, Matt. 18:6, Col. 3:8).

Divine anger is expressed by *orge* and *thumos*. It however has lost its milieu of a passionate outbreaking of emotion. It is governed by eternal principles and is constant as His love is constant. Thus men are either under mercy or wrath, justification or condemnation, salvation or perdition. This coupling of wrath with the constant blessings which flow from those united in a covenant relation to God demonstrate this theological aspect of divine wrath. Kleinknecht says, "The NT does not contain any trace of those enigmatic, irrational out-bursts of wrath and the divine wrath does not burn for ever. In the NT, a theological concept of *orge* clearly outweighs the psychological one."[7] Being used in these frequent couplings with mercy, love, righteousness gives a clue to the causes which evoke God's wrath upon men. Refusing to stand under the love, compassion, righteousness of God as revealed in the Incarnation and the Cross, man steps under an equally unchanging characteristic of God, His righteous indignation. Romans 9:22,23 is the *locus classicus* which sets in sharp contrast the two activities of God towards men—His wrath and His mercy. Romans 2:4-9 speaks of a treasuring up of wrath. Men's persistence in rebellion and refusal to acknowledge God's acts of mercy are thus accounted in the Divine counsels as are his excercises of faith. The latter renders the verdict of "acquitted," but the former sets the stage for the final eschatological outpouring of Divine wrath. Until that time, though the wrath of God is presently hanging over the obstinate (John 3:36), it frequently is not recognizable. To the contrary, the goodness and mercy of God upon such men are misinterpreted as signs of Divine pleasure. Thus infatuated by a sense of false security, men continue to disregard His revelation in nature or conscience (Rom. 1:17-21), they flout the explicit commands of Scripture (Rom. 2:17-27), and worship false deities (Acts 17:16). Resting in a spurious freedom, they give full play to their natures and reasonings, and continue a reckless plunge away from the correcting influences of God. This process they feel is self-initiated and the final expression of the self as it vaunts itself against all restraint. But actually this anti-God direction is an expression of the Divine wrath already at work, a "giving up" (Rom. 1:24, 26, 28). Men are warned to flee from God's wrath, and the avenue of escape is simply repentence, repentence that is decisive and made evident by deeds of goodness and restitution (Matt. 3:2, 8).

Encounter

Japanese concepts of wrath differ little from the classical Gk. concepts—uncontrolled emotion, impulsiveness, an outburst of disapproval conveyed by

---

6 *Ibid.*, p. 78.

7 *Ibid.*, p. 83.

words, looks and action. The "slave" character in the word no doubt conveys little of the disparagement nuance found in earlier forms to the average Japanese today, but the historical emphasis upon controlling one's emotions, especially anger, has made the Japanese people extremely cautious and sensitive towards outward displays of anger. The man who never becomes angry is invariably the "good" man; the man who becomes easily angered is shunned and held in disrespect. In fact this human emotion has been so suppressed that it is almost impossible to detect another person's displeasure. This can be disastrous to the naive foreigner who blithely stumbles through committee meetings and daily interactions with Japanese. He imagines that there is no resistance to him or his ideas. The common phrase, "One can be sitting atop a volcano about to erupt in Japan without ever knowing it," is alas, the common experience. This has worked some difficulties for their own daily interaction as well. Not being able to detect disapproval everyone assumes it is ubiquitous; this leads to an overemphasis upon trivial formalities and attention to decorum in an effort to placate the unseen threat to all relationships. More, it actually has driven the Japanese people away from themselves. Overpoliteness, decorum, formality, extreme care in propriety camouflage and confuse genuine affection; it thus becomes the strange paradox that only those who become angry with you (like your closest relatives) are those you begin to understand and can trust.

Biblical wrath is set forth neither as an emotion nor a sudden outburst of displeasure but as a corallary to the holiness, righteouness, mercy and love of God. Affronts to the holiness of God must be answered by divine disapproval. Man's wrath is dangerous and cannot work out the purposes of God. But it is not categorically rejected as evil. Righteous indignation, hating what God hates, expressing displeasure at impiety should be hallmarks of the Christian as much as their counterparts. When anger is released as a means of protecting the self and its claims, the Biblical view of wrath differs little from the Japanese; it is an undesirable human emotion which must be curbed and checked. But when this anger is jealous for His Name and for others being wronged, it has its place as a legitimate human emotion. But the emotion bristles with danger, so the injunction is to let it fade away with the setting sun.

CHAPTER III
CONCEPTS OF RELIGIOUS EXPERIENCE

FAITH 信 仰 *SHINKŌ*

Japanese Concepts of Faith

Chinese character etymology

Shinkō is comprised of two characters: 信 (trust), and 仰 (look up to, revere). *Shin* has two components: 人 (man) and 言 (word). *KCJ*: Trusting man's word—the unity of man and his word. *Kō* has two components: 人 (man), and 卬 (man in prostrate position looking up). *KGJ*: One person looking up in respect toward another. The added radical for man on the left emphasizes the aspect of relationships between men. *KGJ*: Two people facing each other, the one kneeling and looking up to the other.

Semantic changes in Japan

The word was employed in classical literature refering to belief in the Buddha's teaching. *Shakukyō*: "I recommend faith and reciting of sutras."[1] The "*shin*" character is one of the five Confucian virtues. It conveys the concept of mutual trust, e.g., *Rongo*: "When friends talk together and fellowship together, there you have "faith."[2] *Junshi*: "To believe the truth is faith; to doubt the doubtful, this is faith also."[3] The Japanese indigenous word to which *kō* was affixed is *aogu*. It simply meant, "to look upward." *Manyōshū*: "I look to your gate as I would *look up* to heaven."[4] *Kokkinshū*: "Respect the past as you would *look up* to the sky,"[5]

Modern range of meaning

Shin

KCJ: (1) truth (*makoto*), (2) believe something is true, (3) have faith (*shinkō suru*), (4) news (*tayori*), (5) sign (*shirushi*), (6) proof (*shōmei*), (7) trust, turn over to (*makasu*), (8) extend (*nobiru*).

KJ: (1) without deception (*azamukanu koto*), (2) without doubt (*utagawanu koto*), (3) have faith (*shinkō suru koto*), (4) news (*otozure*).

DNKJ: (1) without deception or falsehood, (2) think something is true, (3) have faith (*shinkō suru koto*), (4) news, report (*otozure*).

---

1 *DGK*, p. 936.
2 *DGK*, p. 925.
3 *DGK*, p. 925.
4 *DGK*, p. 71.
5 *DGK*, p. 71.

Kō

   KCJ: (1) look up (*aogu*), (2) respect (*uyamau*), (3) drink poison (*doku o nomu*), (4) to say (*ōse*), (5) invoke the help of a higher power.

   KJ: to look up, face upward (*ue o muku*).

   DNKJ: (1) esteem (*tōtobu koto*), (2) request, seek (*kou, motomeru*), (3) esteem a teaching (*oshie o aogu*).

Shinkō

   KJ: (1) believe and esteem something (2) aspect of religious activity which is in the consciousness (3) the affection born from fear or admiration of that which is holy.

Modern English parallels

   Seeing is believing (*Hyakubun wa ikken ni shikazu*). Live by faith (*shinkō ni ikiru*). Religious life (*shinkō seikatsu*). Pious (*shinjinbukai*). It staggers belief (*shinjiru ni shinjikirenai*). An arrow of conviction will even go through a rock (*Ichinen iwa o mo tōsu*).

Buddhist concepts

   Buddhism employs the word *kie*, tr. of the Sk. *sarana*, for denoting this religious aspect of response towards a religious object. It means "to take refuge in" or "to worship."[6] Using the verb "suru" with *shinkō* gives stress upon man's activity in faith. It literally means "doing faith" or "practicing faith." Hence from traditional rites in the normal life of a Japanese, faith could simply be a matter of observing prescribed Buddhist memorials for the deceased—offering rice before the family altar each morning. The more scrupulous one is in these traditional customs the more he would be called one who practices faith. Another aspect of faith, stemming from Shintō as the religion of gratitude, is the appreciative type of faith—termed *onkei shinkō*. Faith, then, is a matter of appreciation or gratitude toward local tutelary gods or deceased ancestors for present blessings received. In the new religions, another aspect of faith is that of obtaining a felt need, such as healing from sickness, financial help, etc. This is called *goriyaku shinkō*. Another aspect of Buddhist faith is a proper frame of mind—called *shinkyō shinkō*. That is, the religious object is not of major consequence; if the heart is pure one may have faith in the head of a sardine.[7] This explains the comparative tolerance of Buddhism towards other religions. The *excercise* of faith is stressed more than the object of faith. The common proverb, "Many roads leave from the foot of the mountain toward the summit, but the moon seen from the top is the same," underscores this indifference towards objects of faith.

---

6 *BD*, p. 173.

7 The proverb, "*Iwashi no atama no shinjin kara*" (Men start having faith in something, even the head of a sardine) is rooted in an old custom of fixing the head of sardine above the door for good luck.

Biblical Concepts of Faith

Old Testament concepts

Two Hebrew words are used chiefly to convey the concept of faith; *amen*, and *betach*. *Amen* is discussed under TRUTH, but its verbal form in the *niphal* conveyed the thought of man's relationship to God. "Thou didst find his [Abraham's] heart *ne-eman* before thee and didst make with him a covenant." (Neh. 9:8). This refers to the promise of Gen. 15:6 when Abraham responded in faith to God's promise. Thus, "faith as interpreted by the OT is always the response of man to the primary activity of God."[8] OT faith is not a single act but the whole gamut of man's relationship to the faithful God. The *hiphil* of *amen* is rendered fifteen times in the LXX as *pisteuien*. It is a recognition of the claim contained in the Name of the one trusted, and this claim is binding upon the one who trusts God. God originates the relationship and man's acknowledgment of God's acts is simply recognizing the implicit demand for obedience. Whitehouse maintains that the core of the Heb. concept of faith is that of firmness. He says:

> To believe is to hold on to something firmly, with conviction and confidence. Faith is the criterion of right relationship. It is not quietistic fatalism but finds its life and activity in the object believed, the Living God.[9]

Girdlestone points out the revelatory character of faith:

> The man who believes God is he who, having received a revelation from Him, realizes it and acts upon it as true. The man who trusts God is he who casts all his hopes for the present and future on God.[10]

Amen, Bultmann points out, is not used concerning false deities or political relationships. It is a special relationship between God's people and Himself, founded on the covenant. The second word, *betach*, conveys the sense of security and can be excercised in riches (Psa. 49:6), one's ability (Hab. 2:18), or even idols (Isa. 42:17, Jer. 46:25). Bultmann stresses that though this word occurs more than *amen*, the primary meaning of *amen*, i.e., conveying the idea of one's whole relationship to God, is assimilated into *betach*:

> This can be recognized from the notable fact that it is one of the most significant features of the linguistic development of the other verbal stems that they become assimilated to the meaning of *amen*, involving a more or less pronounced change in their meaning.[11]

Hence in conclusion we see the key concept of faith—"a relationship to God which embraces the whole man in every part of his outward behavior and his inner life."[12] This concept emerges in other Heb. words as well, denoting a

---

8 Rudolph Bultmann, "Faith," *Bible Key Words*, tr. Dorothea M. Barton, P. R. Ackryoyd, and A. E. Harvey (New York: Harper and Row, Publ., 1960), III, 1.

9 W. A. Whitehouse, "Faith," *TWBB*, p. 75.

10 Girdlestone, p. 104.

11 Bultmann, *Bible Key Words*, III, 32.

12 *Ibid.*, p. 15.

particular form of existence and "life of the people of God...who stand in active relationship with God; it embraces this relationship in its whole wide range and penetrates to its utmost depths."[13]

New Testament concepts

Key Gk. word in the NT for faith is *pistis*. In the Gk. world it was not a technical term in religion. It was faithfulness to one's word. The way was paved for its adaptation in the NT for religious usage by its usage in respect to reliance upon divine oracles. In Judaism, the word was used to convey loyalty and obedience and was tinged with a sense of merit; the faithful are those who have fulfilled all the commandments and as such come into a special bargaining position with God. However the NT baptized the word *pistis* with its own meaning; in general it meant "turning towards the God disclosed by the preaching."[14] It has the following range of meaning: (1) put faith in the words of God (John 2:22, Acts 24:14), (2) obedience to revelation received (Rom. 1:8, I Thess. 1:8), (3) trust in a person, or his help (Acts 3:16; 14:9), (4) hope in something that is not quickly discernible or predictable (Heb. 11:1-6, Rom. 4:18, I Thess. 1:3), (5) loyalty (Heb. 12:1, II Thess. 1:4, Rev. 2:13). But specifically, though the word embraces these aspects, it had its technical meaning of *faith in the message of Christ*—the missionary message which declared what God had done in Christ. This faith or faith's object is summed up in the Rom. 10:9 formula, recognizing Jesus as Lord and accepting the miracle of the Resurrection. Stating the Resurrection as part of the credal statement of faith was not to the end of eliciting mental assent, but it is "the fact of salvation on the strength of which Jesus became Lord."[15] The Rom. 10:9 formula contains the whole gamut of the work, death, resurrection, and Lordship of Christ. This is to be the object of NT faith. Thus accepting the NT *kerugma* was accepting the central figure of history which establishes Jesus as Lord. It involved a personal relationship with this Lord, just as *amen* in the OT embraced a personal relationship with Jehovah. NT faith is linked with terms such as repentence, forgiveness of sins, obedience. Hence, "in every case, *pistis* is seen to be the act in virtue of which man separates himself from the world and turns around completely towards God in response to God's eschatalogical deed in Christ."[16] And this faith is not static, ending once admission to the Christian community has been achieved. Faith is active. Believers are the believing ones, "constantly relating themselves to God's act of salvation."[17] Thus some may be weak, others strong in faith, according to personal growth. Faith is worked out in each life. Though faith is the character of the Christian life, by no means can it be subsumed as a work of man. Works do not lead to salvation; to the contrary they lead to pride and status-establishing. It is a continual proclivity in man to rest in some personal

---

13 *Ibid.*, p. 33.
14 *Ibid.*, p. 62.
15 *Ibid.*, p. 71.
16 *Ibid.*, p. 85.
17 *Ibid.*, p. 89·

accomplishment, even his strong faith. But Pauline faith is a rejection of anything but childlike trust in the finished work of Christ. It an expectant faith, not in the gnostic sense of escape from the situation of historical life, but a return to a historical involvement in culture and society to live out this continual submission to the saving acts of God in Christ. John stresses faith, not as a renunciation of this world, but as a "shattering of the world's criteria and appraisals."[18] John employs the preposition "in" more than "unto," for he emphasizes this personal intimate aspect of faith; to believe in Christ is to come to Him, to love Him.[19]

Encounter

The two characters *shin* (trust) and *kō* (look up to) conjoined together to render the word "faith" is no doubt a case of coining new words by adding characters. Theoretically in Buddhist or Shintō faith, the word *shin* alone would cover the concept, for there is no place to which the believer is to look. If the religious object is within, the *hotoke* within man's heart (Buddhism) or in nature (Shintō), there is no "looking up" needed. But with the bringing in of the English word "faith," with its object firmly fixed on God and Christ, a new word was needed. However the original concept of trusting man's word as found in the Chinese character, and common usage in the milieu of Buddhist rites, have no doubt divested the word of any significance of looking beyond oneself to some object of personal trust. It is almost synonymous with being religious or pious or scrupulous in observing rites. Thus when Japanese frankly confess they have no faith, they are simply saying that they are not very zealous in any religious activity. That they have no trust in a personal God goes without saying, for such a concept has not entered their thinking.

Biblical faith, as expressed in the Biblical use of *amen* and *pistis*, speaks of a special relationship, a relationship to God which embraces the whole man. It is a vital cohesion to Christ in which all the blessings which Christ has gained in virtue of His exaltation become common property with those joined to Him, and conversely, all the rebellion, sin and unworthiness of the believer become Christ's possessions as He suffered for him on the Cross. Here again we see the great cleavage. Japanese faith is a mental activity or religious rite performed by man, not particularly related to any living object. Biblical faith is a joining in living adhesion to a Person. If Niebuhr's conclusions are valid, viz., that most cultural changes are brought about by men motivated by faith in an Absolute standing above culture, could it not be demonstrated that lack of this vital faith in some Absolute value beyond nature is responsible for the failure to develop a truly *vital Japanese cultural tradition*?

---

18 *Ibid.*, p. 103.
19 *Ibid.*, p. 99.

PRAYER 祈 *INORI*

Japanese Concepts of Prayer

Chinese character etymology

Inori is one character with two components: 礻 (god), and 斤 (approach). *KGJ*: Make an approach to the divinity; hence make a request. *KCJ*: Seek and approach God. There were other terms for the divine in the Chinese vocabulary, *viz.*, *Shang-Ti*, the supreme ancestor to whose ways each emperor must conform to retain the mandate of heaven; *Tao*, the cosmic unifying force of nature; *T'ien*, heaven. The component 礻 when joined with *mōsu* 申 is the word for *kami* in Japanese. In Chinese it was *shen*, the general term applied both to the "mysterious element in the universe"[1] and also to the human soul, "enclosed in the body as a sheath."[2] This twofold aspect of *shen* suited it perfectly for rendering the Japanese indigenous concept of the *kami*, for it signified at once the numinous in nature and the sage aspects of human nature. Hence the concept of prayer was not one of approaching a Wholly-Other but addressing the numinous of nature.

Semantic changes in Japan

In the *Genji Monogatari*, *inoru* is used in the sense of want and covet.[3] In the *Taketori monogatari* (11th century) we find the sentence: "To pray and fix one's request."[4] Ōno points out that the *i* of *inoru* stems from the *uy* of *yuyushii* (cf. PURITY), a word which conveyed the sense of *awe* before the mysterious aspects of nature. *Noru* he traces to the idea of "conveying something you know to someone who doesn't know it."[5] It is actually saying with one's lips one's name or one's country. This word developed into the *norito* of the priests, spoken out audibly before the shrines, hence "letting the god know something he is not aware of."[6] Thus the supplicant does not pray to God (*Kami ni inoru*), but prays *at* gods (*kami o inoru*). That is, he is calling for the god's attention by clapping hands or ringing bells. Having

---

[1] J. W. Inglis, *The Divine Name in Ancient China* (Shanghai: American Presbyterian Mission Press, 1910), p. 17.

[2] *Ibid.*, p. 18.

[3] *DGK*, p. 286.

[4] *DGK*, p. 200.

[5] Ōno, *Nihongo no...*, p. 62.

[6] *Ibid.*

secured the attention, he makes his requests known and seeks for material benefits in daily life.

A synonymous word, *negai*, Ōno traces from the *negi* (priest) of the shrines whose task it was to placate and appease the gods so as to receive blessings from them.

Modern range of meaning

KCJ: (1) request the help of the gods or Buddha for protection, (2) request, wish for (*negau*, *nozomu*), (3) tell (*tsugeru*).

KJ: (1) act of praying, making a request (*inoru koto*).

DNKJ: (1) act of praying (*inoru koto*), (2) one's request (*kigan*).

English idiom parallels

Prayer is answered (*inori ga kanau*). Prayer meeting (*kitōkai*). Humbly implore (*o-negai mōshiagemasu*). May....be done (*Neguwaku wa ...aran koto o*).

Buddhist concepts

Logically, Buddhism "does not have prayers in the sense of setting up a personified object to pray to. Buddhism could not help becoming a religion without prayer."[7] This will appear quite anomalous as one beholds thousands of Buddhist worshippers in Japan, bowing down, rubbing the 108 beads *juzu*, chanting "*Namu myōhō renge kyō*" (Adoration to the sutra of the Lotus of the excellent law). Takenaka resolves this difficulty:

> Silent meditation, sitting in contemplation, all work as a prayer; it is concentrating the mind and senses on some particular *teaching* (italics mine). The chanting of the sutras can be regarded as a form of prayer in the sense of a confession of faith. Prayer is not a petition, but an expression of conversion to Buddhism and conviction of attaining buddhahood... for this reason prayer in Buddhism differs from that in Christianity which has an unmistakeable faith in an eternal God.[8]

Of course, with the co-mingling of Buddhism and Shintō, Buddhism followed the pattern of the *norito* of the Shintō priests by praying for enhancements to daily life. The words used are *kitō*, defined by *BD* as: "Praying to either Buddhist or Shintō divinities, for some specific purpose. *Kitō* are particularly popular with the esoteric Buddhists and involve elaborate ritual."[9] More to the point of Buddhist prayer, giving the sense of reverence, is the word *namu*, tr. of the Sk. *namas*, defined as: "To pay respect to, to revere, etc. Commonly it is used with regard to the Buddhas or three treasures."[10]

---

[7] *EBu.*

[8] *EBu.*

[9] *BD*, p. 175.

[10] *BD*, p. 209.

Biblical Concepts of Prayer

Old Testament concepts

Twelve Hebrew words are rendered *prayer* in the OT, but actually many of these words do not specifically mean "to pray," but belong to the sphere of prayer. Greeven finds in the Gesenius-Buhl lexicon only one word— *atar* translated "prayer." Over sixty occurrences in the OT give it the sense of "to pray," as asking God or entreating Him (Gen. 25:21, Exod. 8:28, Job 22:27). *Shaal* is literally "to wish," wishing for the peace of Jerusalem (Psa. 121:6). *Chanan* means to "seek the favour of another" thus in the *hithpael* means to present oneself acceptably before one. Greeven says concerning this aspect of prayer: "All prayer seeks to awaken God's favour and thus to turn His goodness, grace and mercy to the petitioner."[11] *Halel* brings out the joyous aspect of prayer, meaning to praise, extol, glorify (Psa. 113:1). The original meaning of *halel* is "bright," "then (came to mean) make clear, and afterwards to exclaim in a loud tone."[12] There is a sound reason why men should so exult in God:

> God has ordained for His works this remembrance with praise (Psa. 111:4); the recollection of His goodness should be proclaimed with praise (Psa. 145:7).... public praising of the acts, the mighty acts, the miracles, the faithfulness and lovingkindness of God.[13]

The word *hishtachuwa* brings out the prostrate posture of prayer corresponding to the Gk. *proskeuo* (to bow the knee). It is the gesture of respectful greeting to superiors; hence in the sphere of prayer it speaks of a worshipful attitude (Gen. 22:5). However, posture is not fixed in the OT; a person may fall on his face (Josh. 5:14), spread forth his hands (Isa. 1:15), or lift them up.

Concerning prayer itself, there is a development in depth of prayer in the OT, as Lambert asserts. The first period, which he calls the "patriarchal period," was the age when men simply called upon the name of the Lord (Gen. 4:26; 12:8; 13:4). McEwen says there are traces of primitive magic and charms in these early prayers, but adds "prayer in the OT is far removed from magic."[14] This he and Lambert associate with the offering of sacrifices with prayer (Gen. 12:8) and Jacob's bargaining (Gen. 28:20 ff.), but Greeven is more to the point in stressing that OT prayer was primarily directed to Jehovah as the One God, who enters into covenant relations with His people. Thus OT prayer is linked with faith, faith in who Jehovah is—the God who has made Israel His people and is the bountiful supplier of their needs. Moreover the patriarchs excercise intercession for others, as Abraham intercedes on Lot's behalf.

The OT is not indifferent to means and places for prayer, "for at the sanctuaries one may hope to draw near to God and to reach Him in prayer."[15]

---

11 Heinrich Greeven, "*euchomai*," *TDNT*, II, 785.

12 Girdlestone, p. 220.

13 Greeven, *TDNT*, II, 787.

14 J. S. McEwen, "Prayer," *TWBB*, p. 169.

15 Johannese Hermann, "Prayer in the OT," *TDNT*, II, 792.

But though sacrifices and offerings can accompany prayer, the Psalms reveal a spiritual sacrifice—thankful praise (Psa. 50:23) which is more efficacious than bullocks (Psa. 69:30, 31).

The Exile becomes a turning point in the development of OT prayer, for the exiled Israelite no longer can find support and encouragement in prayer t rough altars and sanctuaries. Lambert says:

> Chastisement drove the nation to seek God more earnestly than before, and as the way of approach through the external forms of the temple and its sacrifices was now closed, the spiritual path of prayer was frequented with a new assiduity.[16]

Daniel was noted as a man of prayer (Dan. 6). Prayer for the nation is found on the lips of Ezra and Nehemiah (Neh. 2:4, Ezra 8:21). Hence the Psalms, many of which were written during the exile or after it, bring us to the highest pinnacle of spiritual prayer in the OT. Here are men, cut off from their homeland, oppressed, without national unity, without the facilities for common worship. But they find consolation, strength and deliverance through the one means left open to them—prayer. Thus the songs of the Psalter have been the treasury of the ages, used by men everywhere to express their deepest aspirations.

New Testament concepts

There are many words used in the NT to convey different aspects of prayer. *Prosuke* is a petition to God (Phil. 4:6, Eph. 6:18), *euche* is either a prayer (James 5:15) or a vow (Acts 18:18). *Eucharistia* is giving of thanks, from which we have the term eucharist. *Deesis* is used both in the secular and religious sense of a "petition."

But more important in developing NT concepts on prayer is the teaching and practical demonstration on prayer given by Christ to his followers. By his life He demonstrated that prayer could be offered anytime, anywhere. He glances towards heaven and gives a blessing or a sigh; He gives thanks at meals, prays for assurance (Matt. 11:25), and even crys out in prayer in the moment of His being rejected of God as the sin-bearer of the world. His whole relationship to God was simply a matter of communion and prayer. Greeven says:

> The prayer of Jesus is so much an attitude that the individual acts are secondary; yet the Christ who is in such constant touch with God can also turn to the Father in petition and intercession and intercede for His own.[17]

What distinguishes NT prayer from every other prayer pattern is "the certainty of being heard." There is no pleading to be heard; Jesus' use of "Our Father" in His instructions on prayer gave new insight into the ever-ready willingness of God to succor and help those who seek His aid. Giving such samples of concise prayer, not only outlined the scope of prayer—for God's rule to be effected among men, supply of daily needs, forgiveness of sins, deliverance from

---

[16] J. C. Lambert, "Prayer," *ISBE*, IV, 2430.

[17] Greeven, *TDNT*, II, 803.

temptation—but also was admission that man needed help in formulating meaningful prayer. Man has a tendency to slip into vain repetitions, as if the number of words repeated had some magical efficacy (Matt. 6:5-7). He has a tendency to be self-seeking in prayer; this interrupts, not secures, fellowship (James 4:3). His daily habits in the home, not giving honour to his wife, also stand as hindrances to prayer (I Pet. 3:7). Thus as Paul indicates, the words which fall from man's lips may be no more than a babble, unintelligible and unmeaningful. That is why the agency of the Holy Spirit is needed to make prayer efficacious (Rom. 8:26). McEwen traces this need for intercession or help in prayer by divine agency to the ignorance of men.

> While we know in a general way that God's will for us is the perfecting of our salvation, we are ignorant of what this may involve in daily living, so that we might easily pray contrary to God's will. The Spirit, however, knows not only our mind but also the mind of God, and is therefore able to frame our prayers in accordance with the Divine purpose.[18]

Bevan summarizes the NT teaching on prayer as demonstrated by the example and teaching of Jesus: NT prayer is the highest excercise of man's spiritual powers; it comes natural to the one in right relationship to God; it not only expresses need but trust; it is employed in solitude and in public; it is personal yet intercessory; it is prayed for Christ sake, thus concluded in His name.[19]

Encounter

Japanese concepts of prayer fall within the realm of seeking material blessings in daily life by *acquainting* or reporting through cultic acts such requests to the ubiquitous *kami*, whether they be considered deceased ancestors, tutelary gods, or simply numinous forces in nature. Theoretically, Buddhism has no object to which prayer can be made, but cultural borrowing from Shintō customs has no doubt made chanting *sutras* to the *boddhisattvas* take on this prayer aspect in Buddhist households.

Biblical prayer is directed to God or Jesus Christ. It has many aspects—praise, worship, confession, intercession, petition—all of which are offered in full confidence that prayers are heard and answered. The qualifying phrase, "In the name of Christ," makes Biblical prayer centered not so much in man's needs as he feels them but in the will of God. God knows before the Christian asks what is the very best for him and is not concerned with frequency, length, and audibility. More important is the communing heart which by the act of prayer confesses that the source of life lies outside man and that this life is fullest when bestowed with spiritual fellowship, joy, strength, courage, faith.

Perhaps in no other cultural point is there such sharp cleavage. In Japan, man initiates and calls forth a numinous power to assist him in his earthly

---

18 J. S. McEwen, *TWBB*, p. 171.
19 L. D. Bevan "Prayers of Jesus," *ISBE*, IV, 2433.

goals. In the Bible, God calls Abraham, initiates the covenant and establishes a relationship with him, directed towards the supreme end of man's achieving self-fulfillment through communion and obedience. With the advance of secularism and materialism in Japan, the need for intervention of the *kami* is felt less and less. As Ōno points out, the phrases "I am praying for your happiness" (*Gotafuku o oinori itashimasu*) is used in farewells, at the end of letters, etc., but "of a truth those who actually pray are practically nil."[20] If technology will achieve man's chief end—earthly felicity—why pray? But if man's chief end is to glorify God and enjoy Him forever, and this is spelled out in sacrificial service for others, suffering abuse and persecution in establishing a knowledge of God throughout the world, it is mandatory that man seek the ways and means for this task through the One who called him to it.

---

[20] Ōno, *Nihongo no....*, p. 61.

PURITY, HOLINESS 清 KIYOSA

Japanese Concepts of Purity

Chinese character etymology

Kiyoi has two components: 氵 (water), and 青 (clear). *KGJ*: Clear water; to be perfectly clear. *KCJ*: clear, undefiled water.

Semantic changes in Japan

DGK traces the parts of *kiyosa* from *ki*, meaning "fresh or raw," and *yoshi*, meaning "like." Hence something that is fresh or free from defilement. Ōno points out that in the Nara period *kiyoshi* was used in the sense of a mirror with no smudge on it or the moon with no clouds around to blur the vision. So it became used to denote that which had no defects or spots on it. In the *Manyōshū* it was employed to mean "nothing between" as of two people. Ōno mentions a synonym, *sasayaka* which conveyed in those early periods the idea of piercing brightness. During the Heian period the word was used in the form of *kiyora* and *kiyoge* (*kiyora* occurs 60 times, *kiyoge* 100 times in the *Genji Monogatari*), meaning "pretty." *Kiyora* was innate prettiness; *kiyoge*, external. In the *Genji Monogatari* we have the words, "Everything has been cleaned" (*kiyome*),[1] meaning simply the cleaning up of a house. In the Edo period, a person who removed bodies of beasts or executed criminals was called a "*kiyome*," for he removed the cause of defilement, or death. In *Makura no Sōshi* (A. D. 1000) we read: "Send them to the palace to *clean up*."[2] Even today this aspect of clean in *kiyoi* continues; i.e., *asagiyome* from *asa* (morning) and *kiyome* (clean), means "morning cleanup." But the general meaning as from the character and from early usage has been the idea of spotlessness, lucidity, clearness, as of pure water.

Modern range of meaning

KCJ: (1) clear, spotless (*kiyoi*), (2) the part below the eyes (*me no shita no bubun*), (3) rest room (*benjo*), (4) clear rice wine (*sunda sake*), (5) clear water (*sunda mizu*), (6) clear voice (*sunda koe*).

KJ: (1) without spot, cloudless, pure, (2) nothing left, (3) blameless, without fault, (4) piercing, sharp.

DNKJ: (1) without spot or impurity, (2) clear, cloudless, (3) fresh, bracing.

---

[1] *DGK*, p. 505.
[2] *Ibid*.

English idiom parallels

Man of moral purity (*hinkō hōsei na hito*). Chaste (*junketsu*). Keep oneself pure (*junketsu o mamoru*). Sanctification (*seibetsu*). Cleanse from sin (*tsumi o kiyomeru*).

Buddhist concepts

Buddhism employs the same character but in a different combination. Equivalent concept is in the word *seijō*. Another word, *shōjō*, is the tr. of the Sk. *vodana*, meaning "purification" or "purifying." But this is a "cleansing from the stain of illusion..."[3]

Shinto concepts

More pertinent to the discussion of purity in Japanese thinking is the development of Shintoistic ideas concerning the numinous in nature. Ōno says that essentially before the Nara period, the Japanese people were animistic in their thinking. And this animism engendered a feeling toward the numinous of awe or terror rather than "purity". The word *yuyushii*, which today simply means something "big" or "tremendous," conveyed this concept in the early periods. "Anything impressive in nature was considered to have a spirit within it"[4] and hence awe-inspiring, or *yuyushii*. *Yuyushii* is thus the Japanese equivalent to the "taboo" of Polynesia. Man is not to touch *yuyushii* things but to keep his distance from them. There were no words or expressions at that time for confessing one's sins to a deity;[5] rather the concept of the numinous was one of fear and awe. Thus "respect" is the better attitude— to nature, to the emperor, to one's superiors.[6] Ōno points out the de-cultic tendency of Japanese words to prove the basic irreligious temperament of the Japanese. Thus *yuyushii* today means simply "big." *Imaimashii* meant in the Nara periods, "don't touch," in the Muramachi period, "facing an evil omen," but today it simply means "frustration," the inability to avoid an undesirable experience. *Matsuri*, which means simply "festival" today, was used in the *Manyōshū* to mean something offered to the *kami*. Then from the Heian period it began to mean simply entertainment before the gods: "More than showing faith in the god, it became a sort of entertainment before the gods, and thus today."[7] *Matsurigoto* meant in the Meiji period the carrying on of politics or government and also making some food offering to the gods for prosperity.[8] *Itsukushimi*, which today means "condescending love," meant before the Heian period, "the mysterious or marvelous effect of the gods upon the emperor,"[9] and after referred to the nobility, indicating noble birth. Similarly *"iwai,"* which today means "celebrate," originally meant divination, as in the *Manyōshu*. From observing these religiously oriented words undergo semantic change,

---

3 *BD*, p. 295.
4 Ōno, *Nihongo no...*, p. 46.
5 *Ibid.*, p. 61.
6 *Ibid.*, p. 72.
7 *Ibid.*, p. 59.
8 *Ibid.*
9 *Ibid.*, p. 61.

Ōno notes a marked tendency to divest words of their religious content. His conclusion:

> The Japanese are perhaps the one race of people which have little or no religion. Buddhism was a ruling religion for 1000 years, adapted first by the nobility and later by the common people. It was a religion which hated the present world and sought escape from it. How much did Buddhist thought penetrate Japanese thinking? Hardly at all. There is a present anti-religious attitude among the Japanese people not found in any other country in the world.[10]

Hence in the religious sphere, the concept of purity or holiness is one of clarity or without spot. This is not in reference to a deity for there never has been this concept of sin before a deity; rather the central idea has been one of awe before the numinous in nature. Other words which have had this religious milieu have gradually been profaned through usage so that they have lost their original concepts. Thus the one word left (*ki yoi*), upon which Christian concepts of holiness must be built, is not one of relationship but of personal cleanliness.

Biblical Concepts of Holiness

Old Testament concepts

Key Hebrew word denoting holiness is *qodesh*, and is traced etymologically to the meaning of "divide" in the sense of marking something off from secular use, hence "to separate." Rankin defines it as "devoted—as a person or utensil—to God."[11] Snaith dismisses the nuance of "bright" (as held by Gesenius) in the word, following the view of von Baudissin, Smith, *et. al.*, that the word essentially means "separation." It stands for the basic difference between God and man, pointing to the concept of the Wholly Other of Rudolph Otto. "God is separate and distinct because He is God."[12] Robinson sees in these words the primitive taboo concept and traces the slow advance through the OT to the concept of ethical purity as maintained by the Eighth Century prophets. But Snaith's point is just the opposite; things and men are not holy because taboo; things are taboo because they are holy. Primarily *qodesh* refers to Jehovah alone. And this holiness was manifested to His people, for He was not the inactive God of the philosophers, but the God of Isaac and Jacob, active in His creation. Snaith stresses this point:

> God was from the beginning transcendent in that He was different from man, but He was by no means transcendent in that He was remote from man. 'I am God, and not man: the Holy One in the midst of Thee,' (Hosea 11:9).... transcendence does not mean remoteness. It means otherness.[13]

---

10 *Ibid.*, pp. 45-46.
11 O. S. Rankin, "Saint," *TWBB*, p. 215.
12 Snaith, *Distinctive Ideas...*, p. 30.
13 Snaith, p. 49.

Thus, maintains Snaith, the word used in reference to Jehovah means more than a relation or merely a static separation between God and man. Rather He manifests His holiness in the garb of a light (Job 3:4), a flame (Isa. 10:17), or cloud (I Kings 8:10), or the Shekinah glory. Snaith sums up his development:

> We are here once more merging into the realm of the 'numinous' as described by Otto, with its Awfulness, Overpoweringness, Urgency, Wholly Other, and Fascination.... In them we get that element which is fundamental to true religion, that creature feeling in the Presence of Deity.[14]

Procksch's view approaches Snaith's. *Qodesh* in the adjectival form he says simply means "divine" (Isa. 5:16; 6:3, Hos. 11:9) but the verbal form conveys this sense of active holiness. In the *Niphal* form, it denotes "the self representation of His Holiness in Israel in the face of the Gentile world."[15] God may sanctify His name before the nations (Ezek. 36:23), or restore holiness to Israel (Ezek. 20:12; 37:28), or declare the sabbath holy (Gen. 2:3). Holiness is bound up with the *Name* of God, a term which implies His innermost essence. Robinson sees three aspects to the moral character of God, as developed in the OT: (1) He is *just*, as demonstrated by the decalogue, His judgment of sin, etc., (2) He is *loving*, as shown by Hosea, and (3) He is *holy*, as shown by Isaiah. "What Isaiah does is, however, to lift the idea of the righteous and loving God of Israel to a new majesty of conception by His repeated emphasis on the divine holiness."[16] However true this may be, we cannot however accept Robinson's development theory—*viz.*, "The earlier idea of holiness which etymologically may mean 'separation' is that of inaccessability, perilous, and unknown power, involving mysterious taboos, and superstitious fears."[17] For Jehovah was active in holiness before Isaiah's time. Because He dwells with His people, they are to be holy (Deut. 7:6; 26:19, Jer. 2:3). This meant they were to have no contact with false gods and idols (Deut. 6:4). Hence from the outset, "the sphere of ethics is taken up into that of religion."[18] The Ark of the Covenant becomes central in this holy relationship between Jehovah and His people. For there within the Ark, as memorials of the rebellion of Israel — the manna, Aaron's rod that budded, and the broken tablets — stood tokens of man's sin; yet over the Ark were the cherubim, symbolizing the Presence of the Holy One of Israel looking down upon these emblems, whose holiness is only satisfied by the sprinkling of blood of a sacrificial victim. Procksch maintains that the Ark was central in holding the nation together as a fighting unit; "That God's war, which the Ark symbolizes, is holy, derives also from the fact that the warrior is in a state of *qodesh*, being allowed to eat the consecrated temple bread which otherwise only the priests as holy persons may eat" (Matt. 12:3 ff.).[19] But in the prophetic era this element diminishes.

---

14 *Ibid.*

15 Otto Procksch, *"Hagios" TDNT, I,* 90.

16 Robinson, p. 69.

17 *Ibid.*

18 Procksch. *TDNT.* I, 92.

19 *Ibid.*

God is holy and is contrasted with human creatureliness. Isaiah's experience of the *numen tremendum*, the fearfulness of the Holy God is described in his vision in the sanctuary; he cannot but confess the *Trisagion* (Isa. 6:3) as he senses the holy chasm between himself and God. Thus his immediate need, as one living in a corrupt society, is for atonement. But now in the post-exile period there comes the increasing tendency to close this gap between God and men through appointed means of securing holiness, *viz.*, the law and the sanctuary. "The danger of a materialization of the concept is obvious, and Jesus had later to combat this (Matt. 23:17, 19)."[20]

New Testament concepts

Key Gk. word for conveying the holiness concept in the NT is *hagios* with its cognates. *Hagios*, states Snaith, is the nearest equivalent to the OT *qodesh*, for there is a sense of moral purity in *hagios* (from the cognate *agnos* meaning pure or chaste), not found, for instance in *heiros*, purely a Gk. term for a cultic "holy" devoid of moral significance.[21] *Hagios* is predicated of God in the NT, as giving the description of God's immermost nature, while omnipotence and glory stand as the external counterparts to inner holiness (Rev. 4:8 ff). Jesus addresses God as Holy Father in John 17:11. He prays that His Name should be *hallowed*, that is, made distinct from the creature in the world (Matt. 6:9). Jesus Himself is described by the Synoptists as the "Holy One," from the circumstances of His miraculous birth (Luke 1:35), and because, having received the Holy Spirit at baptism (Matt. 3:16), He is bearer of the Spirit (Luke 4:34, Mark 1:24). John sees Him also as the Holy One of God (John 6:69), who not only bears the same holy nature as God Himself but has become in His exalted position the dispenser of the Spirit to men (I John 2:20). In Acts 3:14, he is called the Holy One, looking back to the Holy Servant of Jehovah of Isaiah, anointed by God for the divine mission of saving a lost world. "As the Servant of God, Jesus is the holy sacrifice which, itself innocent, is offered vicariously for the guilt of the people of God (cf. I Pet. 1:18 ff.) to open up access to the sanctuary."[22] In the book of Hebrews, Christ is pictured as both priest and victim, entering the Holy of Holies, figurative of His entering the abode of God in heaven by virtue of His atoning death, to make effective the New Covenant (Heb. 9:24). But from this exalted position He has poured forth His Spirit upon the Christian community to set them apart as a holy community, a temple of flesh and blood, where He can indwell them by means of His Holy Spirit (Eph. 2:21). In Corinthians this temple is termed a living organism (I Cor. 3:16). The sacrifice of this church-temple is not an animal victim offered daily, but Christ offered once for all (I Cor. 5:7). Paul the missionary ministers in this church-temple, preparing Gentiles for acceptable service to God (Rom. 15:16). Baptism is an external rite but signifies

---

20 *Ibid.*, p. 94.

21 Snaith takes Otto to task for divesting *qodesh* of its moral character, calling it simply *numinous*. To be consistent, Otto should have then equated *qodesh* with the Gk. *heiros*, not *hagios*. Cf. his note, Distinctive Ideas..., p. 45-46.

22 Procksch, *TDNT*, I, 102.

a union with Christ whereby the Holy Spirit as agent renews the moral and spiritual faculties of the believer (Tit. 3:5, Rom. 6:3, Col. 2:12).

Encounter

Japanese concepts of purity or holiness find their reference point in man. Usage of *kiyoi* in classical literature and its modern range of meaning indicate not a religious purity but a spotlessness, lucidity, clarity in man. Defilement is through physical contact; any purification rites in a religious milieu such as the *"oharai"* (sweeping away) before Shinto shrines at New Year's are directed to the end of removing such spots and defilements from man *for man*, that is, to return him to his pristine purity and oneness with nature. When approaching the area of the supernatural, the feeling is not one of sinfulness or unworthiness but of awe and gratitude. Hence there is no incongruity between having geisha houses in the city of Ise, locale of the Grand National Shrine, nor of visiting worshippers standing intoxicated before the outer shrine.

Biblical concepts of holiness point to the basic separation between God and His creation. Hence the emphasis is not so much on purity but on division, setting off, separation. But since God is free from every aspect of creatureliness and is holy in His innermost nature, it behooves men who approach Him to be ethically and morally pure. Biblical holiness is active. God actively demonstrated His holiness among the people of Israel and before the nations. Jesus Christ comes as the Holy One, actively showing by His life and work the full content of holiness. Christian holiness is not secured through religious rites but through the inner working of the Holy Spirit in the believer, calling him out from a profane world, investing him with a standing before God in holiness, and slowly working *out* of his character those anti-God qualities and working *in* those graces which make him fit for close communion with a Holy God.

EVIL 悪 *AKU*

Japanese Concepts of Evil

Chinese character etymology

Aku is one character with two components: 亜 (channel and sluice gate), and 心 (heart). *KGJ*: When the heart is choked up, ill feeling results. That which is offensive to human sentiment is intrinsically evil. Evil is a human emotion. *KCJ*: That which is detestable to look upon. And that which is detestable or ugly is hated. Later developed into the meaning of "evil." That which is evil is that which is offensive to human sentiment.[1]

Semantic changes in Japan

DGK defines evil as a wandering from the normal path or customs of men. This no doubt stems from the Buddhist influence during the Nara-Heian periods emphasizing "the path" (*michi*). The Japanese word to which this character was affixed is *warui*, which Ōno says has the basic meaning of "inferior"; it conveys the idea of something which looks bad, that is, "bad looking." The Chinese word "*aku*," Ōno says, has more to do with essence.

Modern range of meaning

KCJ: (1) bad (*warui*), (2) ugly (*minikui*), (3) poor, shabby (*somatsu*), (4) error (*ayamachi*), (5) stain, impurity (*kegare*), (6) hate (*nikumu*).

KJ: (6) bad thing (*warui koto*), (2) bad person (*warumono*), (3) trickster (*itazuramono*), (4) natural evil, (5) evil in human relations, (6) injustice.

DNKJ: (1) bad (*warui*), (2) bad person (*warumono*), (3) immoral thing (*fudōtokuteki na koto*), (4) legal offense (*hōritsu ni taisuru ihan*), (5) wicked thing (*yokoshima na koto*).

English idiom parallels

Harbor ill feelings (*akkanjō o idaku*). Have a bad influence on (*akueikyō o oyobasu*). Sink into vice (*aku ni ochiiru*). If worst comes to worst (*saiaku no baai*). Become dissolute (*mimochi ga waruku naru*). Idleness is the devil's workshop (*Shōjin kankyo shite, fuzen o nasu*). Bad company is the ruin of a good character (*Shu ni majiwareba, akaku naru*).

---

1 Hence the counterpart: the good man, *chüntzu*, does not offend public sentiment nor flout decorum.

Buddhist concepts

Aku in Buddhism is the tr. of the Sk. *akusala*, defined by *BD* as: "Evil. Demerit. Sinfulness. One of the three moral qualities, *viz.*, good, bad, and neutral. Deeds which have strong character, whether good or bad, affect the stream of our present life, and may produce a result in a future life. But the resulting event is always neutral in the moral sense."[2] The technical words expressing cause-effect in a bad sense are *akuin-akka*, defined by BD as: Evil deeds cause bad results... bad retribution is produced by evil deeds. This means that there is no place where man can escape the consequences of evil actions. Evil consequences fall upon the doer of evil."[3] The so-called "ten-evils" (*jūaku*), are "three of the body, four of speech, and three of thought."[4] Zen emphasizes man's transcendence beyond the duality of good and evil, as expressed in the phrase, *fushizenshiaku*, defined as "No thought of good or evil. Freeing oneself from the duality of good and evil, and dwelling in absolute self-identity."[5] The word for "satan" or "devil" in Japan has this character within it. It is *akuma*, which literally is "bad spirit." Thus *diabolos* is so rendered in the Japanese Bible. However the Buddhist counterpart to this word is *akuryō*, "evil spirit of the departed." These are vengeful spirits bent on wrecking vengeance. "It is popularly believed that these malevolent spirits can be pacifed by certain mystical chants and prayers."[6]

Biblical Concepts of Evil

Old Testament concepts

Key Hebrew word for evil is *ra* and "conveys the factual judgment that something is bad, displeasing, harmful. Quite generally it means anything that causes pain, unhappiness, or misery, including the discipline of punishment sent by God.[7] It also meant "harmful" in the cosmic sense of an antagonistic force pitted against man and causing him pain, as for instance in the difficult verse, "I make peace and create evil" (Isa. 45:7, Job. 2:10). This is what Dungan calls "physical evil":

> Disease, individual and national calamity, drought, scarcity of food, may not always be charged to the account of intentional wrong. Many times the innocent suffer with, and even for, the guilty. In such cases, only physical evil is apparent.[8]

Robinson rejects the view that evil and good are presented in the Persian mold of an absolute dualism. There is a dualism in the Bible, but it is conditional and subject to the final authority of God.[9] Robinson sums up three modern

---

2 *BD*, pp. 4-5.

3 *Ibid.*, p. 5.

4 *Ibid.*

5 *BD*, p. 65.

6 *BD*, p. 228.

7 Kenneth Grayston, "Evil," *TWBB*, p. 73.

8 David Dungan, "Evil," *ISBE*, II, 1041.

9 Robinson, p. 182.

views on the problem of evil: (1) evil is a reflection on the goodness of God (the position of J. S. Mill), (2) evil, or suffering is due to causes or factors beyond the province of God's providence, (3) evil or suffering points to the lack of a teleological principle in the universe. None of these views finds acceptance in the Biblical picture of evil and suffering. Rather we are met with a firm conviction that life and its issues, good and evil, are under the sovereign control of an Omnipotent God. The prophets saw that life in its entirety was under the control of God. Robinson says:

> A man's thoughts are his own, yet their issue is God's, and even moral evil is made to serve His purposes (Prov. 16:1, 4)... Clearly therefore, there is nothing in the world of human thought or act which is beyond the sovereignty and control of God.[10]

Thus the Bible goes beyond all three views stated above. As with Job, men may question the goodness of God in the face of inexplicable suffering of the innocent. But the OT prophets answer such questionings with:

> (1) Wait! (2) There may be life beyond death for the righteous; (3) Life is a dark mystery; (4) Life is the bright mystery of a divine purpose higher than our grasp; (5) the suffering of the innocent may avail for the guilty.[11]

That is, no man within a segment of life can forsee the end from the beginning. What men term "good", such as wealth, fame, pleasure might in the final analysis prove "evil"; what they term "evil" may avail for a nation or people for "good." Evil is allowed of God to test and refine man, as Israel's history of suffering well attests. Suffe ing may be vicarious, as the Suffering Servant of Isaiah vividly portrays (Amos 3:6, Joel 2:12-14).

But the OT emphasis is upon *moral evil*, a term meaning that evil springs from personality and is traceable to some moral defect in that personality. The OT prophets emphasis upon the sovereignty of God did not for a moment deter them from laying the responsibility for sin at the door of men's acts. Elijah challenges the people to free choice and roundly scores those who choose wrongly. That is, "moral evil in the OT is seen as sin; related to God it is the transgression of the law... this way of conceiving sin, by preserving intact the personality of both man and God, maintained the reality of moral evil."[12] The OT traces human sin and its fruit, moral evil, back to the Garden situation in which man, exposed to the temptation which freedom gave him, attempts under the subtle suggestion of the serpent to bridge the gap separating the creature and Creator. In his assault upon this freedom-in-dependence situation, Adam fell into the grossest idolatry, the idolization of the self. Thus moral evil springs from the human heart, because men repeat in their individual lives the denouement of the Eden temptation, balking at freedom-in-dependence and asserting freedom in independence.

---

10 *Ibid.*, p. 182.

11 *Ibid.*, p. 172.

12 *Ibid.*, pp. 182-183.

New Testament Concepts

One key Gk. word employed in the NT for denoting evil is *kakos*, with which Arndt lists the range of meaning as (1) morally bad, evil (Matt. 24:48, Phil. 3:2), as the actions of men (Rom. 13:3), or in the neuter sense of that which is contrary to law (John 18:23, Rom. 7:21); (2) harmful, injurious [physical evil], (James 3:8, Rom. 14:20). Another word is *poneros*, which means (1) poor, in the physical sense (Matt. 6:23); (2) wicked, in the ethical sense, both of persons (Matt. 18:32, Luke 19:22, Acts 17:5) or things (Col. 1:21). It is used to denote an *evil one*, such as Satan (Matt. 13:19, John 17:15). The NT carries on the incipient ideas of the OT. The simple onlookers of Job's temptation and Joshua's prayer closet (Job 1:6, Zech. 3:1), which Robinson identifies as simply "prosecutors" (Heb. *hassatan*, adversary), are seen as a developed host of spiritual powers drawn up in hostile confrontation to the purposes of God. This is spiritual wickedness in high places (Eph. 6:12), against which the Christian is pitted in mortal combat. Man's present state of lying in the lap of the evil one (Gal. 1:4, I John 5:19)) is traced theologically from (1) rejection of Divine truth, (2) pride, (3) idolatry, (4) moral wickedness, (5) reversal of established moral order (Rom. 1:21-32).

Encounter

The Japanese language has two words for evil, differentiating moral and physical evil. Calamities, misfortunes, are traced not to moral evil (except in an involved cause-effect process of Buddhist thought) but to natural disturbances. They are termed *wazawai*, or *fuun*. When evil befalls anyone, the common explanation is *"un ga warui"* (he was out of luck). This harks back to a Buddhist concept of "destiny" (*shukumei*), a word meaning "that which is determined by previous existences." Hence physical evil and suffering are traced either to the *un* of Buddhism or the working of vengeful spirits (deceased ancestors who have been neglected at the family altar). Moral evil is rendered by the Japanese word *aku*. It is almost synonymous with ugly.

Biblical evil is either physical or moral, the former being of a probationary nature allowed by God, the latter being traced to the sin of man. Sin or rebellion against God, the Fountain of goodness, has caused evil to flow from man's heart. This evil expresses itself by inflicting pain and suffering on fellow-men (Mark 7:20-23).

RIGHTEOUSNESS 正 義 *SEIGI*

Japanese Concepts of Righteousness

Chinese character etymology

Seigi is comprised of two characters: 正 (straight, upright), and 義 (good, righteous, decorous). *Sei* has two components: 一 (straight line), and 止 (foot). *KGJ*: line and foot together convey idea of moving in a straight line. From walking developed the concept of uprightness and righteousness. *KCJ*: that which is the straight part below the knees — the shins; from this the concept of righteousness developed. *Gi* has two components: 羊 (sheep), and 我 (self). *KGJ*: Sheep was an offering; radical for "self" conveyed the idea of perfectness. So *Gi* is a perfect or unblemished offering. Later developed into the idea of goodness, then righteousness. *KGJ*: sheep radical conveyed the sense of beautiful more than sacrifice. Self radical was used only for the sound of *ga* or *gi*. *Gi* meant the dance or ritual performed at the ceremony; hence the two ideas together give the sense of a graceful, dancing figure. Later developed to mean "decorum," and "ceremony." Thus the same character is found in "manners" (*reigi*).

Semantic changes in Japan

Japanese indigenous word is *tadashii*, meaning straight. The righteous man is the one who walks straightly through life. Righteousness in the Confucian tradition, whether in China or feudalistic Japan has developed along horizontal lines; righteousness is tantamount to right relationships or correctness in human relationships. In Japan, as the *Daigenkai* observes, it is a righteousness between lord and vassal, between parent and child. It is one of the five Confucian virtues (*gojō*). From *Rongo*: Do not pervert the right for one's own ends.[1] Confucius is quoted: "To see the right and not do it is lack of courage."[2] From *Sengokusaku*: "The person who uses evil to punish right will be destroyed."[3]

Modern range of meaning

Sei

KCJ: (1) correct (*tadashii*), (2) to correct (*tadasu*), (3) straight (*massugu*), (4) true (*makoto*), (5) investigate crime, (6) ask, enquire (*toitadasu*), (7) commandment (*imashime*), (8) always (*tsune*), (9) ordinary (*heibon*), (10)

---

[1] *DGK*, p. 450.

[2] *Ibid*.

[3] *DGK*, p. 1077.

law standard (*nori*), (11) chief of something, (12) truly (*masa ni*), (13) tax (*mitsugi*).

KJ: (1) correct (*tadashii koto*), (2) chief (*omo na mono*), (3) standard (*hyō-jun*).

DNKJ: (1) correct (*tadashii koto*), (2) standard (*hyō jun*), (3) square (*shi-kaku*), (4) chief responsibility (*shunin*), (5) chief matter (*omo na mono*), (6) true (*makoto no mono*).

Gi

KCJ: (1) true method (*tadashii sujimichi*), (2) good, correct (*yoi, tadashii*), (3) concern for one's country or public society, (4) moral relationship between a ruler and his subjects.

KJ: (1) according to principle (*ri*), (2) to be concerned with humanity without concern for personal profit, (3) moral principle, reason (*dōri, riyū*).

DNKJ: (1) that which is consistent with one's actions (*kōi no michi ni au koto*), (2) that which is in accordance with social reason (*seisai no ri ni kanau koto*), (3) moral principle (*dōri*).

Seigi

KCJ: (1) the right way in which a man should walk, (2) the right meaning or interpretation, (3) right argument, (4) in logic, that which is fair and impartial.

KJ: (1) correct (moral) reasoning (*tadashii dōri*), (2) correct or right significance (*tadashii igi*).

DNKJ: (1) right justice (*seitō naru gi*), (2) right way of reasoning (*tada-shiki sujimichi*), (3) correct significance.

English idiom parallels

Be open and above aboard (*hyōri no nai*). Sense of justice (*seigi no nen*). Honesty is the best policy (*Shōjiki wa saizen no saku*). An honest person will be taken in (*Shōjikimono ga baka o miru*). A clear-cut person (*take o watta yōna kishō*).

Buddhist concepts

Gi is tr. of the Sk. *artha* defined as: (1) Principle, (2) Meaning, (3) The distinctive features of a substance, (4) In Buddhist logic, the predicate of the premise.[4]

Biblical Concepts of Righteousness

Old Testament concepts

Key Hebrew words for rendering the concept of righteousness are *sedeq* and *mishpet*. *Chesed* and *chok* are also used but these words infuse an emotional element (*viz.*, lovingkindness and grace) into the concept. LXX translators preferred *eleos* over *dikaios* for rendering these Hebrew words. But the OT concepts of God are juridical; conversely all legal concepts are endowed with religious significance. Quell says:

---

4 *BD*, p. 75.

One may say that law is the basis of the view of God in the OT in so far as it is theologically developed, and that conversely the endowment of legal concepts with religious meaning contributed to an ethicising of law.[5]

Jehovah not only posits law but He is bound by it. This serves as the basis of hope for the Israelite. God is not capricious but is bound by the laws He Himself promulgates. Jehovah is the source of all law; they are "righteous because He is righteous."[6] He, thus, is the righteous Ruler (Psa. 7:11, Jer. 12:1). His acts demonstrate His righteousness (Judges 5:11). Girdlestone traces the word *sedeq* etymologically to the idea of "stiff" or "straight." Snaith finds the nexus of OT righteousness in the holy character of God, in the words of Isa. 5:16: "The Holy God is sanctified in righteousness." The Lord being holy demands right conduct of His worshippers. Thus man's right conduct finds its norm in a religious milieu, not a social one. "Jehovah by His very nature demands right conduct from His worshippers and will be content with nothing less (Amos 2:7; 4:2).[7]

Carrying over this basic concept of righteousness to the province of society, the righteous man in the OT is the "one who seeks justice before the judge, defending and vindicating his cause against those who are full of malice and deceit."[8] The pious man then is the one acknowledged by Jehovah, the one pronounced righteous by Jehovah, the highest tribunal in human affairs. "Thus *sedeq* comes to have the sense of the pious and *sedeqah*, the *conduct* which is vindicated before the public tribunal and thus leads to pardon."[9] That is, Quell finds the concept of piety in the word. But Robinson denies this:

> The idea of righteousness is not to be confused with that of morality or that of holiness. Morality is properly actual rightness of conduct judged by the customs of the society. Holiness is properly the un-approachableness of God. But the primary conception in the idea of righteousness is not actual rightness, nor Godlikeness; it is forensic, a product of the primitive court of justice.[10]

Girdlestone holds that the righteous man was the one who exhibited love to his neighbor, because love is the fulfilling of the law. He says: "No distinction between the claims of justice and the claims of love is recognized in Scripture: to act in opposition to the principles of love to God and one's neighbor is to commit an injustice; because it is a departure from the course marked out by God in His law."[11] Though Robinson cannot see the logical outcome of his conclusion, namely, that if OT righteousness is largely to do with acquittal in a legal sense, there necessarily follows a propitiatory aspect in Biblical sacrifices finally culminating in the Cross, we must concur with his conclusion that "the righteous man is not the man morally perfect, but he who is acquitted at the

---

5 Gottried Quell, "dike" *TDNT*, II, 174.

6 *Ibid.*, p. 176.

7 Snaith, p. 53.

8 Quell, *TDNT*, II, 177.

9 *Ibid.*

10 Robinson, p. 168.

11 Girdlestone, p. 101.

bar of God.''[12] The antithetic element in "righteous" becomes apparent; guilty, is the status of the man who is condemned before God.

New Testament concepts

Key Gk. word is *dikaiosune* with its many cognates found in the NT. *Dike* is found only three times in the NT, but it is always used in the sense of penal justice or punishment. The word is found personified on the lips of the barbarians of Melita; the goddess *Dike* has overtaken Paul and administered judgment through the viper (Acts 28:4). The righteous man (*dikaios*) in the Hellenistic world was the "one who conforms, who is civilized, who observes custom.''[13] With Theognis, it was the man who fulfilled his duty in society. So with Aristotle.[14] It denoted a scrupulosity to all forms of social decorum. The word was also used in the sense of an innate quality of human nature. In the LXX, the concept leaves the mere human plane; the righteous man is the one whose life is in conformity to the commands of God. The Rabbis mention that perfect attainment of righteousness is possible and such people should be given the highest places in society. This idea emerges in the NT, as when Pilate's wife calls Jesus "that righteous man" (Matt. 27:19). It denoted the perfect obedience of Jesus to the will of God (Acts 3:13, Acts 7:52). Men who do God's will are called "the righteous" (e.g., Abel, Heb. 11:4; Lot, II Pet. 2:7). Righteousness (*dikaiosune*) was something to be earned by the Israelite of the first century. Quell says:

> Every act of obedience earns merit for the Israelites in the sight of God... A man's standing before God is settled by striking a balance between his good deeds and his transgressions. If the former outweigh the latter, he is acquitted at the last judgment.[15]

This connecting of righteousness with the will of God as the norm is thus found in the NT; righteousness is harmony with God's will, doing what is right before him. But in Matthew there is a break with current Judaistic views of righteousness; it is doing the will of God for His sake and not for the approbation of men. Paul is the advocate of a new type of righteousness, a righteousness not earned but given in response to faith. Righteousness attainable through law-keeping is man's righteousness and compared with the perfect righteousness of God is a net loss (Phil. 3:8). He rejects the optimism of the Rabbinic tradition. The righteousness which avails is that which is God's own, which He confers in judicial acts upon those who qualify for it by faith in the atonement. This righteousness is not merely a static moral quality, but dynamic, active in men, just as God's wrath is. It is bound up with the resurrection of Christ as well; the historical fact of the Resurrection verifies that all legal demands standing against men have been met. But Quell leaves the law court in further developing the NT concept of righteousness. Since we are

---

12 Robinson, p. 168.

13 Quell, *TDNT*, II, 182.

14 Gottfried Quell and Gottlob Schrenk, "Righteousness," *Bible Key Words*, tr., J. R. Coates (Harper and Row, Publishers: New York, 1951), p. 10.

15 *Ibid.*, pp. 32-33.

presently justified (that is in departure from the Judaistic concept that the
verdict of righteousness is only given to the pious at the last judgment), the
believer as being incorporate in Christ shares in the power of a new life; his
physical organs can be in fact weapons of righteousness in the conflict with
evil. The man possessing God's righteousness is under His rule. "When a man
is declared righteous he enters the service of righteousness, becoming so to
speak, its property; his faith in God's righteousness is obedience and leads to
obedience."[16] Girdlestone upholds the same view:

> The process of Divine acquittal is so blended with the entrance of spiritual life into
> the person acquitted, that, though they are theoretically distinct, one cannot be fully
> stated or even comprehended without reference to the other....the ideas of righteous-
> ness, justification, and acquittal all cluster round one verbal root, and are seen to be
> parts of one whole.[17]

Such views of Girdlestone and Quell approach the Catholic view of justification which is an infusion of sanctifying grace; manifestations of this invisible operation take the form of faithful observance of church legislation
and participation in the sacraments, leading to final verdict of acquittal in an
eschatalogical milieu of rewards and punishments. This then leads us to consider
the final cognate of *dikaiosune*, the verb *dikaioo*, meaning "to set right,"
"make valid." From the legal aspect it connotes holding a thing to be right,
reasonable, suitable. It is used in the LXX in the sense of "acquit," "pronounce
righteous," but such pronouncement is reserved for those who truly are
righteous (Exod. 23:7, I Kings 8:32). The word is used in the sense of "proved
to be right" in Rom. 3:4, also in the sense of "self-justication" in Luke 10:29.
With Paul it means the opposite of being condemned (Rom. 8:34). It refers not
to the infusion of moral grace but absolution of the guilty. And such action,
though superficially would seem to flout all legal procedure, is valid "on the
grounds of God's justifying action in the death and resurrection of Christ."[18]
Such "justifying" is neither wholly objective in the Cross nor wholly subjective
in the experience of the believer. It is a justifying objectively made possible by
the historic act of the Cross, but made subjectively personal through faith. But
this acquittal is tantamount to a present salvation; the event is a continuing
present. Thus Paul employs the perfect and present tenses for describing this
justiying act (Rom. 3:24). Hence the sharer in this Divine act of acquittal is
continually being justified; this continuing act of acquittal thus carries with it
the hope of final forgiveness before the judgment seat of Christ.

Encounter

Japanese concepts of righteousness find their basis in man's situation as a
social being. It is straightness, but a straightness which from the very beginning

---

[16] *Ibid.*, p. 33.
[17] Girdlestone, p. 158.
[18] Quell and Shrenk, *Bible Key Words*, I, 61.

was found in man and excercised among men. The word appears in the key concept of the feudal samurai tradition—loyalty (*chūgi*). A righteous man is one who is loyal in his relationships in society. Modern range of meaning gives it the sense of an absolute norm, perhaps from the influence of Western thought. But the interchange of the character in other words, for example, *reigi* (manners) or even (with the human radical added to the left) in *kaigi* (conference), has repeatedly brought the word down to the social level.

Biblical concepts of righteousness posit the norm of righteousness in the holy character of God. God does not do the right: what He does is right; all pronouncements of right and wrong find their criterion in the nature of God. The interplay of holiness and righteousness in the OT leading to the legalistic view of righteousness is lifted to a suprahuman level in the NT by its rejection of human righteousness as a creditable measure of man's true condition before God. Rather, the NT presents a righteousness as a gift of God made available to men through the satisfaction of forensic claims against men accomplished at the Cross. Biblical translators have attempted to present this distinctively vertical dimension of righteousness by employing the generally vaguer word "*gi*," (the second character of *seigi*), but it takes many years for Japanese Christians to divest *gi* of its social ramifications and pour into it the divine content.

SIN 罪 TSUMI

Japanese Concepts of Sin

Chinese character etymology

Tsumi is comprised of two characters: 罒 (net), and 非 (criminal). *KGJ*: Trapping the criminal. Present character has 罪 instead of 辠, which preserves the sound of net. Change was effected because the character for sin was similar in appearance to the character for emperor.

Semantic changes in Japan

The Japanese word, *tsumi*, to which the above character was affixed stems from the word *tsutsushimi* (prudence). One must be prudent about certain acts for they are despised by men. Hence they are called "*tsumi*."[1] DGK develops the word from *sashisawari* (a bad thing), or something distasteful. Ōno says that *tsumi* does not occur in classical literature in the sense of moral wrong or impurity or in the sense of sinning against divinity. In the *Genji Mono-gatari*, the phrase "Because I am a *sinful* person, I may have to wander in the world"[2] refers to the fact that the person has been found *guilty* of a crime. So in the *Manyōshū*: "He fell into *sin* and left the capital."[3] It means that a crime had actually been committed, so the offender was banished. Ōno maintains that concern in Japanese thinking is not with sin but moral faults, impurity. *Togame* (fault) literally means "something protruding" and the verb form is "to hit something." If one had some moral fault and was called to task for it, he would be blamed, or found out. That is, the emphasis is upon moral defects and their coming to light, upon fault-finding by one person against another. The person so blamed or discovered would then sense shame (*haji o kiru*). This, says Ōno, is the nearest approach to the English equivalent of conviction of sin. A sense of shame comes to one when his moral fault is discovered and reprimanded by another. A man's name always has *shi* (Mr.) affixed to it in Japanese newspapers until the man is arraigned in court. Immediately such polite appellations are dropped by the reporters. There has never been nor is there today any sense of guilt before an Absolute God in Japanese thinking. Hence the word sin is always used in the legalistic sense; a person at fault and proved guilty in a public court becomes a sinner. In Shokyo: "When there is no proof of sin, lighten the sentence."[4]

---

1 *GS*, p. 2938.
2 *DGK*, p. 1331.
3 *DGK*, p. 2938.
4 *DGK*, p. 2930.

Modern range of meaning

KCJ: (1) crime (*hō o okasu*), (2) bad act against another (*tsugō no warui koto*), (3) wicked heart (*yokoshima na kokoro*), (4) judicial verdict that a sin has been committed (*tsumi suru*), (5) blame (*togameru*), (6) punishment (*keibatsu*), (7) evil (*wazawai*).

KJ: (1) evil, impurity, something detestable, (2) immoral act (3) act which is against law and will require a judicial sentence, (4) In Buddhism or Christianity, that which is against the precepts of the religion, (5) an unmerciful act.

DNKJ: (1) bad act against morality, (2) what people dislike (*hito ni kirau koto*), (3) crime (*hanzai*), (4) going against the teaching of Buddha (*zaigyō*).

English idiom parallels

Illegality (*fuhō kōi*). Unpremeditated crime (*dekigokoro de yatta hankō*). Juvenile offense (*Jūdai no hanzai*). One's innocence is proved (*seiten hakujitsu no mi ni naru*). Incriminate (*tsumi ni otoshiireru*). Condemn (*tsumi ni sadameru*). Trumped-up charge (*mujitsu no tsumi*). Previous offense (*zenka ga aru*).

Buddhist concepts

Tsumi is not found in the Buddhist Dictionary. The character appears in the word *zaigō*, which means going against the teaching of Buddha. As mentioned in the discussion of *illusion*, the ideas of "wandering," "illusion," and "desire" are more germane to the Buddhist concept of man's moral predicament. Ichikawa says logically in Buddhism sin is "inconceivable and cannot be defined."[5] This logically follows the theoretical atheistic premise of Buddhism, for having no Absolute there can be no normative definition of right and wrong. Mōdai says:

> In Christianity, God as the Creator is presupposed and any resistance to His holiness is regarded as sin, but in Buddhism there is no theory of sin, because it has no objective idea of God.[6]

Biblical Concepts of Sin

Old Testament concepts

There are many Hebrew words for denoting sin in the OT. *ht'* is a frequent word, being translated into *hamartia* in the LXX, and "sin" in the AV. It means lit., "miss a goal or way," used in the sense of "failing to do something in relation to man or God."[7] It was merely a mistake. "The commonest expression for sin in Hebrew lacks the deep religious quality of our word."[8] But it does lay down a line, a norm, or rather it presupposes such a line has

---

5 *EBu.*

6 *EBu.*

7 Kenneth Grayston, "Sin," *TWBB*, p. 227.

8 Gottfried Quell, George Bertram, Gustav Stahlin, and Walter Grundmann, "Sin," *Bible Key Words*, tr. J. R. Coates (New York: Harper and Row), 1951, III, 8.

been drawn, a rule to which man should adhere. *Psh* is rebellion, (Job. 34:37), the active aspect of sin — "a spontaneous human reaction to the holy and the godlike."[9] *Awon* means "warped" or "twisted" and is rendered by the English "iniquity." Sin thus is a perversion of truth or life, a distortion, a crookedness. It has a strong association with guilt. *Shghh* is simply going astray, erring from the right way. All these aspects of sin we find latent in the story of man's Fall. Adam steps over the line clearly defined and commanded by God. He fights against and rebels against this command, finding a "footing in the freedom of will and thought."[10] He perverts the truth of God and becomes twisted in his own thinking concerning God and himself. He errs, wandering away from God and hiding. In a word, sin is defying God with the free will. Quell expresses this aspect of sin:

> The phrases... "Ye shall be as God"... it stirs a longing in the breast of every man, from the simplest to the most mature, and presents him with an apology for sin that is alarmingly persuasive. In this way we are brought with the utmost precision to the religious heart of the problem of sin, which is beyond the reach of abstract thought, and consists in man's incontestable inherent right to defy and reject God.[11]

New Testament concepts

Key Gk. word for sin is *hamartia*, a word taken up from Gk. usage and invested with profound religious significance. It was, in Stahlin's words, the "vaguest and most general profane word for wrong." Yet it served the purposes of the NT writers better than *adikia* (injustice) and *kakia* (evil), for these already had ethical content. *Hamartia* could express the "Godward side" of sin. It is missing God's mark, falling short of His target for the full life. Christ comes and addresses men as sinners. He did not define sin; He showed its effects in men by His parables. The Prodigal Son has left the Father's house and is away from God. "The meaning is plain. Man created for fellowship with God has broken that fellowship."[12] Man is in debt to God (Luke 7:41 ff.) — He has misused God's investments in him for his own goals. Man needs to daily ask forgiveness for sin (Matt. 6:12). The Last Supper again brings out the central purpose of Christ's life—to do away with sin, to establish an eternal covenant through His sacrificial death whereby men's sins will be forgiven. John says this in no uncertain terms. Christ was manifested to take away sin (I John 3:5). He is now exalted and stands as Advocate before God, presenting the credentials of His finished work to assure that men's sins will be forgiven (I John 2:1-3). Paul's whole theology is centered around the supreme act of the Cross whereby men's sins are forgiven them through the merits of their appointed Substitute (Rom. 3:21-25). The purpose of faith in the exalted Christ is to the end of gaining victory over the remnants of sin in the believer and sinful forces arrayed against him in the world (Rom. 6:1-11 ff.). In a word, Christ ushered in a new era, the era where sin's power and claim over man

---

9 *Ibid.*, p. 11.

10 *Ibid.*, p. 30.

11 *Ibid.*, p. 27.

12 *Ibid.*, p. 66.

is broken. The NT does not gloss over sin and moral depravity in the world; to the contrary it states that sin is a basic ingredient in the structure of the world's society. It says that this sin is not some moral aberration but stems from man's rebellion against his Creator and has been dealt with effectively and completely through the mission of Christ. He not only died a vicarious death as the propitiatory sacrifice for sins in the past, but, as the living Head of the Church, He is able to forgive present sins and give strength to meet temptation.

Encounter

The word for sin in Japanese (*tsumi*) brings before the Japanese mind the picture of police stations, law courts, crime, criminals. It is a legal, technical term; a man does not become a sinner until he is so convicted by human court. The *KCJ* defines "sinner" (*tsumibito*) as a "person who has received the verdict of having sinned." More germane to Japanese thinking at this point is the concept of purity. If a moral fault is brought to the surface and discovered by another person, the erring one is gripped with a sense of shame. But there is no conviction of sin. The average Japanese is more concerned about social relations and the maintaining of a harmony with nature. Thus moral impurity is easily cleansed by the wave of the priest's brush at the Shintō shrine (called *oharai*), and this can be done once or twice a year. The cleansing rite has retroactive effects; one's faults fall away, are co-mingled with those of fellow Japanese and flow into an expanse of nothingness, as a river empties into the sea.

Biblical sin is an interruption of man's relationship to his Creator. By falling short of God's purpose for him or trespassing the boundary marked out for him, man falls into rebellious and perverted ways — ways which lead away from God into a labyrinth of self-idolization, pride, and moral perversion.

The preoccupation with sin in the Bible makes it no doubt offensive to Japanese views of pristine man in complete harmony with nature. But the negative illumines the positive. Christians believe that OT sacrifices pointed to, and Christ's work accomplished, perfect forgiveness and deliverance from sin. One reason for the slow advance of Christian missions in Japan may be traced to this failure to understand and appreciate the redemptive work of the Cross. And this stems from an inability to understand or willingness to accept the belief that man in his best state is a lost sinner before a Holy God.

SACRIFICE 犧 牲 GISEI

Japanese Concepts of Sacrifice

Chinese character etymology

Gisei is comprised of two characters: 犧 (unblemished cow), and 牲 (living cow). *Gi* has two components: 牛 (cow) and 義 (righteousness). *KGJ*: a sacrifice to the gods. Having the "sheep" element in it emphasizes the unblemished character of the sacrifice. Something thoroughly prepared. *KCJ*: *Gi* only gives the sound, the sound for the word beauty, hence a beautiful, unblemished cow ready for sacrifice. *Sei* has two components: 牛 (cow), and 生 (life). *KGJ*: that which is offered to the gods. Two characters together are compounded for emphasis — an unblemished sacrifice.

Semantic changes in Japan

Japanese indigenous word which carries the same idea as *gisei* is *ikenie*, which Ōno breaks down into *ike* and *nie*, i.e., "a living feast." It is to give a feast of something recently alive (*ikashita mama de gochisō o ageru*). Ōno traces the word back into the *Kojiki* where *Susano no makoto*'s daughter is offered as a sacrifice (*ikenie*). *DGK* finds the word used in reference to offering an animal before an ancestral mausoleum. *Gensen* further develops this thought; "*Ikenie* is a bullock before which divination is performed; the bullock which yields a favorable verdict is offered on the ancestral mausoleum."[1]

Modern range of meaning

KCJ: (1) sacrificial offering used in festivals for the gods or the ancestors, (2) giving one's life to save another person.

DNKJ: (1) sacrifice (*ikenie*), (2) to disregard oneself and devote oneself to achieve a certain goal.

KJ: (1) living animal prepared for a festival for the gods or ancestors, (2) slain animal prepared for offering, (3) to disregard oneself or devote oneself for a certain cause.

Buddhist concepts

The idea of animal sacrifice is foreign to Buddhism; the words do not occur in the Buddhist dictionary.

---

[1] *GS*, p. 945.

Biblical Concepts of Sacrifice

Old Testament concepts

Sacrifice and sacrificial offerings are key concepts of the OT, given as pictures and symbols of man's approach to God. Jehovah is of too pure eyes to behold evil; there must be some means by which man's sin is dealt with. The forfeiting of a life is grim reminder that sin and death are inter-related, the one leading to the other. Unless there is a substitute provided, man has no way of approach to God. The system also portrayed prophetically the final event of the Cross whereby once for all man's sin problem is solved without compromising the holiness of God. As Girdlestone says, "The system of offerings appointed to Israel may thus be regarded as a book of pictures, sketched in shadowy outline, indicating to God's people the work which was to be accomplished by Divine grace..."[2] Since there are many types of sacrificial offerings outlined in the Levitical code, we shall only briefly mention differences that are pertinent to our discussion. North gives three purposes for OT sacrificial offerings: (1) they serve as gifts to God, (2) they serve as means of entering into communion with God, (3) they are means of releasing life.[3] Firstly, those sacrifices considered as gifts to God were rendered by two words: *korban* and *minhah*. *Korban* was a word meaning simply "present" in the secular sense, as, *e.g.*, Ehud's giving a present to Eglon (Judges 3:18). But it is translated "oblation" in Leviticus and signified a means of approach to God (Lev. 1:2). The abuse of this offering is taken up in the NT; men could avoid family financial obligations by diverting funds to the temple, labelling them *"korban"* and thus securing status (Mark 7:11).[4] But in the intended Biblical purpose, offering gifts to God came from a sense of gratitude for the love and blessings received from God. "It was an acknowledgment on the part of man that the earth is the Lord's and the fullness thereof."[5] Secondly, offerings which effected communion with God were *olah*, meaning lit., "the offering that ascends." Translated "burnt offering" in the AV, it was a sacrifice representing *acceptance*. It did not have sin-expiation as its purpose. Within this group were the *zebah* and *shelem*; *shelem* is a cognate of *shalom*, meaning peace, so the words are translated "peace offerings" in the AV. It was a private or family sacrifice, whereas the burnt-offering was public. This offering spoke of communion with God, "since God and the worshipper were thought to share a common meal."[6] This sacrificial meal would thus engender feelings of thankfulness to God for His kindness and the offerers be thus "stimulated to live in conformity with His law, and to deal mercifully with their poor brethren."[7]

---

[2] Girdlestone, p. 185.

[3] C. R. North, "Sacrifice," *TWBB*, p. 206.

[4] Offering gifts to secure access among men is a fixed custom in Japan even today. Invariably when a Japanese guest is invited to dinner at the writer's home, he brings a gift with him. Or when securing help from an unknown person, gifts are taken in the first approach. Called, "ochikazuki no oshirushi" (lit., "token of approach").

[5] Girdlestone, p. 191.

[6] North, *TWBB*, p. 207.

[7] Girdlestone, p. 193.

Thirdly, sacrifices made to the end of releasing life were called *chattath*, translated "sin offering" in the AV, and *asham*, translated "trespass offering" in the AV, but more properly rendered "guilt offering." The shedding of blood finds atoning significance in the OT, for it represented the forfeiting of life by the victim (Lev. 17:11). The shed blood of the animal was seen to cover (Heb. *kippor*) the sins of the Israelite offerer. Hebert takes up two views of this OT concept of atonement: (1) the covering over of sins is action towards God — the satisfaction view, and (2) the covering over of sins is action upon the offerer; his sins are thus covered, hidden from the view of God — the expiation view.[8] He rejects the former view, pointing out the prophets' stress upon the moral condition of the offerer. Without true repentence, the sacrifice in itself was ineffectual. Also the concept of the wrath of God needing appeasement is difficult for Hebert. However if these sacrifices served as prophetic symbols of the central pillar of the Christian message — the Cross — the satisfaction view, satisfying the judicial sentiment of God offended by man's sin, seems to square with the mysterious element of the Cross, namely, the rejection of Christ by God during His hours on the Cross.

New Testament concepts

We shall discuss only one word out of the many used in the NT to represent the sacrifice of Christ. It is *amnos*, which means simply "lamb." The OT was preparatory for God's final and complete solution for the sin of man. It was inadequate because it did not deal with willful sin nor with the sins of conscience. Christ is presented as the *amnos* of God, the perfect and complete sacrifice for the sins of the whole world (John 1:29, I Pet. 1:18, 19, Rom. 3:24 ff.). By using this "lamb" metaphor, it not only called to mind the sacrificial system of the OT, but it emphasized His patience in suffering (Acts 8:32), His sinlessness (I Pet. 1:19), and the efficacy of His sacrificial death (John 1:36). Jeremias expresses it thus: "As once the blood of the passover lambs played a part in the redemption of Egypt, so by the atoning power of His blood He has accomplished redemption from the bondage of sin."[9]

Encounter

Japanese concepts of sacrifice stemming from earliest ideas of offering freshly slain animals have given way to the concept of food offerings. For there was never a sense of appeasement or covering over of sin but of offering a sacrificial meal to the *kami*. Biblical views find their loci in the holiness of God and the sinfulness of men. To approach God there must be the surrender of a life, the release of a substitute life to satisfy the offended judicial sentiment in God. Divergent views on the atonement in Japanese theological thinking have appeared in two modern translations of Romans 3:25. The *Kōgotai* (Colloquial Version) of 1954, published by the Japan Bible Society has rendered the Gk.

---

8 A. G. Hebert, "Atone," *TWBB*, p. 25-26.

9 Joachim Jeremias, "*amnos*" *TDNT*, I, 340.

hilasterion as *"aganai no sonaemono"* (offering for redemption), following the expiatory view. The *Shinkai yaku* (New Revised Version) of 1965, published by Word of Life Press has rendered the same Gk. word as *"nadame no sonaemono"* (offering for satisfaction or assuaging wrath), following the satisfaction view. However, both translations have blurred over the fundamental differences between Japanese and Biblical concepts on sacrifice. Both use for sacrifice the word *sonaemono*, a word which by historical usage never speaks of a sacrificial victim or shedding of blood but of offering up to the *kami* of rice cakes, fruit, etc. Concentration by these translators should have been more on this word to present to Japanese readers the concept of a living sacrifice. One possible word is *ikenie*, which recalls to Japanese thinking the idea of an innocent person being offered alive. Present profanation of the word *ikenie* in the business world may rule out this word.[10] So better would be the Chinese imported word *gisei*, which has within it the visible pictures of a cow, perfection, and life. Its modern usage in the sense of one person sacrificing himself for others lends itself to the concept of Biblical atonement. Thus the phrase could be *gisei ni yoru aganai* (redemption through sacrifice), leaving the interpretation up to the reader as to whether this was expiation or satisfaction, but certainly fixing the concept of blood sacrifice.

---

10 For example, one business executive may offer his daughter in marriage to another business associate's son, in an effort to foster stronger business ties. Such action would be termed by onlookers as offering his daughter as an *ikenie* for business.

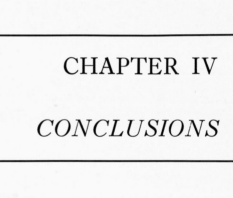

CHAPTER IV

CONCLUSIONS

Conclusions

In our quest for meaningful differences in cultural thought, we have travelled over the roads of both Japanese and Biblical verbal symbols. Now standing back from the roads to view the whole journey in one glance, let us summarize the lessons learned along the way. I would like to confine these concluding remarks to (1) an appraisal of the various routes along the "from-language-to-culture" path, (2) the emergence of a dominant concept in Japanese thinking which appears to color subsidiary ones, (3) how this approach could be employed for learning other languages and understanding their resultant cultural patterns of thought, and (4) as an appendix, some canons for Biblical translators.

Critical analysis of the linguistic approach

Chinese character etymology. — The results of this study are rather marginal and inconclusive. Using our two main sources, the *Kanjigogenjiten* (*Dictionary of Chinese Character Etymology*), and the *Kanwachūjiten* (*Medium Chinese Japanese Dictionary*), we discover sometimes divergent views of the concepts underlying Chinese characters. And as Ōno points out, there are no extant dictionaries in Japanese which give the meanings of the Chinese characters at the time they were introduced. But their very acceptance did reveal a compatible view of life shared by Chinese and Japanese — a substratum of Oriental thought. Conclusions reached in our analysis of the Japanese verbal symbols do not stem, however, from a breakdown of the Chinese characters into component parts, nor of etymological examination of archaic Chinese. What is surprising is that Japanese indigenous views of life approximate some of the ideas trapped within the ancient characers. Another reason why this route of the journey was inconclusive is that already there had been semantic changes within China giving broader and perhaps more abstract meanings to the characters than found in their original component parts. But we have no way to trace these meanings down. Does examining Chinese characters yield therefore, any clue to Japanese thinking? I have already indicated under the Category for THOUGHT how I believe Chinese characters have inhibited the formulation of new ideas. And I would suggest one other effect I believe the characters have had on Japanese thinking. When children learn the different strokes of the characters, Japanese teachers point out the component parts of characters to facilitate memorization. The component parts of most characters are *objects of nature or the human body*, like sun, moon, tree, sky, rain, water, hand, foot, heart, eye, mouth, back, legs. I believe without being aware of it, Japanese children begin to conceive of the ultimate in thought, or the origin of ideas, as being no farther than they can see, touch or feel. Hence, the learning of Chinese characters in itself would form the beginning of a "man in nature" view of life.

The *Semantic Changes in Japan* analysis revealed clearly the impact of Buddhism upon Japanese life: the word for "time" comes to mean the "ephemerity of life"; "end of an age" comes to mean the last age of Buddhist law; "cause and effect" come to mean man's causing an effect through his actions, producing an effect in another life; "knowledge" is not simply learning facts but "awareness" of the Buddha way, the way to enlightenment. But more strange is to observe how Buddhist concepts did not fare well in the Japanese language; many Buddhist words fell out of the vocabulary or were invested with non-Buddhist meaning. This reveals an underlying Japanese *concept-clearing-center* which either resists heterodox ideas, ideas inimical to basic Japanese sentiment, or else generates dynamically a semantic change in words. Buddhist words for "reality" (*yū*), or "voidness" (*kū*), or "impermanence" (*mujō,*), though understandable to the Japanese, just do not find their way into everyday speech. Buddhist de-emphasis upon love (*ai*), or the pejorative use of "hope" (*bō*) (in the sense of desire, craving) strain and tug through the centuries, but these words finally emerge as desirable concepts and are in good standing in common parlance. Words which would suggest a transcendent view of ultimacy, thereby positing Japanese sentiment in the Type II[1] religious category, repeatedly fall out of the philosophical orbit into a naturalist one; wisdom (*chie*) is not the cutting of passions and illusions, perceiving the nonduality of essences, but simply comes to mean "clever," "sharp," "ability to get along in life." Buddhist "illusion" (*mayoi*) loses its meaning of the veil over the human heart eclipsing the Buddha nature or wandering from the paths of the Buddha and simply comes to mean "going off from accepted patterns of conduct — a conduct which will insure a happy life." Buddhist "insight" (*funbetsu*) loses its sense of "one of the consciousnesses" and comes to mean merely "discreet," a means to understand people and discern issues in *life*. Buddhist "truth" expressed in *dōri* loses its meaning of "the Buddhist way" and signifies simply "common sense." Truth (*shinjitsu*) is not ontological truth but falls back to earth in the sense of "personal integrity." Thought (*shisō*) is not a philosophical activity making *karma* but comes to mean "simply mulling over of ideas." The technical Buddhist phrase, "to carry about an intermediate cause" (*engi o katsugu*), has survived in common parlance, but only in the pejorative sense of "being overly superstitious." Conversely, Buddhist religious attack upon pleasure-seeking as the fount of man's ills has been repulsed by Japanese

---

[1] A threefold typology of the world's religions is given by Hutchison in his *Language and Faith* (Philadelphia: The Westminster Press, 1963), p. 256 ff. Using a "height" metaphor, he typifies the nature and culture religions of China, Japan, ancient Greece and Rome as Type I — those religions whose ultimacy is found *in* nature and culture; Type II religions such as Buddhism and Hinduism find their ultimates beyond nature or the world, and are characterized by monistic idealism; Type III religions are those which "locate its one God both above and within the common world of men and nature" (p. 258), such as Christianity and Judaism." Japan's stark naturalism has never been lifted into the Buddhist orbit; rather Japanese Buddhism has come down to earth.

quest for pleasure. The word for "pleasure, enjoyment" (*tanoshimi*), is a key word used by Japanese politicians in their seeking election to office.

Giving the *modern range of meanings* of the core words analyzed, as listed in the accepted lexicographical sources, proved to be a valuable clue to the concept lying behind the verbal symbols. Single word translations into English are fallacious and misleading. In meaning ranges not only do we observe the general semantic change tendency to extend meanings from the concrete to the abstract[2] (e.g., "time" takes on the meaning of ephemerity, occasion, etc.; "first" is extended to mean primary, superior, etc.) but these meaning ranges reveal the cultural impact of previous centuries. Without any knowledge that Buddhism or Confucianism had entered Japan, been accepted, and had influenced Japanese thinking, an empirical philologist could, by simply listing modern ranges of meaning of key words, detect essential Buddhist or Confucian ideas and infer that in previous eras, these religions had in fact arrived and been accepted in Japan. Japan's most recent and authoritative dictionary, the Kōjien, revealed in its various definitions another process taking place... the impact of the West. Some meanings of words, words which obviously developed originally from Buddhist or Japanese thinking, are defined in a strictly Western, rationalistic sense. Thus one meaning of "reality" is given as "that which is truly existent" (my translation), "knowledge" is "a clear consciousness of facts and things," etc.

Finding interesting *English idiom parallels* and listing a few of them points to an overall concept of human culture; human beings react to and explain many of life's puzzling experiences in the same way. It would point to a common psyche among men, which, when divested of external accidence of word symbols or even cultural differences, reacts to life in similar patterns. Otto Jesperson hints at this phenomena in his *Mankind, Nation and Individual*:

> It would naturally not befit me to take a side in the controversy, but it is important to insist that in the world of language, there is a bond of human nature which can bring about the same related effects in many different places where all thought of imitation or borrowing is absolutely excluded.[3]

The dominant concept in Japanese thinking which colors subsidiary ones

We are approaching the Japanese man. Consistently he has rejected some ideas and accepted others — ideas which came across his thinking path through centuries of cultural interchange with other nations. Religious words flowing into his vocabulary survive for awhile and pass out. If they do remain, they are reoriented according to his basic Japanese *concept-clearing-center*. What is this basic concept which effects dynamic semantic changes in the language?

Our transcultural comparison with Hebrew-Christian thought sharpened up contrasts throughout the comparative study. We learned that Hebrew and Christian writers of the Bible took up verbal symbols from the cultures around them and infused them with new meaning and content. We noticed that they

---

2 A maxim explained and upheld by Havelock, Henle, and others. Cf. Henle, p. 45.

3 Otto Jespersen, *Mankind, Nation and Individual* (Bloomington; Indiana University Press, 1946), p. 186.

often avoided words bristling with cultural implication, words like *ahebh* (love), *eros* (love), and *eleos* (mercy). They employed somewhat colorless words in their place, like *chesed* (faithfulness to a covenant, i.e., steadfast love), *agape*, (be content with), and *charis* (graciousness). They invested these words with a semantic change that lifted them above the "man-in-the-cosmos" (Type I) context to a transcendental level, the level of a Personal God who invests history with meaning and direction (Type III). Common words of those cultures, words which already had meanings and associations that would delay or confuse this semantic change were bypassed; new words, sometimes featureless words, were chosen to be the new symbols of these dynamic concepts. God and His revelation in Christ became the *concept-clearing-center* for the Hebrew-Christian verbal symbol system.

In the same way, the Japanese people have consistently revealed a basic *concept-clearing-center* by the way words have undergone semantic changes upon Japanese soil. This clearing house, this one dominating concept is *man-in-the-cosmos*, or *man-in-nature*.[4] This is not peculiar to Japan; Eliade finds this a dominating theme in most non-Christian religions. He expresses the concept as "man participates in the cosmogony." All of the symbols of nature religions (Type I, according to the Hutchison typology), point to this "repetition of the cosmogony" in the life of man. There is an intimate relation between man and the cosmos. Eliade finds this in Japan, pointing out the coincidence of her yearly festivals with the seasonal changes, the equinoxes and the New Year. He sees in the Japanese New Year celebrations a repetition of time from the beginning; the year begins with man's purifying himself, being reborn as it were in the cosmogonic cycle. This *man-in-the-cosmos* concept is the Japanese ultimate, and this concept, says Eliade, creates a man-god, "for what is involved is creating man and creating him on a suprahuman plane, a man-god, such as the imagination of historical man has never dreamed it possible to create."[5] Does our linguistic analysis point to this dominating *man-in-the-cosmos* concept of the Japanese man? We notice that "beginning" is not nature's beginning, but man's beginning; "end" is not the bringing of external forces to bear upon history; the "absolute" is characterized by impermanence and flux, not transcendence; the "real" is not hidden essence but "that which appears"; "cause and effect" are the inflow and outflow of dynamic thought processes of man, man participating in the cycle of nature; "knowledge" is observing phenomena; "error" is not sin but creating disharmony; the "beautiful" is that which is natural; "nature" herself is not even characterized by a word in early literature, she stands not outside man as an object; rather man is a participant

---

4 Interestingly enough, when asked in our final interview as to what is the one dominating concept in the Japanese cumulative cultural thought pattern, Prof. Ōno's answer went something like this: "You in the West have based your relations on "contract." There is a gap between you as men and between you and your God. Thus, you based your relations on the "logos" concept. Men write contracts, God deals with you through a covenant, through an authoritative word. We in Japan have no gaps, no contracts. We deal with each other without contracts. There is nothing dividing us and nature. We are one as a people; we are one with nature. This is the dominating Japanese concept determining and affecting all others.... etc."

5 Mircea Eliade, *Cosmos and History* (New York: Harper and Row, 1959), p. 149.

in nature; "hardships" and "suffering" are an interruption of this harmonious blend and so to be avoided; gradations in society are observed, yet not so much out of profound respect for superiors but out of fear of them, lest one's walk through life and nature be put in jeopardy; Buddhist sadness and melancholy are adapted into national sentiment not because nature is evil but because nature is full of vicissitudes and change: summer gives way to winter, leaves fall, as do one's endearing relationships; "faith" is not belief in a transcendent God but a synonym for scrupulosity in observing rites, the rites that enhance one's daily intercourse with nature, lest there be a quarrel; "purity" has no reference to a Holy God but to the removing of discordant factors in the life, those blemishes that keep man from his oneness with pristine nature; "prayer" is not to a personal God but *at* the gods, calling at numerous forces abiding in the mysterious cosmos, seeking help for the daily walk; "righteousness" is not in a vertical dimension; it is a judgment of men; there is no "sin" unless it appears on the legal records; "sacrifice" is not appeasement but a sharing of a meal with the numinous in nature. Popular Buddhist movements, like the *Sōka Gakkai* with its eleven million members, talk little of theoretical Buddhism but offer ways and means for problem solving, healings, political solutions, economic prosperity.

Thus by merely observing the present day meaning of Japanese words and noting their semantic changes we can detect this *concept-clearing-center — man-in-the-cosmos concept* — in the Japanse mind. Thus to say that the Japanese are Buddhistic, Confucian, or even Shintō, because these systems have been accepted, is *non-sequitur*. Nor can the normal Japanese man be fully understood by examining the tenets of these religions. Rather, if any system of thought enhances the Japanese walk through life, it will be accepted; if any symbol is antithetical to this dominating man-in-nature concept or attempts to lift man out of nature, it will soon fall out of the vocabulary as a meaningful idea or undergo radical semantic change.[6]

Some suggestions on adapting this linguistic approach to the understanding of other cultures

First, it is my earnest hope that the semantic approach for compiling an idiomatic bilingual dictionary will not only assist my fellow missionaries in

---

6 It must be left to someone else to determine why a Type I religious orientation in Japan has been so persistent in coloring or even rejecting Type II or Type III religious concepts, while the Type I religious traditions of Polynesia (Phillipines, South Sea Islands), have readily accepted Christianity and abandoned many of their Type I social practices. A possible answer might be found in this direction: When Type II religions arrive upon a Type I religious culture, they give a transcendental dimension to Type I concepts and social practices. Hinduism and Buddhism throughout Southeast Asia have left virtually untouched the primitive animistic practices of those countries (e.g., the *nats* in Burma, the boat festival of Thailand, remain today and are part of the Buddhist cultic). Then when Type III religions arrive there is an immediate conflict, not so much with Type I practices as such, but with Type I practices fortified with a transcendental philosophy. When Type III religions arrive and confront pure Type I religions (as in the Philippines) there is no philosophical conflict, and the social superiority of Type III may prepare the way for a shift in the "concept-clearing-center."

Japan in their language study but also serve as a possible model for classifying lexical material in other languages.[7] I have already stated the reasons why I believe this approach is more realistic to the actual learning of idiom in the target language. To the skeptical and highly theoretical linguists I can only say, "Give it a try." For the understanding of cultural patterns of thought, it may appear at first as extremely laborious and time consuming. It did take some years of work finally to compile these idioms and find their English equivalents. However, if the basic thought categories listed here served as temporary means for categorizing lexical data, since the intellectual, emotional, and religious concepts investigated seem quite basic, the researcher could use these thought categories as a starting point. With an informant, he could go through several monolingual dictionaries of the language he is analyzing and list the meaning ranges. If he were not facile enough in the language to give good translations into his mother tongue, he could seek the aid of those more qualified. To discover semantic change, he will no doubt have to follow the procedure I did — seek the help of qualified scholars within the cultural tradition to determine how the words were previously used. Within a short period of time, I believe he could come up with a linguistic analysis, which, though not conclusive, could point to important gaps in his thinking and those of the people he is trying to understand. And the importance of such research is not merely academic. Henle says:

> If Whorf and his followers are right, the study of languages takes on new importance in the social sciences. Its place in psychology is greatly expanded, and it becomes of primary significance in all studies of culture.[8]

Notes to Bible translators

Applying the findings of our conclusion, namely, that peoples of different cultures have through the centuries developed a *concept-clearing-center*, which either resists alien ideas or dynamically effects semantic changes in their original meanings, what canons can we propose in the area of Biblical translation? Perhaps in most primitive tribes where Bible translation is being undertaken at this present time, the translators are perplexed with the serious problem of how to lift words and phrases out of a Type I religious milieu (man-in-nature) and put them into a Type III context (transcendent God intervening in history).

Canon I.

Follow the canons followed by the Biblical writers themselves; they employed words not too heavily colored with Type I connotation, and poured new meaning into them from the Biblical context. That is, a term bristling with

---

[7] For the full list of general Thought Categories (we have only examined 33 out of 222), see *Handbook of Japanese-English Idiomatic Equivalents* (Tokyo Kōdansha Int'l., 1967).

[8] Henle, p. 2.

indigenous cultural meaning may be just the reason for its elimination, and a vaguer word, because of its freedom from Type I associations, may be the reason for its choice.

Canon II.

If a choice must be made, words which are from a Type I context are to be chosen over those with a Type II nuance. That is, in Japan, for example, it would be better to select indigenous Japanese words than to employ Buddhist terms for conveying the Biblical message. For in Type I settings culture and history are bound up together. Type II is wholly "other-worldly"; its verbal symbols either are not fully understood or they would be confused when put in a Type III context. Type III into Type I is exactly the pattern to be followed, God intervening into history to give it new meaning.

Canon III.

Rather than assuming that single verbal symbols could convey Biblical truth, greater emphasis should be placed upon the style and understandability of the *context* of a Biblical passage.

Canon IV.

When it is impossible to find a word for a key concept, like *God*, or the *Holy Spirit*, without bringing into the Bible Type I or Type II meanings, the translator must coin a phrase or word. Perhaps the greatest tragedy of Protestant missions in Japan was the choice to render Jehovah and Elohim of the OT into the strictly Type I Shintō word, *kami*. Better that a new word be coined and confusion prevail for a generation than polytheistic ideas be kept alive under the aegis of monotheism's accomodation to indigenous words.

Canon V.

Missionaries themselves and national Christians must be very careful to put existential meaning to words and ideas of the Bible. Biblical concepts must be acted out before each generation so that Biblical love, Biblical righteousness, Biblical truthfulness will be understood by visual and not only conceptual means. Greater stress must be put upon work with youth, Christian homes must be established so that, in very fact, the *written* Word becomes *flesh*.

BIBLIOGRAPHY

General Linguistics

Bloomfield, Leonard. *Language.* London: George Allen and Unwin Ltd., 1962.

Gleason, H. A. *An Introduction to Descriptive Linguistics.* New York: Henry Holt and Co., 1955.

Hayakawa, Samuel I. *Language in Thought and Action.* 2nd ed., New York: Harcourt, Brace, and World, Inc., 1939.

Henle, Paul (ed.). *Language Thought and Culture.* Ann Arbor: The University of Michigan Press, 1965.

Landar, Herbert. *Language and Culture.* New York: Oxford University Press, 1966.

Sapir, Edward. *Language.* New York: Harcourt, Brace, and World, Inc., 1949.

Sturtevant, E. H. *Linguistic Change.* (First Phoenix Edition) Chicago: The University of Chicago Press, 1961.

Etymology — Chinese Characters

Kajitsuka, Shigeki, *et. al.* (ed.). *Kanwachūjiten.* Tōkyō: Kadokawa Shoten, 1966. (First published in 1959.)

Tōdō, Akiyasu. *Kanjigogenjiten* (Etymological Dictionary of Chinese Characters). Tōkyō: Gakutosha, 1965.

Etymology — Japanese Words

Ochiai, Naobumi (ed.). *Gensen.* Vols. I, II, and IV. 2nd ed. revised, Tōkyō: Okura Shoten, 1927.

Ōno, Susumu. *Nihongo no Nenrin.* Tōkyō: Yuki Shobō, 1960.

Ooshiki, Fumihiko (ed.). *Daigenkai.* 2nd ed. revised. Tōkyō: Toyama Sho, 1956.

Japanese Dictionaries

Shimmura, Izuru (ed.). *Kōjien.* 17 ed. revised. Tōkyō: Iwanami Shoten, 1965.

Ueda, Mannen and Matsui Kanji (ed.). *Dainihonkokugojiten.* 11th ed. Tōkyō: Fusanbo, 1956.

Buddhist Terms

Japanese-English Buddhist Dictionary. Tokyo: Daito Shuppansha, 1965.

Japanese Culture

Gulick, Sidney Lewis. *The East and The West.* Tōkyō: Charles E. Tuttle Co., 1962.

Nakamura, Hajime. *Ways of Thinking of Eastern Peoples*: *India-China-Tibet-Japan.* Honolulu: East-West Center Press, 1964.

Biblical Studies — Old Testament

Girdlestone, R. B. *Synonyms of the Old Testament.* Grand Rapids: Wm. B. Eerdmans Publishing Co., 1948. (First published in 1897).

Harkavy, Alexander. *Students' Hebrew and Chaldee Dictionary to the Old Testament.* New York: Hebrew Publishing Co., 1914.

Orr, James, *et al.* (ed.). *The International Standard Bible Encyclopaedia.* Revised. Grand Rapids: Wm. B. Eerdmans Publishing Co., 1949. (Original copyright 1929 by The Howard Severance Co.)

Robinson, H. Wheeler. *Religious Ideas of the Old Testament.* 2nd ed. London: Gerald Duckworth and Co., Ltd., 1959.

Snaith, Norman. *Distinctive Ideas of the Old Testament.* London: The Epworth Press, 1962. (First published in 1944.)

New Testament

Arndt, William F. and Gingrich, F. Wilbur (ed.). *A Greek-English Lexicon of the New Testament.* A translation and adaptation of Walter Bauer's *Griechisch-Deutsches Worterbuch zu den Schriften des Neuen Testaments und der ubrigen urchristlichen Literatur.* 4th revised, 1952. Chicago: The University of Chicago Press, 1957.

Kittel, Gerhard, *et al.* (ed.). *Theological Dictionary of the New Testament.* Translated into English and re-edited by Geoffrey Bromily. Vols. I, II. Grand Rapids: William B. Eerdmans Publishing Co., 1964.

_____. *Bible Key Words.* Vol. I. Containing four books: I. *Love,* II, *The Church,* III. *Sin,* IV. *Righteousness.* Translated and edited by J. R. Coates. New York: Harper and Row, Publishers, 1951.

_____. *Bible Key Words.* Vol. II, Containing four books: I. *Lord,* II. *Gnosis,* III. *Basileaia,* IV. *Apostleship.* Translated and ed. J. R. Coates and H. P. Kingdon. New York: Harper and Row, Publishers, 1958.

_____. *Bible Key Words.* Vol. III, containing two books: I. *Faith,* II. *Spirit of God.* Translated and ed. Dorothea M. Barton, P. R. Ackroyd, and A.E. Harvey. New York: Harper and Row, Publishers, 1960.

_____. *Bible Key Words.* Vol. IV, containing two books: I. *Law,* II. *Wrath.* Translated and edited by Dorothea M. Barton and P. R. Ackroyd. New York: Harper and Row, Publishers, 1964.

Richardson, Alan, *et al.* (ed.) *A Theological Word Book of the Bible.* New York: The Macmillan Co., 1964. (First printing 1950)

Trench, R. C. *Synonyms of the New Testament.* Grand Rapids: Wm. B. Eerdmans Publishing Co., 1948. (A reproduction of the ninth edition published in London in 1880.)

General

Niebuhr, H. Richard. *Christ and Culture.* New York: Harper and Row, 1951.

Ramm, Bernard. *The Christian View of Science and Scripturc.* Grand Rapids: Wm. B. Eerdmans Publishing Co., 1955.

General Lexicography

Householder, Fred and Saporta, Sol (ed.). *Problems in Lexicography.* Indiana: Indiana University, 1960.

Katsumata, Senkichiro (ed.). *New Japanese-English Dictionary.* Tōkyō: Kenkyūsha, 1954.

Onta, Akira. *Shinyaku Seisho Girishago Kojiten* (Small Greek-Japanese Lexicon of the New Testament). Osaka: Osaka Bible Seminary, 1964.